Government Beyond the Centre

General Editors: Gerry Stoker and Steve Leach

GOVERNMENT BEYOND THE CENTRE

The world of sub-central government and administration – including local authorities, quasi-governmental bodies and the agencies of public–private partnerships – have seen massive changes in recent years and is at the heart of the current restructuring of government in the United Kingdom and other Western democracies.

The intention of the *Government Beyond the Centre* series is to bring the study of this often-neglected world into the mainstream of social science research, applying the spotlight of critical analysis to what has traditionally been the preserve of institutional public administration approaches.

Its focus is on the agenda of change currently being faced by sub-central government, the economic, political and ideological forces that underlie it, and the structures of power and influence that are emerging. Its objective is to provide up-to-date and informative accounts of the new forms of government, management and administration that are emerging.

The series will be of interest to students and practitioners of politics, public and social administration, and all those interested in the reshaping of the governmental institutions which have a daily and major impact on our lives.

Government Beyond the Centre

Series Editors: Gerry Stoker and Steve Leach

Published

John Stewart and Gerry Stoker (eds)
The Future of Local Government

Forthcoming

Wendy Ball and John Solomos (eds)
Race and Local Politics

John Gyford
Consumers, Citizens and Local Politics

David Wilson and Chris Game
An Introduction to Local Government

The Future of Local Government

Edited by

John Stewart
and
Gerry Stoker

MACMILLAN

First published 1989

Published by
MACMILLAN EDUCATION LTD
Houndmills, Basingstoke, Hampshire RG21 2XS
and London
Companies and representatives
throughout the world

Filmset by Wearside Tradespools, Fulwell, Sunderland

Printed in Great Britain by
Billings and Sons Ltd, Worcester

British Library Cataloguing in Publication Data
The future of local government.
1. Great Britain. Local government
I. Stewart, John, *1929 Mar. 19–* II. Stoker, Gerry,
1955–
352.041
ISBN 0–333–49485–7 (hardcover)
ISBN 0–333–49486–5 (paperback)

*To the Institute of Local Government Studies on its
25th anniversary*

Contents

III WHAT FUTURE?

List of Tables

Notes on the Contributors

Desmond S. King is Lecturer in Government at the London School of Economics and Political Science. He is the author of *The State and the City* (with Ted Gurr) and *The New Right: Politics, Markets and Citizenship*, both published by Macmillan.

Steve Leach is a Senior Lecturer at the Institute of Local Government Studies, University of Birmingham. He has written widely on local politics, policy planning and other issues of concern in local government. One of his most recent publications, written with John Gyford and Chris Game, is *The Changing Politics of Local Government*.

Graham Mather became General Director of the Institute of Economic Affairs in 1987, having previously been Head of the Institute of Directors Policy Unit. By profession a solicitor, he was a member of Westminster City Council from 1982 to 1986. He writes, broadcasts and lectures regularly on economic and public policy issues. He is a member of the Monopolies and Mergers Commission.

Stewart Ranson is Professor of Education in the School of Education at Birmingham and chairs the Centre for Education and Management Studies at the Institute and the School. He has written widely in the field of the changing policies and government of education. He is author of *Politics of School Reorganisations*.

Kenneth M. Spencer is a Senior Lecturer in the Institute of Local Government Studies, University of Birmingham. He has written on social and economic policies and on local government management issues. He is currently undertaking research and consultancy projects on the management of social housing.

Tony Travers is Director of Research, Greater London Group, London School of Economics and Political Science. He has been consultant at various times to the Confederation of British Industries, the Chartered Institute of Public Finance and Accountancy, the Association of County Councils, Coopers & Lybrand, KPMG Peat Marwick McLintock, Price Waterhouse, ECC Quarries and others. His books include *The London Government Handbook* (edited with Michael Hebbert) and *The Politics of Local Government Finance*.

Kieron Walsh is Senior Lecturer at the Institute of Local Government Studies, University of Birmingham. He has written books and articles on a range of topics in the field of management, organisation theory and industrial relations, particularly in the public service. Has made a particular study of the impact of competition and market processes in local government. He is author of *Marketing in Local Government*.

Hywel Thomas is a Senior Lecturer at the Centre for Education Management and Policy Studies (CEMPS) and School of Education, University of Birmingham. He has published several papers on economic aspects of education management and is co-editor (with Tim Simkins) of *Economics and Education Management: Emerging Themes* (1987). He is the principal author of *Financial Delegation and the Local Management of Schools: Preparing for Practice* (1989) and author of *Education Costs and Performance: A Cost-effectiveness Analysis* (1990).

Preface

This book was written in an environment of change and uncertainty. We would like to express our thanks to the authors who, to a very tight writing schedule, produced their chapters almost on time! The final draft of the book was prepared in March 1989 and in a number of cases authors have had to speculate about the detailed outturn of legislation and regulations so we hope that readers will make allowances if necessary.

The speed with which the book was produced also reflects the contribution of others. At the Institute of Local Government Studies Fay Buck, Barbara May and Kathy Bonehill all performed wonders. We thank them for their efforts. Steven Kennedy at Macmillan was as helpful and patient as ever. Thanks also to Theresa, Deborah, Bethany and Robert.

The book is dedicated to the Institute of Local Government Studies at the University of Birmingham or, more particularly, to the people who have worked there. Twenty-five years ago the Institute was established as a centre for research, consultancy and management development in relation to local government. The expertise and knowledge of its staff have helped it gain both a national and international reputation. The continuous contact with local government officers and councillors, government officials and others associated with the local government world has proved that it is possible to meet across the practitioner/academic boundary. Above all else it remains an exciting, stimulating, even hectic, place at which to work.

JOHN STEWART
GERRY STOKER

1 Introduction

John Stewart and Gerry Stoker

> 'Local authorities are in the throes of a revolution. The immediate cause is a wave of legislation changing their methods of raising revenue, their ways of working and the range of their functions. But this, like all revolutions, has deeper roots. The political, financial and social environment in which local government operates began to change some time ago.'
>
> The Audit Commission, *The Competitive Council*, 1988, p. 1.

When auditors write of a revolution in local government clearly something unusual and significant is happening! Since their 1987 general election victory the Conservative Government has introduced a programme of legislation and other measures that will substantially change the nature of local government. This book aims to provide an up-to-date account of the major changes occurring in local government and examine the implications of the programme of restructuring for the future of local government.

The programme of restructuring follows a period in which the consensus about the role of local government has increasingly come under challenge. From the 1970s onwards elements of the Left, Right and Centre of the political spectrum have increasingly challenged the belief that the established form of local government is capable of solving social and economic problems. Scepticism, doubt and a willingness to experiment with other methods have emerged as major themes. Indeed many local authorities have come to the fore, developing new forms of service delivery and initiatives in economic development, crime prevention and in many other areas.[1]

During her first two terms Mrs Thatcher's government was far from inactive in relation to local government. In total some forty Acts dealing with local government were passed between 1979 and 1987. The emphasis of many of these measures and the central thrust of the Government's concern was with increasing the control of central government over local authorities and in particular on restraining local authority expenditure. A fuller examination of the measures and counter actions by local authorities of this period can be found elsewhere.[2] This book, however, is premised on the view that from the mid-1980s the Government's concern about local government became wider in its focus and more far-reaching in its implications. The Government's programme has gone beyond the search for public expenditure restraint to a more broad-ranging attempt to restructure local government.

The measures of the 1979–87 period in many instances weakened or destabilised local government. This made the likelihood of further change greater, and given the nature of the Thatcher style it was likely that a substantial restructuring would be promoted. But it should not be assumed that the Government had a predetermined strategy; rather it learnt its strategy through experience. The commitment to community charge reflects a dissatisfaction with earlier financial measures. The extension of compulsory competitive tendering builds on its initial application to house building and maintenance work. The education and housing reforms build on earlier legislation. The post-1987 programme draws on earlier initiatives. But it transcends the changes of that period because of the breadth and common themes of the restructuring it proposes. Out of a process of trial-and-error a comprehensive programme of reform has begun to emerge.

The Government has not rushed to set out the implications of its post-1987 programme as a whole. However, behind the welter of legislation, White Papers and Ministerial Statements, common themes and directions are emerging. The jigsaw is by no means complete and areas of ambiguity, contradiction and uncertainty remain. Nevertheless, the basis of a coherent programme of restructuring is observable.

Key themes of the programme as seen by the Government are:

● *the fragmentation of local government*
Elected local authorities will increasingly share their service

delivery, regulatory and strategic responsibilities with a range of other institutions and agencies.

- *a commitment to competition*

A range of services are to be subjected to competitive tendering from the private sector. In addition, schools are expected to compete for pupils. Housing departments are to compete with other social landlords for tenants.

- *the separation of responsibility for a service from the act of providing the service*

A local authority will retain responsibility for some services but it will increasingly pass on the doing. It will seek to enable others to act on its behalf to provide services.

- *a closer relationship between paying for and receiving a service*

The rationale of community charge is that it extends the net of contributors to local government. Higher rents and charges for other services are themes of the programme.

- *a greater emphasis on customer choice*

Clients are to become demanding customers. They are to choose from within a market place of public and private sector providers.

- *a greater scope for individual and private sector provision*

Individuals are to become more self-reliant and provide for themselves (supported by public sector subsidies). Voluntary associations are seen as having an expanded role. Private sector provision is set to increase. Local authorities are encouraged to concentrate on those services really 'needed' by the public, abandoning unnecessary functions and allowing scope for individual and private sector provision.

- *producer interests within local government are to be challenged*

Public sector trade unions and professional groups are to have their influence checked. As too are the welfare lobbies and client groups with which they have forged alliances to expand public services and expenditure. Competition, choice and community charge provide counter-measures to the perceived dominance of producer interests. More flexible employment contracts, pay and working practices are to be demanded of service producers.

- *a commitment to developing more 'business-like' management*

Councillors are encouraged to perceive themselves less as engaged in detailed casework and administration and more as directors, giving a strategic vision and clear policy objectives to their local authority. Chief Officers are encouraged to delegate and work through target-setting and performance appraisal. Service deliverers are encouraged to adopt an ethos of commercialism: developing business plans, marketing skills and managing their cost centres.

● **an increased emphasis on new forms of accountability to the centre and within the locality**

Central government will contract with local authorities and other agencies to achieve its policy objectives. It will be able to choose to which organisation to allocate resources and lay down performance targets and criteria. Decisions over local spending above centrally approved levels will be conditioned by the necessity to substantially raise community charge in order to do so. Business representatives are given control over some local institutions – for example Training and Enterprise Councils – and a greater influence in other areas. Parents are given an enhanced role in the management of schools.

● **a challenge to the mechanisms of local representative democracy**

The placing of some officer decisions beyond the direct control of councillors, new rules covering practices and procedures, and the exclusion of many officers from the right to stand for political office in neighbouring councils are likely to make the operation of the institutions of local representative democracy more problematic.

The new legislation and other measures are framed to produce radical change. The programme, however, is so broad in its agenda and so wide in its scope that it is far from certain how the reforms will work out in practice. What the cumulative impact will be is a matter for debate. There is no doubt that the role of local government is going to change but in what way and how the process will be played out remain open questions. The Government's agenda pushes change in a number of directions. Whether the legislation will achieve the desired effects and how different parts of the legislation will affect each other remains to be seen. The aim of this book is to provide a basis for an assessment of the likely future role of local government in the light of the overall impact of the Government's proposals.

Part I of the book examines in detail some of the key areas of change. We concentrate on the main legislative measures enacted or contemplated by the Government since 1987. Chapter 2 deals with local government finance and Chapter 3 with competitive tendering. Chapter 4 deals with education and Chapter 5 focuses on the housing legislation. Chapter 6 deals with the Widdicombe reforms. Chapter 7 is a 'round-up' of the other major measures undertaken or proposed by the Government.

Part II of the book examines the implications of the Government's programme for the future of local government. Chapter 8 sets the changes in an historical context and argues that the restructuring of local government is part of a broader process of economic and social development. Chapter 9 examines the organisational and management implications of the Government's programme. Chapter 10 examines the New Right normative arguments underlying government policy. These are contrasted with the Left's perspectives on local government. Chapter 11 sets out to evaluate the Government's programme and provides one scenario for the future of local government based on a further development of present policies. A contrasting assessment and an argument for a different future for local government is presented in Chapter 12.

Notes and references

1. These developments are discussed in J. Stewart, *The New Management of Local Government* (Allen & Unwin, 1986), and G. Stoker, *The Politics of Local Government* (Macmillan, 1988).
2. See Stoker, ibid, ch. 7; and J. Stewart, 'Developments in central–local relations in England and Wales', *International Review of Administrative Sciences*, vol. 53 (1987) pp. 483–505.

I THE AGENDA OF CHANGE

2 Community Charge and other Financial Changes

Tony Travers

Introduction

Local government finance is to be reformed in 1990 as part of a wider set of reforms affecting local authorities during the next few years. Community charge or poll tax will be the most prominent feature of the reform, though changes will also be made to non-domestic rates, grants, capital expenditure, housing finance and charging.

The reform of revenue financing in local government under the terms of the Local Government Finance Act, 1988, will lead to the introduction of a community charge to replace domestic rates. In addition, the non-domestic rate will be replaced by a centrally set national non-domestic rate (NNDR), while the Rate Support Grant will be replaced by a Revenue Support Grant. Capital finance will be reformed by the Local Government and Housing Act, 1989, with significant reforms of housing finance and possible changes in the law concerning charging for council services under the same legislation.

This chapter first considers the pressures for change which led to the reforms of local government finance which take place in 1990. It then examines the Government's proposals for reforming revenue and capital finance, before describing changes to housing finance and charging. Finally, the effects of financial reform on local accountability and on the long-term health of local government finance are discussed.

It is impossible to understand the proposed changes in local

9

government finance in isolation from the efforts which were made during earlier years to reform local authority taxation and grants. Indeed, the significance of the introduction of the only poll tax in the developed world, coupled with a range of other financial changes, requires considerable explanation. Such an explanation is suggested by the regular and unsuccessful efforts to reform local government finance in the 1960s, 1970s and early 1980s.

The background to financial reform

During the late 1970s and throughout the 1980s, attempts to find new methods of raising revenue have been accompanied by efforts to constrain revenue and capital expenditure. These efforts have led the Government to pass a number of laws to change the financing of local government. However, the changes made to grant systems, rate-raising powers and capital controls generally stopped short of a root-and-branch reform.

One further ingredient in the pressure for major reform of local authority finance has been provided by the Conservative Party's interest in abolishing domestic rates. In the party's October 1974 manifesto, the abolition of domestic rates was promised as a lure for householders. By 1979, the commitment had been weakened somewhat, with the promise that domestic rates would go only after other direct taxation had been reduced. Nevertheless, the association of the Conservatives with the idea of getting rid of the rates helped to build up pressure for their abolition.

The process of moving to the abolition of domestic rates had been tortuous indeed. Official and government reports published during the 1960s and 1970s (and for that matter earlier) had failed to come up with a potential new system of local authority finance. Structural and financial reforms were always considered in isolation. Conservative commitments in 1974 and 1979 to abolish domestic rates had to wait until 1990 before this goal was achieved.

The reasons why it took so long to produce a full package of reform derived in part from the resilience of rates. The tax had increased gradually since about 1600, was cheap and easy to collect, and the public was used to paying it. Other taxes looked relatively expensive to collect, while the introduction of any new system would produce millions of gainers and, more importantly, losers. Successive governments felt that it was easier to keep the rates for a few more years, rather than risk unpopularity and expense by undertaking reform.

The failure to examine structure and finance together is more difficult to explain. Political issues, such as public resentment against the regressiveness of rates in the 1960s or against massive rate rises in the 1970s and 1980s were perhaps seen as immediate problems, requiring short-term solutions, and not as the starting-point for all-embracing studies of local government. The Royal Commission on Local Government, 1966–69, could, if it had chosen, have decided to make recommendations about finance as well as structure as its terms of reference did not explicitly rule out the consideration of finance. In fact, although the Commission did discuss finance, it made no proposals for change. It appears that the commissioners assumed that their brief did not include financial proposals.

Moreover, during the 1960s and the early 1970s, growth in the economy was generally sufficient to pay for increases in Rate Support Grant from year to year. So long as rising local government expenditure could be financed out of national taxation, ratepayers could be shielded from the impact of the rising cost of local government services.

Finally, it is worth considering why the Conservatives took so long to get round to fulfilling their promise to abolish domestic rates. It is clear that when the Party originally made its commitment, in 1974, a local income tax was seen as the most plausible replacement for the property tax. By 1979, the Conservatives were fully committed to reduce direct taxation. The idea of giving local authorities the power to set income taxes was inconceivable by this time. After the publication of the 1981 Green Paper, the Prime Minister was reported to be in favour of replacing domestic rates with a local sales tax. But it was argued that having different rates of sales tax within metropolitan parts of the country would lead to border-hopping, as mobile consumers bought goods in areas with low tax rates. Worse still, it was suggested that a local sales tax might offend against EEC rules.

When the Scottish rating revaluation made the Government spectacularly unpopular in 1985, the final search for a new local tax was made. The Conservatives were by now well into their second term, and had a majority of over 100 in the House of Commons.

Siren voices from right-wing think-tanks, notably the Adam Smith Institute, pressed for a flat-rate poll tax, on the grounds that it was 'fair' that everyone within an authority should pay the same price for a similar basket of services. Moreover, by spreading the burden of paying for local authority services over all adults within an area, the consequences of increasing local government spending would be felt by the whole electorate. The Prime Minister was convinced.

The need for 'fairness' and 'accountability' underpin the wholesale reform of local government finance proposed in the Local Government Act, 1988. It is clear from various official documents published in the 1960s and early 1970s that fairness at this time was taken to mean that local government should be redistributive. Local taxation was criticised for being regressive, while reforms such as the introduction of rate rebates were intended to reduce such regressiveness. Services provided by local authorities, particularly education and social services, were expected to assist poorer individuals and areas.

The present Government has interpreted fairness in a different way. Surely, it is argued, it is fair that everyone living in an authority's area should make a contribution towards the provision of local services. Everyone enjoys the benefit of using refuse collection, street cleaning, street lighting, and roads, and has the insurance offered by fire and police services. Thus, it is fair that all adults should contribute towards the cost of these services. Of course, the vast majority of adults are also electors, and can therefore vote at local elections.

Strengthening the link between paying for local government and voting in local elections is at the heart of the Government's drive to strengthen local accountability. Government interest in strengthening accountability started in the late 1970s, as efforts were made by Labour and Conservative governments to reduce local government revenue spending.

The Conservatives became convinced that weak accountability allowed councils to spend in ways and on things which the majority of their electorate would find unappealing. Such irresponsibility was possible, it was argued, because many local authorities were able to raise the rates without most local people feeling the impact of the increase. Non-domestic ratepayers paid over half of any rate increase in most urban authorities, while a large proportion of domestic ratepayers were protected by rebates in urban areas.

Community charge and NNDR went a long way to solving the problem of weak accountability. NNDR would be set by the Government, and be outside of local authority control. Community charge would be paid by virtually all adults, and would reflect any marginal change in spending by an authority. Thus, in the eyes of the Government, the new system of revenue finance would improve fairness and strengthen accountability.

Much less effort was made between 1979 and 1989 to control and reform capital expenditure. For a start, capital spending accounted for only about one-tenth of local authority spending. In addition, although control was poor, sometimes there was massive *under* rather than over spending. But, as authorities accumulated capital receipts from the sale of assets such as council houses, and the Government found it increasingly difficult to target resources or to achieve precise control over borrowing, it was decided to accompany the reform of revenue financing in 1990 by a reform of capital financing at the same time.

Changes in the Housing Revenue Account (HRA) and in the potential use of charges, like the introduction of community charge, were intended by the Government to improve accountability and to move towards a more market-oriented kind of local government. The consultative document which first described the HRA changes talked of moving towards a more businesslike system of housing finance. The possibility of increased charging for local authority services, under provisions in the Local Government and Housing Act, 1989, was also part of the ideological drive towards a greater market influence in local government.

Taken with the new requirements for services to be put out to compulsory competitive tender from August 1989 (see Chapter 3), the HRA and charging initiatives are clear evidence of the Government's desire to improve efficiency and effectiveness in local government. This drive for greater economy, efficiency and effectiveness is indicative of the strong desire within the Government to change the culture within local government from one of mass public providers towards a kind of publicly-run holding company for local services.

The reform of revenue and capital finance in 1990: outline of proposals

The 1986 Green Paper 'Paying for Local Government' outlined reforms to the financing of revenue and capital expenditure by local authorities. The proposals became best known because of the Government's intention to replace domestic rates with a flat-rate poll tax, to be known as 'community charge'. But the introduction of a national non-domestic rate and a Revenue Support Grant will also be important for local government, because the way these income sources are distributed among authorities will affect the community charges levied. The three elements of the new system will be as follows:

1. *Community charge* is a poll tax, to be set by each authority and levied on all adults, with a small number of exemptions. The main groups of exempt individuals are: people living full-time in hospital or nursing homes; diplomats; visiting armed forces; nuns and monks; the severely mentally handicapped and people with no fixed abode. The elderly in hospitals and residential care will thus be the largest single group of exempt individuals. Despite these exemptions, the overwhelming majority of Britain's 38 million adults will pay the tax, as compared with the existing total of 18 million domestic ratepayers. A rebate system will operate, though there will be a maximum level of rebate so that no one will pay less than 20 per cent of their local charge.

2. *National Non-Domestic Rate* (NNDR) will replace the existing non-domestic rate. There will be a single, common, rate poundage charged on all non-domestic properties. Initially, the poundage will be set so that the total yield of NNDR – in 1990–91 – is the same in real terms as the yield of the non-domestic rate over the whole country in 1989–90 (the last year of the old system). The poundage will be set on rateable values which will be revalued in 1990 for the first time since 1973. Thereafter, the rate poundage will be increased in line with the Retail Price Index, or less if the Chancellor of the Exchequer so determines. The total yield of NNDR will be allocated among local authorities on the basis of adult population.

3. *Revenue Support Grant* (RSG) will replace the Rate Support Grant. The new RSG will effectively be allocated in two parts, although there will be a single grant figure paid to each authority.

The first part of the new grant will equalise between authorities so as to take account of their varying needs to spend. Needs assessments will be determined by the Government after negotiations with the local authorities' associations. It is the Government's intention that the new needs assessments will be simpler and stabler than those in the pre-1990 system. Any grant which remains after this needs equalisation process will be allocated among authorities on the basis of their adult population.

Allocations of NNDR and RSG will be made before the start of the financial year and will not be changed thereafter until the next year's allocations. This method of paying fixed grants and NNDR will be in marked contrast to the pre-1990 system, when for each year up to 1989–90, grant allocations varied with spending, and were often changed during or after the end of a particular year. Moreover, because NNDR and RSG will be fixed in advance, any marginal changes in spending within a year will fall wholly on the community charge. The Government stated its intention to make grant allocations as stable as possible from year to year, particularly by having simpler and more stable needs assessments within the new RSG.

NNDR and RSG allocations to individual authorities are likely to be different from authorities' existing receipts from non-domestic rates and the Rate Support Grant. The extent of these differences will be considered below. Gains and losses which result from the net effect of the new allocations of these elements of income will generally be introduced over a four-year period. This short-term arrangement is known as 'safety netting'. The overall proportions of local government income derived from community charge, NNDR and RSG will be broadly 25 per cent, 25 per cent and 50 per cent respectively.

In addition to the reform of revenue financing, the Government intends to replace the existing capital controls system in 1990. The Local Government, Planning and Land Act, 1980, introduced a system in which the Government gave each authority an annual capital expenditure allocation. In later years, authorities were allowed to top up these allocations with a proportion of their accumulated capital receipts. But, for a number of reasons, including the build-up of massive levels of capital receipts, the 1980 system was considered unsatisfactory by the Government. The fact that many authorities found creative ways of avoiding the full impact of capital controls further encouraged the Government to seek reform.

The Green Paper 'Paying for Local Government' outlined a new system of capital finance which would have involved the Government in setting limits on the use of external finance by individual local authorities. After consultation, the Government accepted that such a system of external financing limits would be impractical for local authorities. Instead, it was decided to introduce a system of 'credit allocations', which would give the Government power to put a limit on all transactions involving credit within a year, regardless of when payment to finance the new capital good fell due to be paid.

Legislative power to introduce a new system of capital control, and also to reform the Housing Revenue Account were included in the Local Government and Housing Act, 1989.

Distributional impact of the reform of revenue finance

As stated above, the effect of the new grant and non-domestic rate arrangements will be such as to lead to a radical redistribution as compared with the current allocation between authorities. Many city authorities will receive a lower income from the new NNDR than they do from their existing non-domestic rate. On the other hand, rural authorities – particularly in the north of England – will lose grant under the new arrangements. The combined effect of changes in grant and non-domestic rate will lead to changes in the amount which has to be raised from domestic taxpayers, i.e., community chargepayers.

Because the community charge will, on average, raise less than a quarter of current income, it is inevitable that changes in the distribution of grant and NNDR will have major consequences for the size of each authority's community charge. On the basis of the Department of the Environment's estimates, the top five gainers and losers, on the basis of 1988–9 spending, would have been as shown in Table 2.1.

These figures show the gain or loss to the community charge-payers in each authority because of the redistribution of grant and non-domestic rates. So, for example, the local taxpayers of South Buckinghamshire would expect to pay £203 per adult less in

TABLE 2.1 Gains and losses because of redistribution of grant and non-domestic rates, 1988–9

Top 5 gainers (£ per adult)		Bottom 5 losers (£ per adult)	
South Buckinghamshire	203	Greenwich	318
Westminster	200	Tower Hamlets	310
Chiltern	196	Lewisham	264
Elmbridge	194	Southwark	253
Epping Forest	135	Hackney	238

Source: Department of the Environment, unpublished figures.

community charge in the fully introduced new system than they now do in domestic rates (assuming that the existing total domestic rates paid is expressed as a per capita amount). Similarly, the loss of £318 per adult in Greenwich shows how much higher the community charge is expected to be, as compared with the current rate bills.

The Government could reduce the levels of gain and loss by changing the needs assessments within the new Revenue Support Grant. It is almost inevitable that losing areas, particularly those in inner London, will, in the end, find themselves given higher grants than would have been the case if the 1988–9 or 1989–90 needs assessments had been used. The final levels of gain and loss as between districts will depend upon decisions about grant and NNDR made during 1989 and 1990.

Generally, it has been predicted that local taxpayers in the South East, South West, the West Midlands and outer London will gain, while those in the North, North West, Yorkshire and Humberside and inner London will lose. The gains and losses will be phased in over four years, from 1990–1 to 1994–5. During this four-year period, 'safety nets' will operate, requiring gaining authorities to contribute to a pool of money from which losing authorities will draw resources. These safety nets will also offer protection from the financial effects which will flow from reforms to the housing revenue account and from the break-up of the Inner London Education Authority.

The use of safety nets to make shifts between authorities take place in a gradual fashion will have the effect of leaving some authorities with higher charges than would otherwise have been the case and others with lower charges. For example, if an authority raises domestic rates equivalent to £200 per adult in

1989–90, this will be the starting-point for its safety net, though possibly some allowance will be made for inflation between 1989–90 and 1990–1, which might raise the starting-point somewhat above £200 per adult. If, under the new system, a community charge of £300 per adult is required in 1990–1 to finance the authority's expenditure – assuming no change in spending from 1989–90 – then the safety net will protect chargepayers by contributing £100 per adult to the authority's income. This safety net will then fall to £75 in 1991–2, to £50 in 1992–3, to £25 in 1993–4 and to zero in 1994–5. Protection will therefore be gradually reduced. For authorities which gain from the move to the new system, and which consequently contribute towards safety nets, their contributions will fall from year to year.

The shift of NNDR and RSG from one authority to another, and the consequent effects on individuals is only part of the distributional effect which takes place in 1990 and beyond. Within every authority, even in those where there is little or no gain or loss because of inter-authority shifts, there will be considerable shifts of burden from individual to individual. In general, domestic ratepayers will in most cases gain, because their domestic rates bill – for the whole household – will be replaced by a single community charge bill. Non-ratepayers, including spouses, adult children and elderly relatives living at home, will in most cases have to make a direct payment towards local government costs for the first time.

It is difficult to be precise about effects on individuals because it is impossible to know with certainty who contributes towards existing rate bills. In some households, a single adult may pay the whole bill, where in others it may be shared. Moreover, in the new system there will be some households where one person, e.g. a father or mother, pays on behalf of all adults in the home, while there will be others where each adult pays separately.

The only practical way of examining the changing impact of moving from domestic rates to community charge is to compare existing household bills with those expected by households under the new system. Table 2.2 shows, for households with different rate bills and different numbers of adults, the effect of moving from one system to the other. All figures are for 1988–9, and show the average position for England Wales. The average domestic rate bill in that year was about £450, while the average implied community charge would have been about £250.

TABLE 2.2 Effects, by household, of moving from rates to community charge, 1988–9

Existing rates bill:	£112	£225	£450	£675	£900
Adults in household					
1	−138	−25	+200	+425	+650
2	−388	−275	−50	+175	+400
3	−638	−525	−300	+25	+150
4	−888	−775	−550	−325	−100

These figures in Table 2.2 show the gain or loss to households with different numbers of adults in an authority where the average rate bill was £450 and the community charge would have been £250. Where a negative number is shown, this indicates that the household would have paid more in community charge than it did in rates in 1988–9. Take, for example, a two-adult household living in a home with a rate bill at the average (£450). Under the new system, each adult will pay a charge of £250, adding up to £500 for the household. Thus, the total amount paid under the new system will be £50 per year more than at present.

A single adult living in a home with the average rate bill would pay £250 under the new system instead of £450 as at present, a saving of £200, while three adults in the same average rate bill property would pay £750 under the new system, a loss of £300. Four adults in the £450 rate bill home would lose £550.

Columns to the left of the average show households with rate bills below the average: £225 is half the average, while £112 is one-quarter of the average. Columns to the right of the average show households with rate bills above the average: £675 is 50 per cent above average, while £900 is double the average.

It is clear from the columns on either side of the average that households living in properties with rate bills below the average will fare badly as compared with those which have bills above the average. For example, a two-adult household which paid half the average rate bill would lose £275 because of the introduction of the new system. Many couples living in council properties or in terraced houses would fall into this category. Three- and four-adult households lose even more.

On the other hand, a couple living in a property with a rate bill 50 per cent above the average would gain £175, while even three-adult households in such a property would lose only marginally. Couples living in smaller detached houses or in substantial flats could thus expect to gain.

Table 2.2 makes it clear that single adults will do very much better out of the introduction of community charge than multi-adult households will. Equally, households with above average rate bills will tend to gain at the expense of those with below average bills. Thus, a single adult living in a substantial property can expect large gains in the vast majority of cases, while three or more adults living in terraced houses or council homes will lose in most cases.

Social security arrangements will underpin the community charge, although the details of how individuals' entitlements will be calculated have not yet been finalised. No one will pay less than 20 per cent of their local tax bill. Thus, even the poorest individuals will pay something towards the cost of local authority services. Income Support for those paying this 20 per cent minimum will include a notional element covering 20 per cent of the national average community charge.

Because Income Support will cover only 20 per cent of the average charge, individuals living in authorities with higher than average charges will have to make a net payment to local authorities from their own income, i.e. from sources other than the Income Support allocated for that purpose. For example, two pensioners living in an inner London borough with a charge of £500 per adult would, assuming their incomes were low enough to qualify, each pay 20 per cent of £500, i.e. a total of £200. Each of them would receive income support deemed to cover 20 per cent of the national average community charge, i.e. 20 per cent of £250. Thus, this element of Income Support would be £100, or just under half of their total bill. In low-charge authorities, the notional income support would, of course, exceed 20 per cent of the local charge.

Having looked at shifts of resources between authorities and at movements within authorities, it is obvious that movements between authorities would skew the average position shown in Table 2.2. In authorities which gained because of the shifts of resources between authorities, there would be many more households which would gain. Where the authority as a whole lost NNDR and grant, more households would lose.

A final piece of analysis to test the effects of introducing

TABLE 2.3 **Relationship of rates and community charge to net household income, England, 1986–7 prices**

	Ranges of equivalent net household income (£ per week)										
	Under 50	50– 75	75– 100	100– 150	150– 200	200– 250	250– 300	300– 350	350– 400	400– 500	500+
Gross:											
Rates	6.07	6.17	6.72	7.32	7.95	8.31	7.72	9.27	9.95	10.54	13.64
Comm. charge	6.00	6.36	7.27	8.03	8.12	8.01	7.59	7.36	7.09	7.42	7.00
Net:											
Rates	1.64	3.04	5.94	7.18	7.90	8.29	8.71	9.27	9.95	10.50	13.62
Comm. charge	1.63	3.13	6.31	7.64	7.91	7.89	7.52	7.31	7.03	7.34	6.89

community charge is shown in Table 2.3. This table shows the relationship of rates and community charge to net household income, in 1986–7 prices.

These figures suggest that gross rates (i.e. before rebates are taken into account) are significantly more progressive than gross community charge would be. Gross rates in households whose incomes fall between £50 and £75 per week have been less than half the rates due in households with incomes of over £500 per week. Gross community charge in households with incomes of £50 to £75 per week would have been only fractionally lower than those with incomes of £500 per week. It should, of course, be noted that fewer than 10 per cent of households would have had net equivalent incomes above £200 per week; most households fall in the first five income bands.

Net rates and community charges shown include the effects of rebates. Because of rebates, many lower-income households would pay less in rates or community charge than they would under the 'gross' payments schedule. Nevertheless, it is clear from the net payment of rates and community charge that community charge will be more onerous for relatively lower income groups and considerably less of a burden for households with the highest incomes.

The overall effect of introducing the community charge, coupled with the changes to non-domestic rates and RSG, is, on the basis of earliest indications, likely to be profound. Not only will all adults – with a small number of exemptions – have to pay for local government, but there will be a significant shift of burden onto individuals with relatively lower incomes. Moreover, the movements of resources between authorities which will take place because of the introduction of NNDR and RSG will much increase the cost of local services to taxpayers in higher spending authorities.

All marginal spending will fall on the community charge. If an authority decides to put spending up by £1, the full £1 will fall on the charge. Because community charge will make up (on average) only 25 per cent of average revenue income, an increase of spending of 1 per cent (e.g. from £100 million to £101 million) will lead to a community charge increase of 4 per cent (from £25 million to £26 million). This effect is known as 'gearing'.

The Government hopes that the introduction of community charge, NNDR and RSG in this form will much improve the accountability of councillors to their electorates. All spending in excess of centrally assessed 'needs' will fall on the community charge, while any increase or decrease in spending will have a direct impact on virtually the whole of the electorate. Just to be certain, the Government still has a power to cap local tax rates if it feels this to be necessary.

Opponents of the new system have argued that the community charge is unfair because it falls to be paid by all adults, regardless of their income, and it is inherently regressive. The shift of burden onto higher-spending (predominantly inner city) authorities has also been attacked as unreasonable. The Government has retaliated by claiming that it is introducing a new concept of fairness, whereby all the members of a community make a contribution towards the cost of a basket of local government services, and where 'overspending' of assessed spending need must be borne only by local taxpayers. Arguments about what constitutes fairness and about the relative burden of different authorities' local tax bills in the new system will continue for years after the introduction of the new arrangements.

Administrative consequences of the introduction of community charge

The discussion above about the distributional effects of community charge is, of course, separate from considerations of whether or not the tax can be efficiently and effectively administered. A tax on some 38 million adults in England and Wales will inevitably cost far more to collect than domestic rates, which were paid directly by only 14 million householders (a further 4 million paid rates combined with council house rents). In fact, the increase in transactions to collect the community charge will be even greater than these figures suggest, because it will be assumed that all chargepayers pay by 10 instalments each year unless they opt to pay in one or two larger amounts. Relatively few domestic ratepayers made payments by instalments. Thus, the increase in the number of transactions could be from about 75 million to over 300 million.

The Government commissioned Price Waterhouse, a major consultancy company, to calculate the cost of introducing and running the new system. Capital costs of the set-up were estimated by PW to be about £150 million, with an additional £120 million revenue set-up costs. These costs would include buildings, computers and new staff. From 1990–1 onwards, the additional cost of administering the new tax would be of the order of £200 million per year, which would be roughly twice the costs of running domestic rates. On top of these costs, extra benefit payments were expected to cost over £200 million per year.

The first additional expense would be the setting-up of a community charge register in each of 333 district or London borough areas. In Scotland, administration is in the hands of a far smaller number of upper tier (regional) authorities. All adults would have to be canvassed and registered, with a relatively small number of exemptions. Among the larger groups of exemptions are people living full-time in hospitals and residential homes, foreign diplomats, visiting armed forces, the severely mentally handicapped, prisoners, people with no fixed abode, nuns and monks, community volunteers and occupants of some crown properties. Individuals will be registered at their sole or main residence. Students are 80 per cent exempt, and must pay their 20 per cent contribution at their place of term-time residence.

Individuals must, by law, provide information and records to community charge registration officers. The authority may impose penalties on individuals who either fail to provide information or who provide incorrect information. Individuals have a duty to inform authorities when they move from one district to another. There are also penalties which can be imposed on anyone who fails to pay the charge after it has been levied, including an attachment of earnings order, distraint (i.e. removal) of property or even imprisonment. Where one partner in a marriage (or common law marriage) fails to pay his or her charge, the authority can assert joint and several liability on the other partner.

Registering and achieving payment from 38 million adults will be more difficult than the administration of domestic rates. People move around, where property is static. A number of individuals will be exempt from community charge, where few householders were exempted rates. The expected loss on collection of community charge will inevitably be significantly higher than the failure to collect domestic rates. Such difficulties will be particularly acute in inner city areas, where the population tends to be more mobile than in rural and suburban districts. Of course, if 10 per cent of an authority's adults fail to register and/or pay, then the remaining 90 per cent of adults will have to pay 12.5 per cent more than they otherwise would have to. On average, a 5 per cent failure to register and/or collect will add £13.15 to community charge bills, while a 10 per cent failure would add £27.77 to average bills.

The success or failure of authorities to administer community charge efficiently and effectively will be crucial to local government's ability to use the tax as an income source. Central and local government each have a vested interest in making it work as painlessly as possible, so as to avoid political recriminations against themselves. The political reaction to the new tax and its administration will be important both for local authorities and for the Government.

The reform of capital controls, the Housing Revenue Account and charging

At the same time as community charge, the NNDR and RSG are introduced in 1990, capital controls and the Housing Revenue Account will be reformed. Controls over capital expenditure will be replaced by a system which gives the Government more control over the resources available for financing local government capital expenditure.

The new system will give the Government power to make credit approvals to local authorities which will cover all transactions undertaken during the year concerning agreements to acquire capital goods, regardless of when the authority contracts to receive the goods or buildings. The Government will be free to set these allocations taking account of each authority's capital receipts, which will mean that asset-rich districts, particularly in the south of England, will receive little or nothing by way of credit approvals. Authorities will have to devote 75 per cent of their housing capital receipts to paying off accumulated debt, while using the other 25 per cent for capital spending. For non-housing capital receipts, half will have to be used for debt repayment and half will be available for capital spending.

The percentages set for debt repayment and capital spending may be varied by the Government from time to time. If an authority has paid off all its debt, it is possible that the Government will require them to pass on spending power to other public bodies. Authorities will, however, be completely free to use revenue contributions to capital expenditure. The Government has taken a new power to determine where authorities should invest their capital receipts.

It seems likely that the bulk of credit approvals will be directed to those authorities with low capital receipts, and where the potential for receipts is low. Inner city and northern rural authorities might expect to get the larger entitlements under such a scheme, with non-metropolitan districts in the south receiving little or no entitlement. There is no doubt that the new system will give the Government far greater discretion to influence the total and distribution of capital investment.

Reforming the Housing Revenue Account will also have effects on local authority finance. Until 1989–90, authorities were free to subsidise their HRA from the rates, and indeed to transfer any surplus on the HRA to the rate fund. From 1990–1, it will not be possible for authorities to subsidise rents from local taxation. This will affect local taxpayers and rentpayers in a number of (predominantly city) authorities.

Broadly, the effect will be to lower spending by authorities where there is currently a contribution from rates to rents. This reduction of spending should lead to lower community charges, though the relationship between spending reductions and community charge reductions is obscured by the fact that there will also be knock-on effects on the RSG system.

The Government has promised that where contributions from rates to rents are removed, there will be transitional arrangements to cushion the effects on rents by way of a new subsidy. Overall, the effect on the HRA will be to make it a self-contained account which will be more commercial in operation. The Government will have more power than before to influence the level of rents and the management of the HRA. The housing reforms are discussed in more detail in Chapter 5.

The Local Government and Housing Act, 1989 also included powers to allow the Government to make regulations which could be used to increase the number of services for which charges may be made. Indeed, the Act gives the Government the power to force authorities to charge for particular services, or to set maxima and minima for charges, or to give authorities discretion as to whether to charge for a particular service or services. How far the Government would choose to use these new powers remains unclear. Without doubt, it would be consistent with the Conservatives' general approach to local government if authorities were increasingly forced to charge for services, rather than to raise taxation to finance them.

Conclusion

The impact of the reform of local government finance, particularly the community charge, plus the changes to capital expenditure controls and the Housing Revenue Account will affect virtually every adult in the country. The cost of local government is being transferred from some groups of people to others. Domestic ratepayers will generally be better off, non-ratepayers will be worse off. Many council rentpayers may lose out, while community chargepayers gain. Within inner London, the breakup of ILEA will further shift burdens around.

The non-domestic ratepayer will not be left out of this redistribution of burden, though the new National Non-Domestic Rate will, in effect, be a national tax. Non-domestic ratepayers in many parts of London and the south of England will find their rate bills rising enormously following the introduction of the common rate poundage and because of the effects of the rating revaluation. On the other hand, bills will fall for many ratepayers in northern regions. Retailers will pay more in many cases, while manufacturers will pay less.

The Government's hope is that accountability will be improved. There will be 38 million local taxpayers instead of 14 million paying rates directly. Any marginal spending will fall wholly on those taxpayers. Surely, the argument goes, this will make local government spending more ordered because it will no longer be possible to finance local government spending by simply forcing up non-domestic rates or by relying on a minority of domestic ratepayers to pay for high expenditure. Opponents argue that the turbulence caused by the change will itself be inflationary and that spending departments will never let local authority spending fall precipitately.

The effects on accountability will be mixed. By spreading the cost of domestic rate-borne expenditure over all adults, it is likely that the Government will be successful in forcing local authorities to take greater care about their spending and taxing policy. Marginal spending decisions will lead to a direct effect on all adults. Although many councillors do not agree with this way of raising resources, on the grounds that they believe it to be regressive and unfair, it is widely conceded that more effort will be made to ensure that the entire population understands the benefits of local services. The test of changes in accountability will come in local elections after 1990. If turnouts improve and if there are significant changes in local voting patterns, the Government will certainly assert that accountability has been altered, presumably for the better.

On the other hand, the actual change from one tax to another will weaken accountability, as would be true of any change from one tax to another. Community charge bills in 1990 will bear no obvious relationship to 1989 rate bills, because the burden of local taxation will shift around so much from individual to individual. Even in the years after 1990, there will be distortions caused by the removal of safety nets. Many authorities will have their contributions to safety nets gradually reduced between 1991 and 1994, allowing them either to cut their community charge without affecting spending or to increase spending without increasing their charge. Other authorities will be in the opposite position. The certainty that community charges and spending by authorities will be moving without relation to each other for several years will severely impede the search for accountability.

The fact that on average three-quarters of revenue income will be derived from central sources, i.e. NNDR and RSG, will be a further potential way in which accountability may be weakened. Year to year changes in NNDR and RSG, in total and by authority, will affect authorities' total income from these sources. Changes in central income will be reflected in disproportionate effects on community charge. Imagine, for example, that in Year 1 an authority spends £100 million, financed £75 million from NNDR and RSG and £25 million from community charge. In Year 2, spending remains at £100 million, but income from NNDR and RSG falls to £72 million. In order to maintain spending, the charge will have to increase to £28 million, an increase of 12 per cent. The gearing of changes in central income and their effect on community charge will have significant effects on accountability unless an effective way is found of minimising real changes in income from central government.

In the longer term, the move to a flat-rate tax which may prove difficult to increase from year to year, will have implications for the ability of authorities to fulfil their obligations to provide services without proving unduly unpopular with the less well-off members of the electorate. It is the Government's intention that the new system of local government finance will intensify pressure on councillors to spend resources sparingly.

But spending departments, particularly those responsible for education, social services and the police are unlikely to take kindly to reductions in spending, or even to restrictions on increased spending. Changes resulting from the Education Reform Act, 1988 (see Chapter 4) will inevitably lead to considerable additional expenditure in 1990 and beyond. The Government has already announced that it will remove the limit on the proportion of education spending which may be supported by specific grants. Pressure to control local spending by use of specific grants will intensify if community charge appears to hold down spending below the level deemed acceptable by spending departments.

In the long term, the introduction of the new system of local government finance, with only a quarter of revenue income raised from a locally determined tax, and with capital spending under greater central control, must weaken the financial base of local authorities. The Layfield Committee, in its 1976 Report, argued that local accountability was threatened by a high grant percentage. Under the new system of finance, over three-quarters of local revenue income will come from central sources. The consequences of such a high dependency on central sources is likely to lead for greater pressure for central control.

Community charge could, then, lead to a reduction in local control. On the other hand, the Government has regularly argued that by introducing a new local tax which will ensure accountability, it will in future be possible for the Government to stop interfering in local decision-making. If there were to be a reduction in central involvement in local authority affairs, it would reverse many years of movement in the opposite direction.

The results of this massive reform to the financing of local government will take some years to become clear. If the Conservatives stay in power, we may see what these results are. If any other party takes office in the early 1990s, it is likely that community charge in its original form will not survive long. The regular, minor changes made to local government finance throughout the late 1970s and early 1980s may give way to regular and major reform in the 1990s. Local authority finance cannot yet be said to have reached a stable new system.

3 Competition and Service in Local Government

Kieron Walsh

The introduction of competitive tendering is part of the approach of those who look to the market to provide new ways of delivering local authority services. In theory it would be possible to have competitive tendering for almost every service that the local authority provides, from the collection of the community charge to the provision of education.[1]

The Government's attempt to introduce market disciplines into the operation of local authorities through the introduction of competition services has two main components: the requirement to subject some services to competitive tender and the imposition of internal trading. The tendency is to focus upon the requirement to put work out to tender, but it may be that the greater longer-term impact will arise from the requirement to operate on a trading basis which will introduce an ethos of commercialism within the authority. It is quite possible to envisage the local authority of the future as a set of contracts, and a network of internal and external trading.

This chapter is concerned with the development of the policy of competitive tendering in local government over the last ten years and the likely impacts of the Local Government Act 1988. I start by examining the origins of the policy in the thinking of the new right and in the activities of certain local authorities. I go on to examine the form that the policy has taken in the Local Government Planning and Land Act 1980 and the Local Government Act 1988. We will see that the Government has slowly tightened the rules, as it has done in other areas of policy such as trade-union legislation. Rather than attempt to change things completely all at once the Government has developed and, indeed, learnt its strategy as it has gone along. I shall argue that, from the Government's perspective, competitive tendering has the virtue that it can gradually be extended and can be changed to meet varying circumstances. The impact of competitive tendering will be considered under four headings: the financial implications, the effects on the management of local authorities, the impact on the role of the politician, and the impact on staff and industrial relations.

The pressure for competition

The pressure for the introduction of competition in local government has come from within the Conservative Party, from the various 'think-tanks' of the new right, from the private sector and the academic world, and from within local government itself. The idea is relatively new, and even those who argued for a reduction in the role of the state before the 1980s still tended to assume that when the state did provide services it should largely do so by directly employing the necessary staff itself. The private sector took the same path in the 1950s and 1960s, tending to employ its own staff for the provision of ancillary services.[2] Contracting out fits easily into the new market-oriented philosophy of conservatism that has developed under Mrs Thatcher, and its value as a strategy was enhanced by the public sector strikes of 1979, which gave powerful ammunition to those who wished to reduce the influence of the producers of public services.

The support for competitive tendering grew through the early 1980s, particularly on the Conservative backbenches, and a number of its major proponents, notably Michael Forsyth and Christopher Chope entered Parliament and became ministers. Each Parliament since 1979 has favoured competitive tendering more strongly and there has been some feeling that the Government has not moved as quickly as it might. The various think-tanks of the new right, particularly the Adam Smith Institute, the Institute of Economic Affairs and the Centre for Policy Studies, have pressed for legislation on competitive tendering, and there has been a strong overlap between the politicians and the think-tanks, with the Adam Smith Institute publishing two of Michael Forsyth's pamphlets.[3] The private sector has actively lobbied for the extension of competitive tendering through their trade associations, which have built up good links with government departments. Some academics have supported the move to competitive tendering, working on the *Public Service Review*, a newssheet supporting privatisation.

There have been two sources of pressure for competition and trading at work within local government – the Chartered Institute of Public Finance and Accountancy (CIPFA) and individual authorities. The influence of CIPFA has come through the approach that it has taken towards the means of accounting for direct labour work. *The Manual of Principles of Financial and Management Control for Local Authorities Carrying out New Construction by Direct Labour*, produced in 1969, had recommended that Direct Labour Organisations (DLOs) should compete for a representative proportion of their work. In 1975 CIPFA published *Direct Works Undertakings – Accounting* which recommended that local authorities should run their DLOs as trading organisations, that tendering should be adopted for the vast majority of contracts and that accounts should be based on value rather than cost. These principles were accepted by the Labour Party[4] and a Government report on the running of DLOs in 1978 argued that they should 'act as trading bodies and charge on a formal contract basis,'[5] that they should make a rate of return on capital and that there should be limited tendering. The same report carried the principle of competition further by stating that DLOs should also be allowed to compete for some kinds of work in the private sector. The approach to the operation of DLOs established by the Local Government Planning and Land Act 1980 followed this model closely, while denying local authorities the right to compete for private sector work.

Competitive tendering and internal trading for services other than construction had different roots. There had been no significant advocacy of competition from professionals or Government before 1979, but, following the public sector strikes of that year, in which a number of authorities used contractors to carry out services, some, such as Southend, decided to put services out to tender, arguing that the contract resulted in a considerable saving. Other authorities, notably Wandsworth, followed the example and tenders were invited for services such as school meals, school cleaning, road sweeping, grounds maintenance and building cleaning. The Local Government Chronicle survey in 1988 found that between 1981 and 1988 131 councils contracted out services and claimed savings of £42 million.[6] But most contracts are small and the total value of work put out is less than £100 million. Most of the authorities contracting for services were Conservative controlled and in the south-east of England. The Local Government Chronicle surveys show that the advance of contracting has been slow, has not affected the mainstream of local authority services and has not been taken up by the majority of authorities. It is clear that left to themselves local authorities are not likely enthusiastically to adopt competitive tendering.

Why competition?

The Government's basic reason for introducing competitive tendering for local authority services is its belief in the efficacy of markets. It maintains that service provision will be more efficient if there is competition, and, even if the level of competition will be limited in the short term, local authorities will need to control their costs since private sector competitors are likely to target the least efficient. The operation of the market can be mimicked within the local authority by the use of trading accounts and the establishment of client–contractor relationships. The Government points to the savings that competition has produced as the most obvious justification for the policy, but it also makes a clear distinction between provision by public and private sectors, whether or not there is competition. Direct labour organisations are not to be allowed to compete for work in the private sector even if they could do so effectively. Private is viewed as necessarily superior to public, though with no very clear justification. Successful local authority operations could be privatised for example through the use of management buy-outs,[7] or forcing local authorities to form trading organisations into companies. The Government's purpose is to provide a stimulus to the private sector as well as to reduce the role of the public sector.

The introduction of competitive tendering is not only about efficiency; it is also about power. The Government sees competition as a means of reducing the power both of the local authorities and the trade unions. The policy is particularly aimed at the trade unions and the way in which local authorities are seen as having colluded with them in the distortion of the working of the labour market. Competitive tendering, it is thought, will force local authorities to abandon excessively high pay and over-generous conditions and will make them recognise the nature of the local labour market. National negotiations are a particular target of the Government since they are seen as setting rates that are much higher than some authorities would have to pay if left to themselves. It is highly likely that authorities will begin to break away from national pay and conditions and that local government trade unions will be weakened by competition.

Power and efficiency effects are intertwined. Powerful unions are able to establish national uniform minimum rates and build on them at the local level, but their power depends either upon a tight labour market or institutional protection of their position. Clearly in conditions of high unemployment the labour market for relatively unskilled jobs will be loose and the unions will have to fall back on their institutional position. Until the late 1980s the Government had done little to change the institutions of collective bargaining in the public sector but it is now clear that they are willing to act, as they have already done in the case of the teachers. The Government's desire for differential pay to reflect local labour market conditions has been made clear for example in the debate over nurses' pay.

Competition in the civil service

The policy now being adopted for local government has already been established in the civil service and in the National Health Service. The Government came to power committed to cut the size of the civil service and contracting out has been one of the major means by which the policy objective was achieved. It has, obviously, been easier for the Government to introduce competition for the services it controls itself as opposed to local government, for which legislation is necessary, or the National Health Service in which the Regional and District Health Authorities have some, though limited, autonomy. Contracting for cleaning, laundry and maintenance work was well established before the 1980s, but the Government is now looking to contract out a much wider range of activities. The Ministry of Defence has taken particularly strong action and has a unit charged with forwarding contracting out.[8]

The Treasury has claimed cumulative savings of £22 million from contracting out between 1980/1 and 1985/6.[9] The multi-departmental review of competitive tendering in central government departments found that the benefits largely flowed from better training, more and better supervision, improvements in work practices and a 'generally tougher regime'.[10] The limitations of competition were also highlighted by this review which found that there would be difficulties in introducing competition for professional services. The Government has been enthusiastic in the use of privatisation in the civil service and the resistance has not been great. It may be, as Dunleavy has argued, that the contracting out of functions will be more or less acceptable depending on the 'bureau form'.[11] The structure of government departments will vary depending on the nature of their activity. Some, such as the Department of Social Security, will employ large numbers of staff involved in the direct provision of service; others, such as the Department of Education and Science, may employ relatively few, operating through other organisations such as local authorities. Where those at the peak of the organisation are not dependent for their pay and status on managing large numbers of staff then they are less likely to feel threatened by and to resist competition. Many of those in essentially policy positions will feel themselves little threatened by a reduction in the size of the civil service, particularly in the Treasury. Competition has, as yet, only affected support and peripheral functions, though the Efficiency Unit recommendations on the future organisation of Government[12] would have more far-reaching implications.

Competition in the National Health Service

In 1983 the Government extended the policy of competitive tendering to the National Health Service, requiring testing of the catering, domestic and laundry services. The imposition of tendering was not welcomed enthusiastically by most authorities and progress was slower than the Government wished. The National Audit Office study of competition in the National Health Service[13] found that contracts had been let or tenders issued for 68 per cent by value of the work subject to competition by the specified date. The failure to meet the target was

> due to under-estimation by health authorities of the work involved in the tendering process, demands on management time and the authorities' concern about the impact of the initiative on industrial relations.[14]

The National Audit Office found that private contractors had won 18 per cent of the contracts let overall, though, because they had been more successful on bigger contracts, they had won 24 per cent by value. Some companies that won contracts in the NHS found it more difficult than expected to meet the specification and make an acceptable level of profit, and they have withdrawn from the market.

The development of competition in local government

Local authorities have always engaged in competitive tendering for the provision of many of the goods and services that they need to carry out their functions: for example, the supply of educational materials or the construction of buildings. But authorities have traditionally employed the labour to do most of the work that is required in the course of service delivery. The tendency for authorities to employ their own labour was enhanced by the tight labour markets of the 1960s when it became difficult for private sector companies to provide such services as cleaning. Local authorities were no different in adopting this approach from large companies in the private sector which faced similar problems and adopted similar solutions. The private sector has been faster to move back to a contracting approach as the labour market has become more favourable to them. Local authorities have been neither willing or able to change.

The first move in the Government's initiation of competition in the provision of local authority services was the introduction of the Local Government Planning and Land Act 1980, which required local authorities to engage in competitive tendering for the construction and maintenance of buildings and highways, and to maintain trading accounts which had to make a surplus sufficient to enable them to make a rate of return on capital of at least 5 per cent. If local authorities wished to carry out work by direct labour then they had first to invite bids for the work and were only allowed to carry it out if they won the right to do so in competition. The number of individual failures to make the rate of return has been high; CIPFA figures show that 212 authorities – 56 per cent of the total number of authorities in England, Scotland and Wales which made returns to CIPFA on the performance of their DLOs in 1985/6 – failed to make the rate of return for one or another category of work in at least one year between 1982/3 and 1985/6. But very few authorities failed to make the rate of return in more than one year or in more than one work category, and, generally, authorities have been successful in achieving the required surplus.

The impact of the Local Government Planning and Land Act was limited by the various exemptions that were made. Local authorities were not required to bid for any building maintenance work valued at less than £10 000, or any highways work costing less than £100 000. Small DLOs were exempted from the legislation; emergency work was excluded; local authorities were allowed to allocate extension contracts to the DLO. Various specific types of work were excluded such as the maintenance of street lighting. These exclusions gave the local authority a good deal of leeway. Local authorities were also able to let contracts in a form that was unattractive to some potential bidders, by asking for tenders for very large amounts of work, or combining different aspects of work in a way that makes it unattractive. Local authorities did not have to win the majority of their work in competition except in the case of new construction, which was, in any case, declining as housing expenditure was cut back. The result was that (as shown in Table 3.1) in the years immediately following the implementation

TABLE 3.1 Proportion of local authority construction and maintenance work done by DLOs, 1982–3 and 1985–6

	England and Wales			Scotland		
	1982/3	1985/6	Change	1982/3	1985/6	Change
General highways work	51.6	46.6	−5%	44.3	47.6	+3.3%
Major new construction	12.9	11.5	−1.4%	4.8	6.6	+1.8%
Minor new construction	23.6	25.6	+2%	29.2	30.9	+1.7%
General maintenance work	57.8	53.6	−4.2%	63.4	53.3	−10.1%
Total	43.3	42.6	−0.7%	46.1	40.4	−5.7%

Source: Adapted from CIPFA Direct Labour Organisation Statistics.

of the Planning and Land Act the private sector won relatively little more building and highway work than it had before.

In the shire counties in particular the Act had a relatively limited impact on the amount of work that the authority had to compete for in the early years and most country DLOs were allocated more than 90 per cent of their work. The Federation of Civil Engineering Contractors was moved to produce a report claiming that the competition was 'neither fair nor frequent'.[15]

The fact that many local authorities were able to avoid competition in the early years did not mean that the Act had no effect. There was competition, especially for building work, and some trades, notably painting, were very strongly affected. Some types of authority fared worse than others, with London Boroughs and Welsh Counties finding the greatest difficulty in maintaining their share of the work. But the major effect was through the requirement to keep separate trading accounts for the competitive services. Many DLO managers now saw themselves as having commercial priorities. They were encouraged, as one metropolitan district treasurer put it, to 'Think Profit'[16] and many contrasted that with a service orientation. DLO managers saw themselves as subject to market pressures and behaved accordingly. Many who felt that they could not make the transition to the new values left, and new managers rose quickly to head DLOs.

The impact of the Local Government Planning and Land Act has increased as the Government has continually tightened the regulations. Authorities have been required to tender for increasing amounts of the work that they do, and the areas for manoeuvre have gradually been closed down. In December 1988 the Government announced that the competition free allowance for building and maintenance work should be entirely abolished, the exemption for continuation contracts withdrawn, the exemption for DLOs with not more than thirty employees should be reduced to fifteen employees, and the rules on emergency work made tighter. It estimated that this would expose an extra £400 million worth of work to competition. The Secretary of State has also used his power to stop DLOs doing new building work in a small number of cases.

The requirement to compete was extended by the Transport Act 1985, which required bus undertakings to operate commercially. The Government also extended the requirement to operate on a commercial basis to some local authority airports.

The Government announced its intention to extend competition for local authorities' services in February 1985.[17] It proposed to start with refuse collection, street cleaning, catering, cleaning of buildings, grounds maintenance and vehicle maintenance. The paper also proposed that a 'wider acceptance of the principles of competition' be promoted by the publication of comparative cost information. In the longer term the competitive regime would be extended to other services, such as computing, surveying and architecture. A bill was introduced in June 1987, and received the Royal Assent in April as the Local Government Act 1988.

The Act required competition for a number of defined activities, those in the consultation paper, and gave the Secretary of State power to add other activities by means of an order in Parliament. There were some minor exclusions from the legislation, for very small levels of activity, for work done by staff in tied residences, for emergencies and for staff performing a defined activity as only a minor part of their work. Cleaning of police buildings and maintenance of police vehicles were exempted from competition on security grounds and a number of other minor exemptions were made. If the local authority wishes to employ its own labour to carry out any of the defined activities then it must win the right to do so in competition. A separate trading account must be kept for each activity if it is carried out by direct labour and accounts may not be subsidised and must meet a financial target. Local authorities are to be required to subject activities to competition according to a timetable, structured to ensure that the private sector is not overloaded, and minimum and maximum contract periods have been laid down.

The Local Government Act 1988 is more tightly drawn than the Local Government Planning and Land Act 1980, and many of the loopholes in the earlier Act have been closed. The provisions on emergencies and the exclusion of small-scale activities are tighter, the Secretary of State's powers to intervene more explicit and more extensive and the powers and duties of auditors more clearly stated. The Act also requires local authorities not to 'act in a manner having the effect or intended or likely to have the effect of restricting, distorting or preventing competition'.[18] This catch-all clause is the most powerful in the legislation since it means that local authorities must examine everything that they do to ensure that it is not anti-competitive. The private sector will be able to take action against any authority which they consider to be acting anti-competitively either through the courts or by appealing to the Secretary of State. The trade associations are active in policing the legislation and in taking their case to the Secretary of State and the courts.

The powers of the local authority are further restricted by the contract compliance sections of the legislation which defined a number of matters as being non-commercial and forbid the local authority to ask questions about them or to take them into account in the award of contracts. The matters defined as non-commercial include terms and conditions of employment, the use of labour only sub-contracts and restrictions on the country of origin of materials. The Secretary of State has laid down specific questions that may be asked by local authorities in carrying out their duty to prevent unlawful racial discrimination. A clause allowing local authorities to ask questions about and take into account companies' policies on the employment of people with disabilities was added to the Bill in the House of Lords but rejected when it returned to the Commons, though local authorities will be allowed to discount the extra cost of employing people with disabilities in assessing bids. The limitations on contract compliance will reduce the local authority's ability to vet companies that wish to tender for their work and will prevent it applying contractual conditions such as fair wages clauses.

The reality of the intention to extend the legislation to other services became apparent soon after the Local Government Bill was published when a consultation paper proposed extending competition to the management of leisure facilities. The potential for the extension of competition to other local authority services is great. During the Parliamentary discussion of the Bill, Teresa Gorman, the Member of Parliament for Billericay, proposed its immediate extension to a large number of other local authority activities from pest control to social services. The Government is unlikely to bring further activities under the provisions of the legislation before the next election, simply because of the amount of work involved for local authorities, but there is no necessary reason why, in the long term, competition and trading could not be required for almost every local authority service.

Competition and education

The introduction of competitive tendering is complicated in the case of education by the requirements of the Education Reform Act, and particularly the delegation of budgets to schools. The money allocated to the school will have to include an amount that will enable it to pay for the competitive services. School catering services are still to be provided centrally unless the school can show that it could provide the service more efficiently itself. But for cleaning, grounds maintenance and vehicle maintenance the school will be free to opt into or out of the service that the local authority is providing. Even if it wishes to stay with the authority it can ask for a particular level of service to be specified. Schools may well find that they can find cheap labour, for example to do cleaning, and there are already examples of the use of pupils to do the work.

The school will have strong staffing powers, which it will be able to exercise over DLO staff. The governing body of the school will have the right to 'require the removal from the school of a particular DLO worker'[19] and select a replacement. Schools that opt out of local authority control and become grant-maintained will be allowed to stop using the DLO even if the authority won the tender. The Education Reform Act places great powers in the hands of the headteacher and governors who may well differ from the authority in their approach to competitive tendering. When schools have delegated budgets there will be a strong incentive for those which have below average costs for cleaning or grounds maintenance to opt out of local authority provision, since the funding formula will allocate average costs, and for others to search for cheaper means of provision.

The impact of competition

The first and most obvious impact of competitive tendering is that private sector firms will win contracts. The experience of the National Health Service and the state of the market would suggest that many authorities will be unable to compete with companies paying lower wages and with worse conditions of employment, especially in the case of cleaning. The productivity of private companies is also likely to be higher, partly because of better equipment and training but also because of harsher management than the local authority. The impact will grow over time as private sector firms first pick off the higher cost authorities and then attempt to expand into others. In the first round of contracts the local authorities are likely to be very successful because the private sector is not very extensive or is not yet prepared to take on the large amount of local authority work that will be put out to tender. Cleaning and refuse collection are the services most at risk, because there is a well-established private sector, the work is not complex and many local authorities have high costs.

Whether or not the authority wins the right to do the work, competitive tendering will have a great impact on the way that local authorities operate. The impact can be considered under four headings; financial implications, the effect on staff and industrial relations, changes in the way that local authorities are managed, and developments in the role of the elected member.

The financial effects

Much of the evidence that is presented either to prove or disprove the value of competitive tendering is tendentious, produced by those concerned either to promote or oppose competition. *Public Service Review*, published by proponents of competition, regularly contains lists of the savings that have already been made by authorities that have voluntarily introduced competition. There is no doubt that many of these savings are genuine but they cannot be evaluated since no information is given on how they are calculated. There is no statement of the difference between short- and long-term implications, or the relation between capital and revenue expenditure saving. Little information is given about how savings are achieved. Equally the focus by the trade unions on the failures of contractors says little about the failures of the public service, and ignores the successful contracts. Certainly there are failures but we have no means of comparing them with the present level of success. Neither of these arguments, that competition will always yield savings or that it will always lead to poor standards, takes us very far in the debate over the impact of competition. In general there can be little argument that in many cases competitive tendering will save the local authority money; the question is more one of the price at which the savings are bought. It is possible to accept the fact that there are savings to be made and still to reject competition on the grounds that the price that staff will pay will be too high. Equally it is possible to believe that there will be failings but that they are acceptable, given the long-term gains.

It is clear that there have been savings in many cases; it is equally clear that there have been cases of contractor failure. If we are to discern any pattern then we must look at the more systematic evidence, which is remarkably sparse. The American evidence generally tends to be that privatising services saves money, though a study by the Urban Institute[20] found that it was simply change, from public to private or vice versa, that led to savings, and not contracting out. Since much of the argument for the value of competitive tendering is based upon allowing local market conditions to operate it would be foolish to expect the results in Britain to be the same as in America. In any case the policy has not been extensively evaluated in the United States; Ascher quotes a review by the Urban Institute:

> The amount of independent, comprehensive evaluation of the effects of contracting . . . is quite small except for solid waste collection. Few trials of contracting, including the recent innovations, have been adequately evaluated to permit agencies nationally to learn under what conditions contracting works well.[21]

There is a danger of generalising, as Savas does,[22] from a study of refuse collection to the public service as a whole and to regard the effects as valid for all time.

There are a number of studies of tendering in Great Britain. The Audit Commission's study of housing maintenance found that 'costs tend to be higher when work is not subject to competition',[23] and for refuse collection[24] it found that privatised services had lower than average costs, but that some services provided by direct labour did equally well. Generally the Commission concludes that:

> The most competitive DLOs have costs that are lower than the prices quoted by the average private suppliers; but an average DLO's costs are more expensive to ratepayers than private suppliers. That is, most DLOs are not fully cost effective.[25]

The National Audit Office findings for the National Health Service[26] were that by December 1986 annual savings had reached £86 million and that eventual saving would be between £120 million and £140 million, though there would be some extra costs to set against this. Domberger and his colleagues[27] found results similar to the National Audit Office in their study of domestic services in the National Health Service.

The major studies of competitive tendering in local government in Britain are those by Domberger *et al.*[28] and Cubbin *et al.*[29] which are both concerned with refuse collection. Domberger *et al.* find that:

> costs are lower (by about 22 per cent) where private contracting is taking place. This result suggests that the introduction of private contracting has yielded substantial cost savings – a conclusion confirmed by analysis of the trend in costs in authorities where private contracting has been introduced. Real costs have fallen in these authorities.[30]

They also find cost savings where tenders have been awarded in-house and argue that:

> it is the introduction of competition, rather than awarding contracts to private firms, which is the critical factor in achieving lower costs.[31]

Cubbin *et al.* take this work further and attempt to find the source of the savings. They find that:

> for those authorities with private contractors, the bulk of the savings can be attributed to improvements in technical efficiency – that is, physical productivity of both men and vehicles. Only a small residual remains that can be attributed to other, pecuniary factors.[32]

Overall the evidence suggests that there are large savings to be made through subjecting services to competitive tendering, some of which will come from reducing pay and conditions, some from new methods of working and some from increasing the pace of work and reducing the total labour input.

Results from studies of refuse collection cannot be automatically extrapolated to other services, because the pattern of use of labour, materials and capital will vary as will the conditions in the labour market and the level of skill involved in the work. In catering, for example, the cost of food may be up to 40 per cent or more of total costs, and the most competitive organisation may be the one that can exercise great purchasing power. In cleaning there are certainly great gains in productivity to be made through the use of high-speed cleaning machinery, and the evidence that is available would suggest that private firms have much higher productivity than the public sector. We also lack studies that consider developments over time, and consider whether short-term savings will continue in the future, when, perhaps, DLOs have lost work and ceased to exist.

The claim that there are savings from contracting out because of the competition for the work can be countered by the argument that the initial competitive market will give way to monopoly or oligopoly as time passes and as large firms acquire smaller firms that have won contracts. The initial saving to the authority will be eroded over time as the contractor exploits the local monopoly. In some cases, most especially cleaning, the contracting industry is dominated by a few very large firms and the pace of amalgamation over the last few years has been rapid. Amalgamation may well increase as firms attempt to increase their capacity to offer combined contracts, for example for cleaning, catering and grounds maintenance, and try to buy firms in the relevant industries.

The argument that the efficiency savings that result from competition will be eroded by the growth of monopoly has, in turn, been countered by three arguments. First, there are still competitive pressures even when there is a monopoly because of the nature of the stock market and the labour market for managers. There will be a threat of takeover for those firms that do not use their assets effectively whatever the structure of the industry. Managers will also want to ensure that the firms for which they work perform well so that their value in the market and their own rewards are enhanced. This is likely to be a particularly strong argument in service industries that are technologically simple and where the key skill is the effective management of staff. If a firm has a poor record of performance both it and its managers are likely to be vulnerable.

Second, many of the large firms that are active in the services that will be subject to competition operate through subsidiaries, and they are harsh in the way that they will treat subsidiaries that are failing to make adequate returns. Though they are part of larger firms, individual subsidiaries will be expected to make an adequate rate of return on capital and managers will have detailed performance targets to meet. Third, according to the theory of contestable markets[33] the fact of concentration need not destroy competition which will depend on the conditions for entry to and exit from the market. When the barriers to entry and exit are low then firms will be forced to behave as if there was competition, because otherwise new firms will force their way into the market. It is not the pattern of ownership that is important but the nature of the industry and in most local authority services entry and exit are not likely to be difficult. But it is possible that firms in industries where concentration is high will collude with each other to control potential competition. Much of the justification for competitive tendering assumes a degree of effectiveness in the working of markets which is only weakly supported by the evidence.

A different perspective on the effectiveness of competition is offered by Williamson's work on transaction costs,[34] which compares the advantages of internal organisation of the production of goods and services with those of buying them on the market. Williamson argues that the appropriate form of organisation will depend upon the cost of transactions under the alternative forms of organisation which will depend, in turn, on three variables – bounded rationality, opportunism and asset specificity. Bounded rationality means that we cannot know everything, and that gaining information costs money. Opportunism refers to the presumption that people will pursue their interests whenever the chance arises, and they will do so with 'guile'. Asset specificity refers to the fact that some assets are highly specific to the uses to which they are put while others can be moved quickly and easily from one use to another.

The presence of bounded rationality makes it difficult to write contracts because future circumstances cannot be fully anticipated. The less certain is the future the more contracts will need to be written to allow variation, but contractors will always look to variation as a means of making high profits. Opportunism will be

greater the more difficult it is to state precisely what it is that is
wanted and the standards of performance. Asset specificity is
higher the less there is a market for the labour skills, or the
equipment used in the production of the service. When the local
authority can simply go elsewhere to purchase the same skills or
equipment then the power of the supplier is reduced and purchase
on the market is a more effective way of obtaining goods or
services.

The greater are bounded rationality, opportunism and asset
specificity, the less effective is contracting on the market and the
more effective is internal production. It is easier for an organisation to obtain information on those whom it employs, to change
their patterns of work, and to take sanctions against those whose
opportunistic behaviour will damage the organisation. Most of the
services that are to be subject to competitive tendering do not
come high in the scales of bounded rationality, opportunism and
asset specificity. The greatest difficulties seem likely to arise in the
case of leisure, which is more complex than the other services that
are subject to competition. If we consider the degree of bounded
rationality, opportunism and asset specificity as being high,
medium or low then the position of each of the services that are to
be subject to competition might be as set out in Table 3.2.

TABLE 3.2 Competitive tendering and the Williamson variables

	Bounded rationality	Opportunism	Asset specificity
Refuse collection	Low	Medium	Medium
Street cleaning	Low	Medium	Low
Building cleaning	Low	Medium	Low
Catering	Medium	High	Medium
Vehicle maintenance	Medium	High	Medium
Grounds maintenance	Low	Medium	Low
Leisure services	High	Medium	High

Building cleaning, for example, will not be subject to high levels
of bounded rationality since the use of buildings and their characteristics change only slowly, the likelihood of opportunism is fairly
high since it is often difficult to know whether the work has
actually been done or not, and the assets used, predominantly
unskilled labour, are not very specific. In leisure services, by
contrast, future patterns of demand are relatively unpredictable

creating high levels of bounded rationality, there is the possibility
of opportunism because of the wide variety of activities involved
and the relative profitability of different activity mixes, and assets
cannot readily be transferred to other activities. This relatively *a
priori* classification would suggest that the most difficult services to
subject to tender will be leisure services, catering and vehicle
maintenance.

Williamson's analysis is valuable in emphasising the structure of
information rather than ownership. The ability of the authority to
obtain an effective service on the market will depend upon the
information that it is able to obtain. The more difficult it is to
develop an information system that will allow the client to control
the contractor the more likely it is that internal production will be
more effective than purchase on the market.

The impact on management

Local authorities are changing their patterns of management and
organisation in response to competitive tendering and internal
trading. The major change is the need to separate the role of client
and contractor within the authority. This separation may be made
within a department or by creating separate contractor departments. A few authorities are also creating technical client units to
advise on such matters as specification and contract conditions. It
is becoming increasingly common for authorities to bring together
the various services that are to be subject to competition in a single
trading department, in order to reap economies of scale, gain
flexibility, and concentrate managerial expertise. The effect of
change as a result of competition is being felt most strongly in shire
districts because a greater proportion of their work is subject to
competition compared to other authorities, but all authorities are
facing the need to change their management structures.

The requirements to keep internal trading accounts, meet
financial targets and put in successful bids is leading DLOs to put
pressure on the rest of the authority to make changes. The costs of
central services such as law, personnel and accountancy are usually
recharged to the various service accounts. These central recharges
have mattered little in the past but are seen as an imposition by the
managers of trading departments who often feel that they are
excessive and that they have too little control over the charge or

the way it is calculated. Pressure is being put on central services to justify the charges they levy and on the authority to allow greater freedom for DLOs to decide the level of service that they want and, perhaps, to purchase services outside the authority. The tendency for training services to go their own way is heightened by the fact that they need new skills which may not be available in the authority: for example, cost and management accountancy, marketing and estimating. Competitive tendering is leading to more decentralised control of resources and the development of cost centres in a number of authorities. Authorities are being forced to consider the role of central services, distinguishing between corporate functions, such as committee administration, control, such as internal audit, and support, such as computer services.

Competition and the politicians

As with the officer structure there will be a need to reflect the differences between client and contractor interests in the committee structure of the authority. A committee will face problems if it tries both to let tenders and oversee the DLO's bid. The likelihood of conflict of interest would be great. The tradition committee structure of local authorities is also likely to be inadequate to deal with competitive services because of the need for speedy decision-making. A DLO faced with the prospect of losing money will need to act quickly if it is to take remedial action, and the normal committee cycle is likely to be too slow.

The major development in the pattern of committee operation is the emergence of boards for dealing with DLO affairs. Boards may be sub-committees of policy committees, full committees, or officer-member working groups. These DLO boards are likely to have strong delegated powers and can react more quickly than the somewhat ponderous full committee. They are normally small, in order to make speed of working easier and so that the board can work closely with the DLO manager. The development of boards is a move towards a more executive style of working and a style in which the officers and members work closely together.

The introduction of competitive tendering is likely to affect the way that members' complaints are dealt with. It will be less easy to take account of complaints because of the client–contractor split and the requirement to work to a prior specification. What members see as an unsatisfactory service, perhaps because of complaints that they are getting from their constituents, may be closely in accord with the specification for the work. Changing specifications, even if there is a variation clause written into the contract, will be expensive. It will be difficult to influence DLOs or contractors because they will be at one remove from the client, and subject to a set of pressures that may override the interests of the client.

The contracts that are to be let will vary in length from three to seven years. There may be break clauses written in, but, in the main, the authority will need to ensure that the contract and specification that are developed will be satisfactory over a long period of time. This will mean that major policy decisions will have to be made before contracts begin, because significant changes in the middle of the contract period might lead to high variation costs. If the authority wants to introduce wheeled bins for refuse collection, mechanised street sweeping or new methods of food preparation, then it will be best to do so before the contract starts. This level of forward planning will be difficult for some services such as leisure in which changes in taste are likely to have a major effect. The need to write contracts that will stand for a number of years will require the authority to plan its service much further into the future than it now does. The ability of elected members to influence services will be limited because they will be tied to contracts which they will have to honour whatever the platform on which they have been elected.

The need to plan is even more clear in the case of budgets. Unless there are clauses that allow the authority significantly to vary the level of service, then the cost of the service to be provided will be set for a number of years ahead. The need for budget variations will fall more strongly on the rest of the budget if the trading services cannot be varied. On the other hand the service department may gain some certainty by being clear on the charge that it will face from the DLO, which will only be able to vary its prices within the limitations of the contract. Moreover it may be possible for the service department to force the DLO to bear the impact of shortage of money by varying the amount of work that is ordered. But generally the legislation on competitive tendering will force local authorities to plan their services and budgets over a longer time-period. The role of the elected members in future will involve more work on planning and the development of clear statements of the quality of services that they want to be delivered, whether by DLOs or by the private sector, and the development of effective systems of monitoring to ensure that those standards are delivered.

The impact on staff

The introduction of the competition legislation was intended to have a major effect on the power and influence of the trade unions and the operation of industrial relations in local government. The obvious impact will be on pay and conditions of service and on the level of employment. Local authorities are good employers and offer rate of pay for some of the services subject to competition that will be much greater than those offered by the private sector, particularly in less skilled work such as cleaning. Even when the private sector offers comparable basic pay rates it is unlikely to offer bonus payments, and conditions on sick pay, holidays and superannuation are likely to be inferior. Part-time working is increased as contractors reduce the hours worked by individuals so that they can avoid paying national insurance. Even if the local authority can win the work it will need to reduce the workforce. The experience of local authorities that have tendered is that reductions in staff of between 15 and 30 per cent on average can be expected and in some cases even more. Authorities that win tenders are likely to reduce staff in order to do so. The effects are bound to be great since the services that are to be subject to competition are large employers. There are no accurate figures on employment in the competitive services, but about 700 000 jobs are likely to be affected in England and Wales, with more than 100 000 jobs being lost and possibly 200 000 or more.

The impact of competition is likely to be different for direct and indirect employees, that is administrative, professional and managerial staff. The proportion of white-collar staff in the total workforce in highways and building maintenance organisations rose from 12.4 per cent in 1982/3 to 14.2 per cent in 1985/6, following the Local Government Planning and Land Act 1980. The proportion of indirect employees in the total workforce rose most rapidly where the total level of employment was falling, suggesting the greater vulnerability of manual workers to cuts in the level of employment. The impact of competition is likely to be greater for women, people with disabilities and for workers from minority ethnic groups, since they tend to be employed in those jobs that are most likely to be reduced as a result of competition. A total social costing of the implications of competitive tendering that took account of the implications of job losses for example on social security payments and on revenue from tax as tax payments might come up with a less clear picture of the savings that result from competition.

Conclusion

Competitive tendering is a major weapon in the Government's armoury as it attempts to change local government. It has the virtue of apparent simplicity, and if local authorities argue that there is a great deal of work involved in specifying work for competition, they are open to the accusation that they should have had the necessary information long ago in order to manage effectively.

Competition also has the virtue of forwarding a number of different Government policy objectives. It provides more work for the private sector, it reduces the power of the local authority and it weakens the public sector trade unions. The policy is flexible because the Secretary of State can add further services to the list for competition, and can change the rules for tendering and for trading accounts. Loopholes in the legislation are likely to be quickly closed, and if the Government does not see the policy as having the effects that it wants as quickly as it wants them, then it can easily change the rules. Competition on its own will have a huge effect on the way that local authorities operate; the effect will be even greater when competition is combined with the other changes.

Notes and references

1. See two pamphlets produced by the Conservative Party think-tank, the Centre for Policy Studies: Nicholas Ridley, *The Local Right* (1988), and S. Lawlor, *Away with LEAs* (1988).

2. For a study of the development of competitive tendering, see K. Ascher, *The Politics of Privatisation: Contracting Out Public Services* (Macmillan, 1987).
3. M. Forsyth, *Reservicing Britain* (Adam Smith Institute, 1980), and *Reservicing Health* (Adam Smith Institute, 1982).
4. See, for example, *Building Britain's Future: Labour's Policy on Construction* (Labour Party, 1977).
5. *Working Party on Direct Labour Organisations. Final Report* (Department of the Environment, August 1978) para. 5.3.
6. Local Government Chronicle, *Supplement*, 8 July 1988.
7. The consultative paper, *Local Authorities' Interests in Companies*, produced by the Department of the Environment in June 1988, proposes exempting from the restrictions that will apply to other local authority influenced companies those that are set up 'to provide the service under contract with the authority which they have been providing as officers'.
8. See Institute of Personnel Management and Incomes Data Services Public Sector Unit, *Competitive Tendering in the Public Service* (1986) pp. 13–14.
9. HM Treasury, *Using Private Enterprise in Government: Report of a Multi-Departmental Review of Competitive Tendering and Contracting for Services in Government Departments* (HMSO, 1986) p. 15.
10. HM Treasury, *Using Private Enterprise in Government: Report of a Multi-Department Review of Competitive Tendering and Contracting-out for Services in Government Departments* (HMSO, 1986) p. 34.
11. P. Dunleavy, 'Explaining the Privatisation Boom: Public Choice versus Radical Approaches', *Public Administration*, 64 (Spring 1986) pp. 13–34; and P. Dunleavy, 'Budgets, Bureaucrats and the Growth of the State', *British Journal of Political Science*, vol. 15 (1985).
12. HM Treasury, *Using Private Enterprise in Government* (HMSO, 1986).
13. National Audit Office, *Competitive Tendering for Support Services in the National Health Services* (HMSO, 1987).
14. Ibid, p. 2.
15. The Federation of Civil Engineering Contractors, *Neither Fair nor Frequent: A Review of the Impact of the Local Government Act 1980 on Highway Work by County Direct Labour Organisations* (no date).
16. Phrase used at a private local authority seminar on the Local Government Planning and Land Act 1980.
17. Department of the Environment, *Competition in the Provision of Local Authority Services* (1985).
18. Local Government Act 1988, s.7(7).
19. Department of the Environment, *Education Reform Act: Local Management of Schools*, Circular 7/88 (September 1988).
20. Ascher, *Politics of Privatisation*, p. 17.
21. Ibid, p. 18.
22. See E. S. Savas, *Privatising the Public Sector: How to Shrink Government* (Chatham, New Jersey, Chatham House Publishers).

23. Audit Commission, *Competitiveness and Contracting Out of Local Authorities' Services*, Occasional Paper 3 (HMSO, 1987) p. 2.
24. Audit Commission, *Securing Further Improvements in Refuse Collection* (HMSO, 1984).
25. Audit Commission, *Competitiveness and Contracting Out*, p. 2.
26. National Audit Office, *Competitive Tendering*.
27. S. Domberger, S. Meadowcroft and D. Thompson, 'The Impact of Competitive Tendering on the Costs of Hospital Domestic Services', *Fiscal Studies*, vol. 8, no. 4, pp. 39–54.
28. S. Domberger, S. Meadowcroft and D. Thompson, 'Competitive Tendering and Efficiency: The Case of Refuse Collection', *Fiscal Studies*, vol. 7, no. 4, pp. 69–87.
29. J. Cubbin, S. Domberger and S. Meadowcroft, 'Competitive Tendering and Refuse Collection: Identifying the Sources of Efficiency Gains', *Fiscal Studies*, vol. 8, no. 3, pp. 49–58.
30. Domberger *et al.*, 'Competitive Tendering and Efficiency', p. 79.
31. Ibid.
32. Cubbin *et al.*, 'Competitive Tendering and Refuse Collection', p. 54.
33. The major text on the theory of contestable markets is W. J. Baumol, J. Panzer and R. Willig, *Contestable Markets* (New York, Harcourt Brace Jovanovich, 1982). For a more accessible discussion, see G. Davies and J. Davies, 'The Revolution in Monopoly Theory', *Lloyd's Bank Review*, July 1984.
34. O. E. Williamson, *Markets and Hierarchies* (New York, Free Press, 1975), and *The Economic Institutions of Capitalism* (New York, Free Press, 1985).

4 Education Reform: Consumer Democracy or Social Democracy?

Stewart Ranson and Hywel Thomas

I Introduction

A National Curriculum with national assessment of the performance of pupils, together with greater emphasis on parental choice of schools are the keynotes of Britain's Education Reform Act,[1] which became law on 29 July 1988. Intended to alter the purposes and responsiveness of the education service for the coming decade and the next century, the Act reconstitutes a governance of education which has been in place since 1944. The Act re-defines the relationships between central and local government, between parents and teachers in the unending debate over educational purposes and practices doing so through a set of changes which envisage both the greater use of administrative authority over teachers while at the same time drawing upon the discipline of the market to strengthen the accountability of teachers to parents.

These issues will be explored in stages. The next two sections of this chapter explore the background to the legislation and the changes proposed to the government of education. Section III analyses the apparent tension between a more heavily administered curriculum and a market-influenced approach to school choice. The conclusion critically reviews the values of consumer democracy within the Act and discusses the possibility within the legislation of developing an alternative vision of active citizenship within a social democracy.

II   The pamphleteers of consumer rights and accountability

The challenge to the post-war ruling order in education grew over an extended period, its views increasingly articulated and influential. Three main phases can be analysed: the first phase (1969–75) consisted of a number of 'Black Papers' which attacked the quality of comprehensive schooling and the need to strengthen the voice of parents in education. The second phase (1974–84) developed a 'parents charter', a theory which tied educational quality to consumer accountability, and an initial phase of legislative reform – the Education Act 1980 – which presented parents with extensive information about schools and allowed them limited discretion in choosing schools. In the third period (1984–8) a number of New Right pamphlets[2] promoted the idea of a revolution in the parental power which culminated in Parliament in 1987–8 with the Education Reform Act 1988. Here we wish to draw out the common and developing thread in the argument about the need radically to expand the role of parents in the education service.

This growing critique of post-war education focuses upon failures of achievement, on inadequate and distorted curricula. Standards have fallen is the claim. These failures of education, it is argued, derive from professionals and (local) politicians appropriating control of the service from its proper source – the parents. The 'producers' have taken over and pursue their own purposes at the expense of the needs of the 'consumers' of the service. The Adam Smith Institute's *Omega File on Education* generalises the problem facing education (in common with other public services) as those of 'producer capture', whereby the service comes to be organised more to suit the needs of the producers than the consumers. The professionals create a technical language which serves only to bamboozle ordinary people and they organise the system for their convenience rather than to respond to the demands of the consumers. The result is inertia and resistance to change.

The pamphleteers call for action and change: 'nothing short of radical measures are needed to improve the state-maintained system of education and to placate its growing critics, the parents, the employers, and the children themselves'.[3] The solution lies in new values and beliefs about education and the reconstituting of the government of education to suit.

The values emphasise that the education system must be built upon the principles of public (as consumer) choice and accountability. Individual parents have an inalienable right to choose the education which their children receive. The values articulate beliefs about educational achievement which assert that a system which is accountable and responsive to the choices of individual consumers of the service will improve in quality as a necessary consequence. As in other forms of market exchange, the products which thrive can only do so because they have the support of consumers. Those products which fail the test of the market place go out of business. The astringent experience of the market can be the test of quality in schooling as much as in the production of chocolate bars.

For consumers to fulfil their allotted role as controllers in the market place they require some diversity of product, information about the scope of choice and the quality of performance, as well as the opportunity to choose. If schools were made to respond to the market 'there would be a built-in mechanism to raise the standards and change forms and types of education in accordance with that market demand':[4]

> In short, it supposes that the wisdom of parents, separately and individually exercised, but taken together becoming the collective wisdom, is more likely to achieve higher standards more quickly and more acceptably to the public than the collective wisdom of the present bureaucrats, no matter how well meaning those bureaucrats may be.[5]

Creating this direct accountability between consumer and producer is the secret, it is argued, to renewal in education. To shift from a producer to a consumer-led system will take time, but placing public choice at the heart of the system will release the quality which is at present alleged to be submerged under the weight of administration.

Radical reforms are proposed to the government of education in order to reconstitute it according to these new organising principles and values.

The pamphleteers propose to dismantle the present system of education government. For some, even the DES would become 'superfluous' over a period of time as the routines of the market established themselves. The *Omega File*, however, invisaged a continuing and strengthened role for HM Inspectorate to ensure standards were maintained and teaching was of an acceptable quality. More significantly, for the Hillgate Group the state becomes an essential guarantor of the nation's traditional culture and values, 'safeguarding our educational tradition ... a repository of knowledge',[6] an inheritance that survives only if it is enshrined in durable institutions which have the means and purpose to pass it on.

A variety of strong, increasingly independent institutions are proposed which would provide a differentiated system of education that would allow diversity of choice for parents. The independent sector would be reinforced, the direct grant schools recreated, magnet and city technology colleges established, grammar and secondary moderns restored *de facto*.

The root of the current problems, argue the pamphleteers, lay with the LEAs (local education authority), which should be stripped of their powers and eliminated from the system of government. In time it is proposed that the ownership of all schools and the management of teachers would transfer to independent trusts or boards. This would create self-governing institutions under the control of parent governors and subject to consumer pressures in the market place. The survival of schools

> should depend on their ability to satisfy their customers. And their principal customers are parents, who should therefore be free to place their custom where they wish in order that educational institutions should be shaped, controlled and nourished by their demand.[7]

Strengthening the rights of individual consumers is the secret to improved educational quality.

The pamphleteers' proposals influenced the manifesto of the Conservative Party for the 1987 general election and the early proposals for educational reform of the newly elected government.

III   The Education Reform Act 1988

In the summer of 1987 a series of consultative papers were published which amounted to a radical recasting of the education service. The Education Bill presented to Parliament on 20 November 1987 conformed closely to those papers. The Bill could be seen as the culmination of a decade's campaigning to strengthen the rights of parents in the government of education. Introducing the Bill in Parliament, the Secretary of State said:

> The Bill will galvanize parental involvement in schools. Parents will have more choice. They will have greater variety of schools to choose from. We will create new types of schools. Parents will be better placed to know what their children are being taught and what they are learning ... and the Bill will introduce competition into the public provision of education. This competition will introduce a new dynamic into our schools system which will stimulate better standards all round.[8]

The legislation proposes that parent power in a market place of schools that are given more autonomy to respond to their consumers will improve educational standards. Yet in the transformed system of government the Education Secretary realises the powers of 'control and direction', while institutions are strengthened and the LEA diminished. We review here the changing roles of parental choice, the local management of schools, and central government control of a new national curriculum and the emergent tensions between them.

Parental choice and accountability

Parents are brought centre stage in the establishing of an education market place. Parents are accorded choice, influence over governing bodies, and control – if they choose – of new grant-maintained schools.

Open Enrolment is designed to end the LEA's capacity hitherto to place artificial limits on admission to schools. 'The government is committed to securing wider parental choice within the system of state schools'.[9] To this end schools will be allowed to recruit up to their available capacity defined as physical capacity or 'the standard number' admitted in 1979 (when schools were largely full) or, if it is higher, the number admitted in the year before the legislation takes effect. If a governing body decides it wishes to accept a larger number of pupils it can apply to the Secretary of

State. Moreover, local electors can object to the Education Secretary if they believe an LEA has set the limit too low.

LEA's, therefore, will no longer be able to set an admissions limit up to 20 per cent below the capacity of a school. (LEAs had wanted to plan admissions and thus resources to a school so that they could ensure that all children experienced a broad and balanced curriculum.) An LEA will not be able to manage admissions to a new school serving a new residential area as a means of enabling the local community to gain access to that school as a neighbourhood school. This could occur because the head and governors can choose which children to admit to their school.

How these changes affect a specific school will depend in part upon the relationship between actual enrolment and the standard number in that school and other schools in the same neighbourhood. Where there is a close match between admissions and standard numbers, open enrolment will allow less opportunity for parental choice than in neighbourhoods where there is considerable surplus capacity.

The Government believes that consumer choice depends upon variety of products in the market place. To this end a much greater diversity of institutions is being created for parents to choose between. *City Technology Colleges* will be schools established by the Secretary of State, though sponsored by the private sector, providing a broad curriculum with an emphasis upon science and technology. CTCs together with new *Grant Maintained Schools* (GMS) will provide the conditions engendering competition between institutions and thus the variety of choice that consumers purportedly desire.

GMSs are the means not only of choice but control for consumers. Parents are granted the capacity to acquire control of Grant Maintained Schools, if they can gather sufficient support. The Act will allow the governors of all secondary schools, and primary schools with more than 300 registered pupils, with the support of parents, to apply to the Secretary of State for maintenance by grant from central government and to cease to be owned and maintained by the LEA:

The Government is taking action to increase the autonomy of schools and their responsiveness to parental wishes. . . . The

Government considers that it should . . . respond to the numerous indications it has received that groups of parents want responsibility for running their schools as individual institutions. . . . The Government believes that this proposal . . . will add a new and powerful dimension to the ability of parents to exercise choice within the publicly provided sector of education. The greater diversity of provision which will result should enhance the prospect of improving education standards in all schools. Parents and local communities would have new opportunities to secure the development of their schools in ways appropriate to the needs of their children and in accordance with their wishes, within the legal framework of a national curriculum.[10]

These schools will receive grant directly from the Secretary of State and will form a new type of independent school within the maintained sector and, initially at least, they will retain their existing forms (a comprehensive school cannot opt out and immediately become a non-comprehensive school). Governors of the larger primary schools as well as of all county and voluntary secondary schools can apply to opt out, but only if they already have the support of 20 per cent of parents from a secret postal ballot. As Circular 10/88[11] points out, parents if necessary can override the opposition of governors and pursue their own application according to the same rules. Parents can have a determining influence on the governing bodies of newly formed GM schools.

The proposal has been unpopular with most of what might be termed the 'education establishment'. Concern has been expressed that the grant maintained proposal may be used as a means of introducing selective schooling in areas which have established systems of comprehensive schools. This has not been calmed by assurances – not included in the Act itself – that a school would not be allowed to alter its admissions requirements for a period of five years. There is also anxiety that the government may ensure that grant maintained schools are better funded than their local counterparts, making the opting-out alternative more attractive. If this weakens the ability of LEAs to offer an attractive alternative it would contribute to them 'withering on the vine' and becoming a redundant tier of education government and administration, fulfilling some of the hopes of those, such as Stuart Sexton,[12] who have advised government on this package of measures.

Parents are, therefore, granted more scope for choice and control of schools. Parents are also to acquire increased influence over *school governing bodies*. The 1986 Education (No. 2) Act gave parents an equal representation with the LEA on governing bodies and extended the powers of governors over the curriculum and conduct within the school. Now the Act gives governors responsibilities for school budgets, and the appointment and dismissal of staff as well as the ability to overrule an LEA on redeployment of staff. The Act extends such proposals to the governing bodies of colleges. The representation of college consumers – for example, business and commerce – are increased 'to ensure that the governing body is, and is seen to be, properly independent of the maintaining LEA'.

Local management of schools

The 'local management of schools' initiative contrasts with the centralisation of the curriculum and the creation of new national administrative structures to monitor the performance of schools on the programmes of study. This initiative is an integrated package of five changes which will facilitate greater accountability of schools to parents and the local community.[13] However, the package is also incomplete. It is left to LEAs to define the rules for local schemes of management, although the Secretary of State has the final power of approval and may amend LEA proposals after consultation. As will be exemplified in the following discussion, this local discretion may have a powerful influence in determining outcomes.

Formula Funding   At the core of local management schemes will be formulae for the distribution of resources. The Act envisages that special needs be taken into account in developing a formula, which

> shall include provision for taking into account, in the case of each school ... the number and ages of registered pupils ... and may include provision for taking into account any other factors affecting the needs of individual schools which are subject to variation from school to school.

Summary statements in consultation documents can avoid the complexities of formula funding; however, there can be little doubt that it is an approach which will create great difficulties for an education system which, typically, does not know the costs of individual schools. Even the leading exponents of school-site management in England and Wales (Cambridgeshire and Solihull) have managed their schemes by basing resourcing on historical costs.

The Act does not specify the factors which may be taken into account when defining the needs of individual pupils and schools, reflecting the aim of the consultation paper that these are for the LEAs to determine. On several occasions, civil servants with responsibilities in this field have emphasised that it is for LEAs to propose a formula as part of their delegation scheme. Nevertheless, although the DESs consultation paper[14] states that differential social need and different types and sizes of schools could be taken into account in the formula, Circular 7/88[15] makes clear that the overriding emphasis should be upon the number and age of pupils. Thus an embryonic voucher system is being introduced[16] because parental choice of school will now have a direct effect upon resources allocated.

As the Act requires LEAs to consult with the governing bodies of schools before deciding upon the elements of their formula, what is proposed is not only a major change in the techniques and processes for formulating budgets but also in the cast of characters required to take some part in the decisions. This move to an explicit and public formula-funding approach, defining the unit costs of pupils, will make it almost inevitable that LEAs will have to address the values upon which it has based its decisions. It will mean an end to the considerable discretion education officers have often had in allocating resources to different schools.

The change in the people involved in deciding the distribution of resources is also likely to influence spending priorities. Will the change lead to more or less support for younger pupils? Will governing bodies tend to favour generous support for small schools or will they wish to concentrate support for larger schools? Will the process of consultation lead to more or less support for children from socially disadvantaged backgrounds? Answers to these questions will determine how pupils and/or schools are weighted, a concept which shows that the apparently remote and unexciting concept of a funding formula is not neutral in its effects. They are not intended to be neutral. The purpose of weighting a formula is to ensure that more resources go to groups defined as having greater need, however need might be defined.

Early examples of funding formulae[17] suggest different judgements about special and additional needs. Are these examples of formulae indicative of a diverse pattern of future formula-resourcing, each representing local judgements about educational needs and preferences? (Or will actual decisions of the Secretary of State on LMS schemes ensure more uniformity in formula-funding?) A school system more strongly geared to client choice will still be resourced through political processes which articulate social preferences and it remains to be seen whether the outcome expresses the preferences of those with a vision of consumer democracy or social democracy.

Financial Delegation The formula-determined budget will be managed at the level of the school, enabling governors and teachers to switch spending in ways which reflect their judgements of resource needs. Whether their judgements are always better than those more distanced from the school has rarely been questioned, despite the contradiction suggested by the opposite trend of curriculum policy.

Although there has been limited experience in other authorities such as the ILEA and Hertfordshire, the practice of school-site management has been pioneered in the UK by Solihull[18] and Cambridgeshire[19] as a means of getting better value for money from the educational budget. Local control of the budget has been popular with the schools included in these schemes but there are important differences between them and the government's proposals for a national extension of financial delegation. First, the voluntary principle is lost and will mean that some LEAs will have to introduce financial delegation who may be hostile to the principle. More fundamentally, financial delegation is only one part of the larger package of local management; open enrolment, formula-funding and delegation to governors of powers of appointment, suspension and dismissal reconstructs the relationship between parents, teachers and local authorities in ways which are quite different from the value-for-money emphasis of existing financial delegation programmes.

It is the Government which has added the emphasis on accountability to the idea of financial delegation. The Act will require schools to 'publish information on actual expenditure at each school, which could then be compared to the original plans'.[20] This information will complement other performance indicators from the national assessment.

Local Management of Staff   The Act gives to boards of governors of individual schools the powers of appointment, suspension and dismissal of teaching and non-teaching staff attached to the school and paid from the delegated school budget. These powers radically extend the powers and responsibility of governors re-defined as recently as the 1986 Education Act. They place major limitations on the powers of LEAs over staff, although the LEA remains the formal employer but lacking the power normally given to the employer.

Much of the focus of accountability in the Act is on the teachers, and if they cannot respond successfully, their claim to employment would seem to be forfeit. In a funding system which will be largely pupil-driven, fewer pupils will mean less money and will require schools to dismiss teachers in post. Where this occurs, the Act overrides any local 'no redundancy' agreements with teacher unions, so that the teacher cannot simply be kept in post. Our understanding of the Act and the accompanying 'Notes on Clauses'[21] suggest that a dismissal from a school could well become a redundancy from the authority. Clearly, one might expect processes to be developed within LEAs whereby teachers 'volunteer' to move to another school before being formally dismissed. However, the viability of other schools agreeing to take such a teacher and it is on this issue that concern about redundancy must arise. As with open enrolment, the 'management culture' of the LEA, its relationships with schools and the relationships of schools to each other, is likely to influence the way this change works in practice. Nevertheless, it is difficult to avoid the conclusion that the formula-funding process will lead to teacher redundancies.

The national curriculum and assessment

In the 1987 General Election all mainstream political parties advocated policies designed to deliver a national curriculum for schools. While parties differed as to the structure, content and assessment of such a curriculum, it is an approach to educational provision which reflects a view that there is common set of experiences which is relevant to the preparation of young people for entering the larger social and economic community of which they are a part as well as its future.

Introducing its proposals the Government argued that, despite improvements in curriculum provision in many schools and school systems, in too many schools standards of attainment did not equip young people 'with the knowledge, skills and understanding that they need for adult life and employment'.[22] A national curriculum, linked to regular programmes of assessment, is designed to raise standards by:

(i) ensuring that all pupils study a broad and balanced range of subjects throughout their compulsory schooling . . .
(ii) setting clear objectives for what children over the full range of ability should be able to achieve . . .
(iii) ensuring that all pupils . . . have access to broadly the same good and relevant curriculum . . .
(iv) checking on progress towards those objectives and performance achieved at various stages . . .[23]

However, raising standards is only one part of the Government's purpose. A common curriculum will also facilitate population mobility and the accountability of teachers. It will:

(i) secure that the curriculum in all maintained schools has sufficient in common to enable children to move from one area of the country to another with minimum disruption to their education . . .
(ii) enable schools to be more accountable for the education they offer . . . Parents will be able to judge their children's progress against agreed national targets for attainment and will also be able to judge the effectiveness of their school . . .[24]

The curriculum is defined in terms of subjects, with maths, English and science forming the core. Other foundation subjects include a modern foreign language, technology, history, geography, art, music and physical education. These foundation subjects will occupy about 70 per cent of the curriculum and programmes of study are to be prepared for each subject. Programmes are intended to define minimum content and competencies and are not expected to occupy all the time available to a subject. Pupils will be assessed on their performance within these programmes of study at ages 7, 11, 14 and 16 and, for the core subjects, attainment targets will be set in order to 'establish what children should normally be expected to know, understand and be able to do at around the ages of 7, 11, 14 and 16'.

Despite cross-party support for a national curriculum some of the detailed proposals of the government have received much criticism. One target for criticism is that the Act defines the curriculum in terms of subjects, thus limiting the flexibility of schools in organising the curriculum in ways which cut across traditional subject boundaries. Indicative of the debate over the degree of flexibility allowed by the proposals are the views of Walton[25] and Bolton.[26] Walton interprets the Act as being very restrictive, inhibiting the ability of schools to take ownership of change and innovate in ways which, while working within an LEA's curriculum policy, allow schools to respond positively to local needs. Bolton gives emphasis to the professional discretion allowed by the proposals, suggesting that there is much scope for curriculum flexibility. Indeed, he says, the national curriculum could become a 'Frankenstein' if the 'sensible and constructive professional voice of education did not make itself heard'. He is also less sanguine about current standards and methods which include, he says, too many examples of overly prescriptive teaching, teaching to the exam and 'massive' testing in primary schools.

However, the strongest criticism has been directed at the proposals for national assessment and the publication of results on a school-by-school basis. Murphy[27] offers a six-point critique:

(a) The purpose of the tests is confused – the results are almost certain therefore to be misused.
(b) The attainment targets will not encapsulate more than isolated fragments of the whole national curriculum.
(c) The tests are bound to encourage an extremely narrow approach to teaching and learning, even with respect to the broad aims of the national curriculum.

(d) There is little justification for prescribing attainment targets in relation to fixed ages. Optimum attainment levels should be recorded and rewarded regardless of the age when they are reached by individual pupils.

(e) The assessment system is likely to be dominated by 'nationally prescribed tests' to the detriment of the assessments to be carried out by teachers.

(f) The pressure to keep the proposed system simple is likely to result in the worst kind of norm-referenced tests which will produce results, on a three (or five) point grading scale, which will convey little or no information in relation to the attainment targets anyway.

This critique of the consultation paper and the Act provides a helpful template against which to evaluate the effects of the administrative process which will convert grand policy into practice. It is through these processes that the professional voices will be heard as their expertise is drawn upon to develop the detail of practice. And already some of the criticisms – for example (d) to (f) – must be moderated in view of the recommendations of the Task Group on Assessment and Testing,[28] set up by the Secretary of State to advise on the framework for the national assessment.

The TGAT Report gives considerable emphasis to the role of classroom teachers in the assessment process. Testing is viewed as having diagnostic and formative purposes, complementing the teacher's central role as a facilitator of learning. The Report appears to have resisted the pressure for excessive simplicity, although the process of aggregation to provide published results on school performance will require a simplification of the information available for individuals. It has also avoided the prescription of attainment targets for fixed ages, proposing a series of ten levels of attainment which are less rigorously linked to age.

The Report is less convincing in attempting to control the misuse of the results (Murphy's item (a)), particularly the use of data to evaluate school performance. The Report shows an awareness that summative and aggregated results of the performance of pupils in one school is not the same as in a statement of whether the teachers in that school have been successful or unsuccessful. While summative information on the pupil is relevant – for example, to an employer or a university – it is not the relevant criterion for assessing teacher performance. The relevant criterion for evaluating the performance of teachers and schools is the learning value-added achieved by pupils, a measure which needs to take account of intake differences between schools. The Report recommends that the only form in which results of national assessment for, and identifying, a given school should be published should be as part of a broader report by that school of its work as a whole.[29]

This broader report would comment upon the nature of the socio-economic area from which the school draws its intake. It is not persuaded of the case for adjusting figures to take account of social deprivation.

Yet even the TGAT Report is inadequate framework for measuring the performance of schools. The learning value-added performance of schools can only begin to be properly addressed through information specific to the intake. The previous histories of two comprehensive schools drawing upon the same catchment may still influence recruitment. If one had been selective and the other non-selective, later intakes could still be skewed and influence the outcomes. More attention is needed on finding ways of controlling for the quality of the intake already in the school.

It may be that further change will take place on the means of controlling for differences in the intake of pupils before school performance data is published. Work continues on this problem in the Statistics Branch of the DES; in addition a DES working group, composed of LEA Chief Education Officers, is working on performance indicators; the DES has also recently commissioned management consultants to examine the information base needed for a greater use of performance indicators on schools. Beyond that, further change may be expected as national reports and recommendations are translated into detailed LEA and school plans.

The Report fails to calm anxieties about items (b) and (c) in Murphy's list, although it may be expecting too much of a single report to overcome all the concerns voiced about the national assessments. However, what the Report does show is the beginning of that process of change which policy so often undergoes between declaration and implementation. Indicative of this is evidence of disagreement between the Prime Minister and her Secretary of State for Education – in a private letter from the

Prime Minister's office leaked to the press – about the acceptability of the Report's emphasis on the role of the teacher in testing,
the need for a complex formative approach to the task and the
resource implications of sophisticated assessment procedure.[30]

Summarising the reforms

The several provisions of the Education Reform Act express
related principles of public choice and accountability. What will be
created through the proposed structures and processes of the
national curriculum, national assessment and local management is
a system of locally provided education which, within a national
framework of curriculum objectives, will be more accountable to
parents for the quality of its delivery. Parents will receive information of a more systematic nature about school performance, and
ending the controls on enrolment will enable them to 'vote with
their feet', taking children from schools which, in their judgement,
are not successful. Pupil-related funding will emphasise the
accountability of schools, funds declining in step with enrolment
and leading to the dismissal of teachers. If these new pressures are
insufficient in making LEA-owned schools more responsive to
parents, the third strand of the Government's proposals is to
enable parents and governors to vote for the creation of centrally
funded schools which will be in direct competition with the LEA
sector.

One key question arises about the effectiveness of the education
reforms. How will the tension at the heart of the legislation –
between centralising and decentralising powers – impact on the
effectiveness of the reforms and, in particular, on the role of the
local education authority (LEA)? Will there be any significant role
for local government after the 1988 Act?

IV   Local government after the Act: contradictions

The 1988 Reform Act reconstitutes powers and duties in the
government of education. It will accomplish this in a way that will
create considerable tensions for the LEA now caught between the
markets of consumer choice and the hierarchies of Whitehall

regulation of the curriculum. The Act thus creates contradictions and yet, we shall argue, possibilities for the local government of education.

Market forces are likely to weaken and fragment the LEA. The Act is paralysing the will of a number of LEAs that wish to plan their school provision for the future in a period of falling school rolls. But with the prospect of some schools within an LEA choosing to opt out rather than, for example, lose their sixth form to a tertiary college, many LEAs are now reluctant to publish schemes of reorganisation which their systems require to remain effective.

Even if they do not precipitate opting out, LEAs may nevertheless face the prospect of watching the growth of GMSs and CTCs fragment local public and accountable control of schools. Moreover, market forces may encourage incipient privatisation of education as more schools become grant maintained as a stage before entering the independent (private) sector. LEAs would be left with responsibilities for educating the poor and disadvantaged underclass in society.

Yet the Act nationalises the curriculum and assessment of learning and provides the Secretary of State with an extraordinary array of detailed powers of regulation and scrutiny. Not only can Whitehall determine the content of courses and tests but can intervene at virtually every stage of the government of education: for example, determining the acceptability of schemes and funding formulae, of GMS governors and the articles of government, as well as the statutory control of bodies to advise the Secretary of State.[31]

The effect of these dual organisational changes – of centralising state power especially over the curriculum while placing institutions in a competitive market place of consumer choice – not only formally erodes the position of the LEA but can undermine their capacity to deliver the post-war commitment to expanding educational and social opportunities. By controlling the curriculum and assessment the State now regulates in detail the process of social differentiation, while the practice of consumerism[32] can result in social selection and hierarchy. The combination of social regulation and selection has the same effect: a service ordered more tightly than ever before to achieve social stratification and control.

The 1988 Act, therefore, appears to create contradictions for

the effective operation of the local government of education by
separating power from responsibility as well as by centralising and
decentralising authority. What is intriguing in the new legislation is
the translation of this contradiction from central to local government. Although Section 1 of the 1944 Education Act placed the
LEAs and national policy under the 'control and direction' of the
Minister, he or she was given few powers of direct control. The
distinguishing feature of the 1944 Act was the distribution of
powers and responsibilities between levels of government so as to
form what Briault[33] has called a triangle of tension, of checks and
balances.

However, in the transformed economic climate of the mid-1970s
with a recession and accelerating youth unemployment together
with a growing public challenge about the effectiveness of education, the Government sought increasingly to review and redirect
the service. Wanting to steer the service in a new direction the
DES found the contradiction between its responsibility to control
the service but its lack of power to do so increasingly frustrating.
Since the mid-1970s the DES has sought to extend its power at the
expense of the other 'partners' – the teachers and the LEAs.[34]

The 1988 Reform Act completes this process of centralisation,
while empowering consumers at the same time. The LEA, former-
ly the centrepiece of the government of education, responsible for
planning and maintaining local institutional provision and the
curriculum, is now bereft of many of its traditional powers though
retaining important responsibilities for overall strategy and monitoring quality. The gap between responsibility and authority is
transposed from Whitehall to town and county hall.

Possibilities for the future

The undermining of the LEA as an effective tier of education
government is a disturbing and likely scenario. Yet more hopeful
possibilities for local authorities can emerge even within the
framework of the 1988 reforms.

While the LEA has lost formal and direct control of its
institutions it can, nevertheless, create a new and significant role
within the reformed government of education. The LEA has,
traditionally, been known as the 'maintaining authority': providing

the infrastructure of services and administration required by institutions. Even though the LEA had responsibility for the curriculum (s. 27, 1944 Act) and for the education of the community (s. 7), issues of learning process were regarded typically as professional matters for heads and their staffs in schools and colleges. LEAs developed and administered the framework of education while delegating the content and quality of learning to others.

Now the Act charges LEAs with responsibility for monitoring and evaluating the quality of the national curriculum as it is being delivered in schools. The role of the LEA changes:

from administration to strategic leadership;
from controlling to the management of influence;
from maintaining to enabling;
from providing to monitoring and evaluating.

The primary role of the LEA is now to enhance learning quality and public accountability. The strength of its rationale in both cases resides in the system-dependent qualities of learning and of the public domain.

The LEA can have a vital role in promoting the quality of learning: by developing progression between the stages of learning especially between primary and secondary as well as between 14 and 19; identifying and disseminating good practice in curriculum development and teaching method; encouraging clear and consistent thinking throughout the service about educational values and purpose; making staff development suit the needs of institutions and by encouraging good management. Understanding has developed over recent years[35] about how the quality of learning depends upon the mutual support of institutions. The role of the LEA is to enable and facilitate partnership of learning within an interdependent system. This can be achieved by establishing strategic planning teams to develop shared values, agree programmes and targets, as well as methods of evaluating performance. Intensive in-service training programmes will be essential to achieving partnership in the new education reforms.

Yet this reinforcing of learning quality will only improve public confidence if the authority and its professionals continually seek to involve the public at every stage and become accountable to the public. Even HMI, the priesthood of professional knowledge,

increasingly urges schools to form a partnership with parents,
governors, local employers and the community in order to develop
the quality of education: 'schools cannot afford to be insular; they
are part of society and accountable for their performance'. Evidence of the benefit of involving parents and the community as
'complementary educators' grows year by year: in nursery and
infant classes;[36] in home-school reading schemes;[37] in primary
schools;[38] in secondary school tutor group parent associations and
home-school councils;[39] and in members of the community becoming 'coaches' to young adults making the transition from school to
work.[40] Through such strategies and many more, parents and the
community can develop understanding of schools and their work.
The Government paper 'Better Schools'[41] stressed the important
role of parents in the learning process and encouraged schools to
'reach out and support . . . parents' as 'partners in a shared task for
the benefit of the child'.

The role of the LEA in this context, therefore, is to support and
enable the involvement of the public as consumers but also as
citizens. Citizens need to be involved because education is a *public*
(i.e. *collective*) *good* – a good, that is, in which we are all
interested because of its pervasive significance. It is a good which
because of these collective characteristics cannot be determined by
individuals acting in isolation from each other. The quality of
education, therefore, requires to be the subject of *public choice*
which is *accountable* to the public as a whole.[42]

If choice is to be public choice it requires the opportunity for
citizens to express their view, for their voice to be heard, so that
the inescapably diverse constituencies of education are enabled to
present, discuss and negotiate their account. Public choice presupposes public participation and mutual accountability.

Such an active citizenship requires the necessary conditions for
participation: extensive consultation, the use of surveys as well as
using the authority's outreach staff to listen to the views of the
public. Community polling could be another approach to encouraging public choice.

A constitutive condition, however, for any citizenship is to
provide arenas for active public participation. A model in the
recent past has been the creation of local youth councils which
have enabled young people to debate and make decisions about
youth policy and provision. Some schools have developed com-

munity councils which involve a broader representation in order to make the life of the school wherever possible serve the needs of the community as a whole as well as parents. Some colleges have sought to play an enabling role with community businesses by providing the community with skills and advice and resources to deploy as they choose. The role of the educator is to encourage community groups to take responsibility and ownership for their own learning enterprise.

An education service which seeks actively to involve citizens in its policy-making and become accountable to the community as a whole needs to constitute local community forums or councils. These would enable the several interests – including women's groups, the black and ethnic minorities, and the disabled – within a community to participate, articulate needs and contribute to decision-making. Where an authority has formed a pool of re-sources – perhaps from urban aid funds, EEC or local grants – to support community groups, decision-making about distribution could be delegated to these forums. In this way citizens within the community are being enfranchised to influence and take responsi-bility for their own learning environment. They can negotiate with the providers to use educational resources so as to meet the learning needs of the community as a whole: in access courses, 'women back to work' classes, health courses, community lan-guage and bilingual learning and so on.

The LEA, therefore, can have a major role to play in developing this partnership with an active public which is the fundamental condition for the quality of public education following the 1988 Act. The LEA can develop public choice and accountability by presenting information, evaluating performance and enabling pub-lic discussion about achievement and educational purpose. It requires, for many LEAs, a radical change in their attitudes to the public and a new commitment to involve citizens as partners. In conclusion, we have argued that the Education Reform Act espouses a view of learning quality premised upon extending public choice and accountability. Such objectives can be widely endorsed. But the legislation chooses a conception of the public as private consumers and a structure of divided government that is likely to frustrate the achievement of important aims. Yet if LEAs, governors and teachers can share the aspiration of serving and encouraging active citizenship then the conditions can be created for using the legislation to create a new vitality for learning in the community. Out of this can return a renewed confidence in the institutions of local government and democracy.

Notes and references

The authors would like to thank the editors for their helpful comments on the chapter.

1. Education Reform Act 1988 (London, HMSO, 1988).
2. *The Omega File on Education* (Adam Smith Institute, 1984); *Whose Schools? A Radical Manifesto* The Hillgate group (1986); S. Sexton, *Our Schools – A Radical Policy* (Institute of Economic Affairs, 1987).
3. Sexton, ibid.
4. Sexton, ibid.
5. Sexton, ibid.
6. The Hillgate Group, ibid.
7. The Hillgate Group, ibid.
8. The Secretary of State introducing the Reform Bill in Parliament on 20 November 1987.
9. DES, *Admission of Pupils to Maintained Schools: A Consultative Document*, London, July 1987.
10. DES, *Grant Maintained Schools: A Consultative Document*, London, July 1987.
11. Circular 10/88 Education Reform Act 1988: *Grant Maintained Schools*, DES, 14 October 1988.
12. S. Sexton, *Our Schools*.
13. H. Thomas, *Local Management of Schools*. Open University (forthcoming).
14. DES, *Financial Delegation to Schools: A Consultative Document*, London, July 1988.
15. Circular 7/88 Education Reform Act: Local Management of Schools, DES, 6 September 1988.
16. H. Thomas, 'Pupils as Vouchers', *Times Educational Supplement*, December 1988.
17. H. Thomas with G. Kirkpatrick and E. Nicholson, *Financial Delegation and the Local Management of Schools* (Cassell, 1989).
18. C. Humphrey and H. Thomas (forthcoming) 'An Appraisal of Change', in B. Caldwell and B. Cooper (eds), *Schools at the Center: An International Perspective on School-Site Management* (New York, JAL Press).
19. P. Downes, *Local Financial Management* (Oxford, Blackwell, 1988).
20. DES, *Financial Delegation to Schools: Consultation Paper* (London, DES, 1987).
21. House of Commons, 1988.

22. DES, *The National Curriculum 5–16. A consultation document* (London, DES, 1987).
23. Ibid.
24. Ibid.
25. B. Walton, 'The Impact of the Government's Educational Legislation upon Local Government', *Local Government Studies*, vol. 14, no. 1 (1988) pp. 83–92.
26. E. Bolton, Lecture on 'The National Curriculum' at the Centre for Education Management at the University of Birmingham, 26 February 1988. Extracts reported in *The Times Educational Supplement*, 4 March.
27. R. Murphy, 'Great Education Reform Bill Proposals for Testing – A Critique', *Local Government Studies*, vol. 14, no. 1 (1988) pp. 39–46.
28. DES, *National Curriculum Task Group on Assessment and Testing: A Report* (London, DES, 1988).
29. Ibid.
30. TES, 'What the Letter from No. 10 Said', *Times Educational Supplement*, 18 March 1988.
31. R. Morris, 'New Roles in a New Repertory', *Local Government Studies*, vol. 14, no. 1 (1988).
32. S. Ranson, 'From 1944 to 1988: Education, Citizenship and Democracy', *Local Government Studies*, vol. 14, no. 1 (1988).
33. E. Briault, 'A Distributed System of Educational Administration: An International Viewpoint', *International Review of Education*, vol. 22, no. 4 (1976).
34. S. Ranson, 'Contradictions in the Government of Educational Change', *Political Studies*, vol. 33, no. 1 (1985); and B. Salter and T. Tapper, *Education, Politics and the State* (London, Grant McIntyre, 1981).
35. DES, *Better Schools*, Cmnd 9469 (London, HMSO, 1985); and D. Hargreaves, *Improving Secondary Schools* (ILEA, 1984).
36. B. Tizard *et al.*, *Involving Parents in Nursery and Infant Schools* (London, Grant McIntyre, 1981).
37. The Thomas Coram Home-School reading scheme, Haringey Council, 1981; and P. Widlake and F. Macleod, *Parental involvement programmes and the language performance of children* The Community Education Development Centre, Coventry, 1984.
38. The Plowden Report, *Children and their Primary Schools* (London, HMSO, 1967); and P. Mortimore *et al.*, *School Matters: The Junior Years* (Open Books, 1988).
39. D. Hargreaves, *Improving Secondary Schools*.
40. J. Bazalgette, *School Life and Working Life* (London, Hutchinson, 1976).
41. DES, *Better Schools*.
42. S. Ranson, 'From 1944 to 1988'.

5   Local Government and the Housing Reforms

Kenneth M. Spencer

Introduction

Local government in Britain has played a very distinctive role in the provision of public or social housing. Such housing has been variously targeted on individuals and groups of the population regarded as being in need of decent, modern housing. Particularly since 1919 and the Addison Act, this local authority housing role has continued to multiply with new permissive powers being entrusted at regular and highly frequent intervals. Through to the 1980s there was general consensus that local authorities were the proper and most appropriate bodies to carry out this mammoth national task of reconstituting the housing scene by providing greater choice to poorer households. In the 1980s this consensus has broken, though it was being seriously challenged in the later 1970s because of escalating public investment costs. A great deal was achieved in terms of new building, slum clearance, housing renovation, the provision of suburban dwellings and the considerable improvement in the quality of the housing stock occupied by lower income households.

By 1961 there were 4.5 million local authority owned dwellings in the United Kingdom, a figure which rose rapidly to around 6.8 million by 1980. This period witnessed a growth of the proportion of all housing stock owned by local authorities in the United Kingdom from 26 per cent to 32 per cent. 'Only in this country do public authorities acquire the land, build the dwellings, receive the subsidies, allocate the completed accommodation and collect the rents. No other market economy has so much publicly owned housing.'[1] Perhaps public housing's very success proved its downfall when new political values oriented towards stronger market forces, tightened control over public spending, and reduction in the role of governmental interference were powerfully combined in the Conservative Governments of the 1980s.

By 1986 there has been a reduction to about 6 million local authority owned dwellings in the United Kingdom. The bulk of the reduction was a result of the 'right to buy' legislation of 1980 which offered discounts to sitting tenants wishing to buy their council home. At the same time the new construction of council housing decreased dramatically, so that very little new housing has been added to the council stock in the 1980s. From around 130 000 new council home completions in 1975 the number had fallen to 33 000 by 1985, since when a further decline to under 20 000 completions a year has occurred.

Local authorities often had problems in their housing role including paternalism towards tenants, discrimination in allocations, poor design and layout, and poor management systems. Many allocations (until the 1950s) were based not on absolute need but on prospective tenants' ability to afford the rent charges. It is also worth noting that until the 1980s housing duties as laid down by Parliament and placed upon local authorities were expressed in 'vague (and unenforceable) terms. There is certainly no duty upon a local authority to provide housing, though there is a long list of needs which it has a duty to consider.'[2] Thus local authorities had a great deal of discretion to act in meeting housing needs as perceived locally. Indeed it was possible to argue in 1978 that 'central government thus faces real difficulties when it attempts to ensure that the policies which it favours are carried out'.[3]

Certainly the Conservative Governments of the 1980s have addressed this issue directly and, as we shall subsequently see, have taken very real control of the local authority housing role, through much stronger, directive legislation and through greater control of individual local authorities' housing accounts. In a decade we have witnessed a complete reversal of the power relationship in the public housing service as between local government and central government. Power increasingly is held by the centre at the cost of erosion of local decision-making. The key impetus to this change has been the Government's dramatic measures to both constrain and contain public sector spending on council housing in Britain. During the ten year's since 1979 public spending on council housing in England has fallen by 80 per cent in real terms. Between the financial years, 1988–9 and 1989–90 there is a planned reduction in total housing expenditure of some 21 per cent to a figure of £1.71 billion. Of this housing expenditure an increasing proportion is being channelled through the Housing Corporation to housing associations. Indeed in 1989–90 housing association new homes construction exceeded, for the first time, those built by local authorities. In England government plans indicate that by 1991–2 only 6000 new council dwellings will be built compared with 24 000 by housing associations. It is clear that the Government sees housing associations as the main source of publicly subsidised housing and is directing finance accordingly.

A number of reports in the 1980s have been critical of the local authority housing service, perhaps the most significant being that of the Audit Commission in 1986.[4] However, the report did point out that public sector housing was significantly underfunded so that the problem was not simply one of the quality of management of the housing stock vested in local authorities. Indeed a recently published report sponsored by the Department of the Environment suggested that local authorities were no less efficient than housing associations, despite the latter's higher staffing ratios.[5] Through Priority Estates Projects and Estate Action schemes central government has been targeting resources to managing run-down council estates more appropriately. Perhaps its experience of these projects amongst other things has led it to conclude, fairly or unfairly, that local authorities have problems in managing their estates. We should bear in mind that such project schemes were often aimed at the most difficult estates to manage and that some local authorities had managed to considerably improve their own management of such estates, unaided by extra funding.

The rest of this chapter considers first the driving forces behind the Conservative Governments' housing reforms. It then outlines the totality of the reforms themselves and focuses upon tenants' choice, Housing Action Trusts, rent increases, housing revenue finance, and capital finance for housing and housing associations. This is followed by a discussion of the impact of these reforms on the role, organisation and operation of local government housing services.

Driving forces for change

Clearly the general political consensus about the role of council housing which lasted from the end of the First World War to the 1970s has ended. New values, policies and understanding are providing a major shift of direction, the most significant since the 1919 Act itself. Public housing is no longer viewed as a publicly subsidised commodity but rather as an asset, a trading service. New understanding dominates current governmental thinking on the future of social housing in Britain. There are a number of key driving forces behind the new housing reforms. These are described below.

Many of the driving forces of housing reform are reflected in other government policies affecting non housing issues. These forces permeate much of the thinking and legislation of the Conservative Government. Other forces are more specific to the perceived role of social housing in Britain. We will concentrate on some of these more specific housing issues after first commenting upon some of the wider Conservative philosophies which nevertheless have a clear impact upon the housing scene.

The 1980s has witnessed the development of an increasingly comprehensive new right ideology about competition and choice which is applied to public policy development. Much of the change in social housing runs in parallel with these wider philosophies, including an enhancement of the role of the free market. At the same time individual as opposed to collective choice is emphasised, thus new rights are designated with the aim of increasing the options open to some people. This emphasis on competition and choice also incorporates a growing consumer influence over bureaucracy. Such an alteration of the balance of power between consumers and bureaucracies is a means to strengthening consumer power in public agencies, thus pressing such bureaucracies to behave more in a market-led fashion.

There are also strong forces aimed at developing a more business-like organisation in the public sector. Here the purpose is to replace often inwardly looking bureaucratic and often paternalistic structures and professions. This business-like emphasis is also concerned, where possible, to substitute private capital and market risk for public subsidy. This means putting services on a more self-financing basis, which in turn is aimed at opening up competition and enabling new organisations to enter the market place of public services.

Another key driving force for reform has been central government's strong desire to keep local authorities in check and to tie the range of local authority options in housing policy much more closely to those determined by central government. Much legislation is therefore aimed at curbing independent local discretion which could detract from the achievement of the government's political aims. Thus national agendas dominate local ones to a greater degree than previously.

A prime concern of any government is that of sustaining electoral popularity. Much of the new right philosophy and its reform programme is aimed at targeting new beneficiaries in order to woo groups towards the new right. However many unpopular minority groups find their housing needs outside the broad concerns for electoral popularity.

Finally, central government has been pressing the role of local government as an 'enabler' rather than as a 'sole provider' of services. In part this is built upon models of local government as perceived in the United States of America. The pressures are increasing for local authorities to work with the private sector and with the voluntary or independent sector. It is, nonetheless, important to recognise that enabling and providing roles are not necessarily mutually exclusive.

Many of these pressures, or driving forces, lie behind much of the Conservative housing reform programme. There are issues which can be seen as rather more particular to the housing scene in Britain. Some of these are set out below.

The government clearly sees an ongoing dominance and enhancing of the status of owner-occupation in housing as a key goal of its philosophy of market-led forces. Thus in a property-owning democracy it is up to each individual to make decisions to resolve their own housing needs. As a result of this there has been the strong shift of council housing into owner-occupation through the 'right to buy' legislation of 1980 and subsequently. At the same time other policies associated with the encouragement of owner-

occupation have continued, of which the most important is mortgage tax relief.

Housing policy has also provided a key ground for the Conservative Government to launch a major offensive on key areas of
Labour support on the large council estates. Right to buy was a
first major inroad, which is supported by a right to repair which has
largely failed to achieve its goals. The new offensive is by the right
to select a new landlord if a tenant is dissatisfied with his or her
local authority landlord.

Another specific driving force has been the Conservative view
that council rents have been kept at too low a level to ensure both
proper repair, maintenance and a good housing management
service. Low rents have also kept out competition. Rents have
been kept low, so the government argues, by Labour Councils
because it is council tenants from whom they gain much electoral
support.

Urban municipal council housing in particular is regarded by the
new right as a remaining bastion of socialist policies and socialist
support in the cities. It is these very areas in which the Conservative Government seeks to expand its electoral strength. In some
cases this is attempted through the use of direct and specific
government grants to improve the quality of life on urban council
housing estates, for example, through the use of City Grants,
Estate Action Grants, Inner City Grants.

The future of housing policy generally and social housing in
particular thus provides a key and central challenge to the ideology
of the new right. Housing, therefore, represents a major element
of the Conservative Governments' reform programmes.

The Government's housing reform programme

The 1987 White Paper 'Housing: The Government's Proposals',[6]
establishes a new direction for the local authority housing service
to the end of the decade and into the early 1990s. It sets out the
Government's proposals for action, including a programme of
legislative reform. These proposals have been put into place
through the Housing Act of 1988 and the Local Government and
Housing Act 1989.

The White Paper sets out four key aims for the reform of

housing policy in England and Wales:

To reverse the decline of rented housing and improve its quality.
To give council tenants the right to transfer to other landlords if
they choose to do so.
To target money more accurately on the most acute problems.
To continue to encourage the growth of home ownership.

The Government sees its new policies leading to much greater
private sector investment in housing, the provision of wider choice
for the consumer and tenant and aiming resources at housing
problems in the inner cities and elsewhere. They are seen as vital
elements in the Government's wider programme of reform.

Associated with the four key aims of the reform of housing the
Government has adopted four strategies as a basis for its subsequent legislation. These are, first, to spread home ownership as
widely as possible by ensuring tax relief on mortgage interest,
pressing on with right to buy, ensuring adequate housing land
through the planning system and assisting owners with limited
means to keep their property in good condition. Second, it is
intended to revive other forms of renting by making the letting of
private property an economic proposition, and by helping housing
associations to restructure financially in order to utilise a higher
degree of private finance. At the same time measures are to be
taken to ensure that tenants on low incomes retain help with rents
through housing benefit. Third, the government wishes to change
the housing role of local authorities so that their role as landlord
and provider gradually diminishes as alternative forms of tenure
and tenant choice increase. This means giving tenants greater
rights and a say in their own future. 'Local authorities should
increasingly see themselves as enablers who ensure that everyone
in their area is adequately housed; but not necessarily by them.'[7]
Fourth, scarce public money will be used more effectively and a
new business-like management of the stock will be adopted by
local authorities through the development of a new financial
regime. Housing Action Trusts (HATs) will be introduced on
some of the most intractable of local authority housing estages.

The White Paper's proposals for action include nine main
points.

1. Change the financial system for housing associations so that there is greater reliance upon an injection of private funding. The aim of this is to lever private funding to schemes where some degree of public subsidy is necessary.
2. Change the system of financing for local authority housing in order to improve efficiency in revenue and capital budgets. At the same time central government will be given greater control over housing spending.
3. Introduce private lettings, outside the control of the Rent Acts. These include new shorthold lettings, where the tenant has no security beyond the tenancy period but can seek rent registration, and new assured tenancies, where rents are freely negotiated but the tenant has security of tenure. New lettings by housing associations and by local authorities will fall under the assured tenancy arrangements outside the existing Rent Act legislation, as will new lettings in the private sector.
4. Induce more private sector housing investment, especially for lower income groups which would have higher rent levels (assured tenancies) in order to provide an incentive. Investment opportunities were to be incorporated within the Business Enterprise Scheme,[8] if desired, in order to give investors tax relief at the higher rates.
5. Powers to establish Housing Action Trusts to take over run-down estates from local authority ownership. The purpose is to improve the estate and subsequently hand it over to various permutations of owner-occupiers, private landlords, housing associations and tenant co-operatives. Central government was to identify estates and take action by setting up a local HAT agency on each estate.
6. Give to council tenants the right to form tenant co-operatives to both own and manage their estates or flat block.
7. Provide council tenants with a choice of landlord by giving them a right, both individually and collectively, to transfer to a socially 'approved' landlord of the tenant's wish. Such landlords will be approved and monitored by the Housing Corporation in England and by Housing for Wales and Scottish Homes. The right is for each individual household in council houses to exercise, but for tenants in block of flats this right will be based on a majority decision with a series of sub-lettings for those now wanting the majority landlord. Certain dwellings are exempted:

i.e. those let in connection with employment, specially built or adapted for the disabled and handicapped; or particularly suitable for and used for, housing the elderly. If such dwellings are where a block transfer takes place they will be leased back to the existing landlord.

8. Abolish the subsidy from the General Rate Fund to the Housing Revenue Account. This stops local authorities from subsidising rents through rates. It will dramatically increase costs for many urban authorities where heavy subsidies have been made recently. It will also not be possible to subsidise the General Rate Fund from the Housing Revenue Account without the permission of the Secretary of State. This will stop the practice of a number of local authorities which have used surpluses on that account to subsidise future rate increases.

9. Revise the improvement grant and housing repair schemes in order to target resources where they are most needed by relating grants to household income. Renewal areas will replace the existing dual pattern of General Improvement Areas and Housing Action Areas.

The legislation to enact these changes and give impetus to the reformed housing programme was contained in the Housing Act of 1988, with the exception of points 2, 8, and 9 above which were dealt with in the Local Government and Housing Act of 1989. A number of the key changes are examined in more detail below.

Tenant's choice

The Government's legislation on tenants' choice is seen as extending the rights and choices given to council tenants since 1980. This includes the statutory Tenant's Charter and the 'right to buy' legislation in the Housing Act 1980, later extended in 1984 and 1986. All this is seen as exerting further pressure on council landlords to 'improve the quality and responsiveness of their housing management'.[9] Tenants' choice is clearly intended to complement the right to buy. 'The effect of this will be to open up the closed world of the local authority housing estates to competition and to the influence of the best housing management practices of other landlords'.[10] The purpose is to begin to break the virtual council monopoly of rented housing in some areas.

New independent landlords who have obtained prior approval as appropriate social landlords under the conditions laid down by the Housing Corporation, may bid to take over council housing stock if a vote of the existing tenants so decides.

In maisonettes or blocks of flats tenants' choice is exercised collectively. In the case of houses this can be done collectively by estates, or in groups, but the right also applies to individual households. No council tenant will have to change landlords under tenants' choice unless they choose to do so. The Government also argues that the spur of competition provided by this new right should promote better services and better value for tenants, even where they do not exercise their new rights.

Indeed there is ample evidence that local authority housing management is undergoing fundamental reappraisal and review, partly because it has been recognised as long overdue but also partly because of tenants' choice. As has been pointed out by the Association of District Councils, 'Housing authorities have every reason to give a good account of themselves and there have been encouraging signs over the past year of tenants' desire to stick with their council landlords. This has increased the morale of these providing the service and has confirmed that local authorities have a unique advantage as they are publicly accountable.'[11] This statement accompanied the publication of a guide to housing authorities urging them to examine their policies, alter them where necessary, and go out to fight and win in the tenants' choice stakes.[12]

Some councils, however, have attempted voluntary transfers of their housing stock using voting procedures which parallel those in the 1988 Housing Act. Basically the voting system is that if a majority of tenants eligible to vote, vote 'no', then the application for transfer to another landlord fails. This is clearly not a matter of a simple majority, in that an abstention counts, in effect, as a 'yes' vote to the transfer. At least 50 per cent of all voters have to vote 'no' in order to stop a transfer.[13] Despite this somewhat strange voting system (or because of its unpopularity) votes in Salisbury and Rochford were clear votes against transferring to a housing association. In Torbay, after a confused vote, with 787 tenants voting in favour of transfer, 2210 opposed to transfer and 2209 abstentions, the council was able to declare 58 per cent in favour of transfer (abstentions counting as 'yes' votes). The Secretary of State referred this back for a postal ballot, but the council then decided not to proceed. In Chiltern and Sevenoaks strong votes in favour of opting out to newly formed housing associations were recorded. In both cases it was the existing local authority housing staff who created the new housing association and who would work for it. Thus in these cases an alternative landlord has the same staff but a different legal status independant of the district council.

Many tenants are clearly wary of potential new landlords. With the uncertainties involved, moves to opt out may proceed relatively slowly, at least initially. However, much will depend upon how far local authority housing departments develop a new tenant-oriented system of housing management. The result is likely to be a very varied pattern (as we have already seen). The onus is clearly upon local authorities to improve their services and their management performance. Those least able to do so are likely to lose higher proportions of their tenants to other landlords.

A tenants' choice scenario of 2 per cent per year opting out would equal the rate of right to buy sales each year. Nationally, on this scenario the 6 million council dwellings of the United Kingdom in 1986 could reduce to about 4.3 million dwellings remaining in council ownership by about 1995 (a loss of 28 per cent of the stock). The Audit Commission envisage a scenario of higher sales and higher levels of opting out so that only 50 per cent of the stock in 1986 would remain by about 1993.[14] It is too early at this stage to have a clear indication of the likely proportion of tenants who will use their right to opt for another landlord.

Housing Action Trusts

As with tenants' choice HATs legislation was enacted in the Housing Act of 1988. The proposals were clear.[15] New agencies would be set up by central government to take over and improve the fortunes of run-down estates by a combination of private investment and public subsidy. The HAT would be a single purpose appointed body with significant power and would dispose of the stock on completion of its work, after only a few years, as the agency felt fit, to a combination of owners/landlords.

Following the legislation twenty designated HATs estates were declared throughout England. However the government clearly did not expect the strong backlash it received from the tenants of designated areas. Those in Sunderland, Lambeth and Sandwell have been particularly vociferous against what they see as the imposition of a HAT. Tenants were not consulted about the proposals (the legislation did not include consultation mechanisms or voting systems). Many HAT designated areas have held their own ballots which have rejected designation as HATs. To some extent this has been politically motivated yet nonetheless the government's proposals on HATs appear to be running out of steam, probably because they were ill thought through in terms of consultation, tenants' choice links, and a lack of clarity about what happened to the housing stock of the estate once the HAT was wound up. Many people clearly felt this could be used as a mechanism to turn them from their homes and allow private developers to take over and sell property. This may or may not have been the intention of HATs. The results clearly indicate that local residents and tenants can stop HAT schemes going ahead, though they may lose out on investment in improvements to the stock and to the environment as a result. Because of the confusion and public pressure HAT residents have now been given a right to consultation and a right to vote.

Clearly HATs have been put on the back-burner for a while. Though through a growing emphasis on Estate Action schemes undertaken in consultation with local housing authorities, work on improving some run-down estates does continue and does attract extra central government funding. Thus far the reform to introduce HATs must be regarded as a failure. Tenants in the HATs designated estates to date have firmly decided to remain with the local housing authority.

On 16 March 1989 the Government dropped half of the designated HAT schemes. Plans are in progress for nine areas to proceed. There are several reasons for this. First the Government set aside £180 million for the programme over the first two years, but consultants' reports on the designated estates indicate that costs would be much higher. Clearly the Government had failed to recognise the magnitude of the problems its HAT programmes would have to deal with. Tenants whose houses are proposed for transfer to a HAT will be given the opportunity to vote on the transfers. Tenants whose homes are intended for transfer are in Sunderland (4 estates), Lambeth (2 estates), Southwark (2 estates), Leeds (1 estate), while a further study is being carried out of an estate in Sandwell.

Rent increases

The introduction of assured tenancies for new lettings of rented accommodation apply to new council lettings as well as to housing associations and private landlords. Clearly the pressure is to push rents higher. Rents are discussed in terms of 'affordable rents' which are not precisely defined. However, the general view is that rents will double or more in real terms as a result of various measures in the Government's housing reform programme. The pressures for higher rents come from several sources in addition to the shift to assured tenancies. These are the need to finance the housing service adequately and especially to improve local repair and maintenance standards, the pressure to differentiate local authority rents and make popular homes dearer, the pressure to move towards market rents, the introduction of the new housing revenue financial regime (see later) and the need to increase council house rents so that competition can be placed on a 'fair footing'.

The results of all this will be larger proportions of tenants deciding to buy, most continuing tenants paying some extra rental, new tenants paying higher assured rents, possibly higher levels of rent arrears amongst some low income band groups, and ceilings introduced on eligible rental costs for housing benefit payments. Housing benefit payments themselves will rise, though central government intends local authorities to increasingly take up the costs of these extra benefits through surpluses on Housing Revenue Accounts. These measures are likely to detract from the Government's declared aim of enabling a higher degree of national population mobility.[16] The result is likely to be that council tenants will stay put, as mobility would lead them into the higher assured tenancy rent levels.

Housing revenue finance

The 1989 Act Part VI also provides for more stringent controls by central government over the statutory Housing Revenue Account (HRA) of housing authorities. The Government's considerations are set out in its consultation paper 'New Financial Regime for Local Authority Housing in England and Wales' 1988,[17] and in an explanatory note later attached to the consultation paper. The key reasons for change are basically twofold: first, to regain control by central government over the behaviour of local housing authorities (made more difficult as many were outside the scope of housing subsidy under the 1985 Housing Act); and, second, to find a new source to finance housing benefit. The legislation will bring *all* housing local authorities back into central government subsidy and hence *control*. It will also, over time, transfer some of the financing of housing benefits from the Government to local authority rent payers.

This housing revenue reform is operative from 1 April 1990, but a transition period over three years is introduced in order to minimise the sharp impact of an approximate doubling or more of rents. The Housing Revenue Account (HRA) becomes an independent trading account through a system of ringfencing. This means that Rate Fund contributions will be allowed to be paid into the HRA after 1990, nor will the HRA be able to transfer surplus to the General Rate Fund unless specified by the Secretary of State. A new HRA subsidy will be payable to local housing authorities. This will replace subsidy payable under the Housing Act 1985, and that part of rent rebate subsidy payable to them under the Social Security Act 1985 (which relates to rent rebates required to be granted to tenants of HRA dwellings). The decisions on subsidy levels will be based on a government formula, which can be varied by the Secretary of State for the Environment, and which will include regional rent levels, efficiency and effectiveness measures, e.g. levels of rent arrears, percentage of empty property. Thus the more inefficient housing authorities will be more heavily penalised through loss of subsidy – which in turn will push up rents even more. There will be additional subsidy payments as incentives for good housing management which will be assessed by the use of relevant, though as yet unspecified, performance measures.

The legislation will push rents to reflect property values more closely and, it is acknowledged, in the longer term to achieve market rents for council housing. This erodes the basis of council house financing since 1919. Again this is likely to lead to yet more pressure on tenants to buy their council home. The consultation paper stated that no working balances on existing HRAs could be carried forward to the new 1990 account, but this has been changed so that some working balance can be carried forward.

Clearly the pressure is to increase council rents, to develop the HRA as an essentially trading account, and to take tighter control of local authority financial decisions about their housing. At the same time it will be an incentive for improved management performance by the local authority housing department, and ultimately by the local authority as a whole, because other local authority departmental charges to the HRA are likely to be increasingly challenged by those responsible for the local authority housing service.

It is also intended that over time surpluses on the HRAs are to be used to offset the increased levels of housing benefits to match rising rents. Thus better-off tenants will ultimately contribute towards the rebates of poorer tenants.

The housing revenue reforms are likely to have the greatest impact on local authority housing services of any element of the Government's housing reform programme. It has led the Institute of Housing[18] in its response to the consultation papers on capital and revenue financing for housing to state that the government has to be clearer about what is meant by 'affordable rents', and that the adequacy of the housing benefit scheme, take-up and the poverty trap need to be addressed before a policy of increasing rents on the scale envisaged could be acceptable. The Institute argues that housing subsidy in 1990 should take into account the costs a local authority needs to incur to manage and maintain its stock properly. The Institute called upon the Government to withdraw its housing revenue proposals, hold discussions with others and seek a system to both resolve present anomalies and to redistribute limited resources to areas of growing housing need.

In relation to the new housing capital control system the Institute, whilst welcoming some features, felt that unless it was changed this would result in three things. First, it would lead to a reduced local authority ability to meet housing need. Second, the new system would offer little improvement over the existing system in relation to the need for long-term planning. Third, it would place considerable pressure on local authorities' ability to provide affordable accommodation. However, as we have already seen, the emphasis on enabling rather than providing suggests some of these comments are unlikely to be influential with the Government.

The Association of Metropolitan Authorities[19] in their response to the housing revenue consultation paper stress that its implications and that of the legislation (which lacks much relevant detail) will have a more drastic effect on local authority housing services and public sector rent levels than any other recent legislation. The Association argues that rents are likely to progress to private market rent levels and are likely to be higher than equivalent mortgage repayments required under 'right to buy' provisions. Thus the 1989 Local Government and Housing Act will boost the drift towards greater home ownership on the part of existing council tenants. The general level of 2 per cent council homes sales per year could increase as a result of the legislation. On the other hand the escalating home price inflation of 1987–8, which has created problems for many first-time buyers, could produce a strong pressure on the need to ensure a much enhanced programme of rented dwellings than the government's proposals of 1987 suggest.

Capital finance for housing

In the Local Government and Housing Act 1989 Part IV, central government adopted powers to reform the local authority capital control system. This is against a background of decreasing capital expenditure by local authorities on housing provision – given their new enabling rather than providing role, and given the Government's own emphasis on enhancing the role of the Housing Corporation (including Housing for Wales, which took over from the Housing Corporation in Wales in 1989, and Scottish Homes in the case of Scotland).

The Government aims to create new mechanisms for dealing with high levels of local authority capital receipts (e.g. about £3 billion from council house sales alone expected in 1989–90) and to close legal loopholes. The new system switches to control over borrowing rather than over spending. The two prime aims are, first, to control conventional borrowing and creative accounting and, second, to reduce local authority debt. The new capital finance regime begins on 1 April 1990. Annual credit approvals for borrowing will be notified to each local authority (by service areas of expenditure for England but not for Wales). The Housing Investment Programme (HIP) system is thus abandoned to be replaced by basic credit approvals and special credit approvals for housing capital expenditure. There is a three-year rolling programme of credit approvals – allowing a degree of forward planning. As for capital receipts, the local authority under the existing system can spend 20 per cent a year, with 80 per cent rolled over so that the receipt fund and the value of a 20 per cent proportion increases in size on the basis of sums unspent. After 1990 25 per cent will be spent in the year the receipts are accumulated, but there will be no spillover allowed between different financial years (i.e. the 25 per cent could well be worth less than the 20 per cent in the pre-1990 system). The other 75 per cent of capital receipts from housing must be spent on redeeming debt. This means that after 1990 the carry forward of the 80 per cent unspent capital receipts for re-use in subsequent years – known as the cascade effect – will cease.

Debt payment will be brought forward by increasing the burden of debt charges in the early years through the new 1990 system of payment by equal annual instalments of principal (EIP). Under this system a higher proportion of the principal borrowed has to be paid back earlier: thus reducing resource flexibility by lessening the amount of housing debt which can be pushed further into the future for repayment. The existing HIP financial tolerance level of a 10 per cent transfer between financial years will be abandoned in 1990 and credit approvals will only be applicable to the current years. The legislation also gives greater central government control over the practice of revenue funding of housing capital works. Basically all this tightens significantly central government's controls over local authority capital spending. An immediate impact of these changes is for local authorities to rush into spending their maximum capital receipts allowances before 1990.

Housing associations

The reform programme gives enhanced status to the housing association movement. Such associations owned around 5 per cent of the housing stock in 1989. The Government sees them as the new main engine of publicly subsidised housing in Britain, and argues that by applying pressure on them to seek and obtain private sector funding, the available public money will extend even further in terms of the production of new housing units. The purpose of such mixed funding is to produce homes at the elusive 'affordable rent'. The average grant for mixed funding schemes nationally rose from 60 per cent in 1988–9 to 75 per cent in 1989–90, though regional allocations vary around the national average.

Government's proposed gross expenditure plans for housing associations in England and Wales demonstrate this commitment with a rise from spending of £580 million in 1986–7, to £815 million by 1989–90, and £1328 million by 1991–2. The Housing Corporation grows in power and influence as a result of this and its approval and monitoring role of new social landlords. Directives from the Housing Corporation have, amongst other things, suggested that associations operating in relatively expensive areas need to consider whether they could achieve the same objective in surrounding districts at lower cost. It has identified particular Ministerial priorities in 1988–9 as the relief of homelessness and rural housing. Finally it has argued that Regional Directors will need to protect the more vulnerable elements of the development programme, including small, new, ethnic minority and co-operative housing associations expecting to undertake special needs schemes and rehabilitation in the inner cities.

Housing associations generally recognise the need to retain good working relationships with local authorities, especially in relation to land and planning permissions. It is clear that many housing associations are not keen to push to take over large areas of council housing stock unless asked to do so by the local authority and tenants. Other associations, especially national ones, and new social landlords are awaiting the opportunities presented to them by tenants' choice. However, the pressures on rents remain the same as those within the local authority, as assured tenancies begin to operate for new housing association tenancy agreements. People will be living in very similar dwellings but would be paying a vastly different rents. This is because new tenants would be paying assured rents, whereas existing tenants would continue to pay their rents under the previous system of fair rent registration. Fair rents are significantly less than assured rents.

Impact on the role, organisation and operation of local government housing services

Very clearly the local authority housing service of the future will undergo marked change. Significant amongst those changes is undoubtedly the shift in the balance of choice about council housing to tenants, to the consumers of services. 'Consumers are going to take over. The service will have to be entirely consumer oriented. Housing will no longer be looked at as a welfare service, but as a business with welfare overtones.'[20] This should lead to improvements in the quality of housing management services by local authorities, and the signs are already there that many local authorities are reappraising their performance and seriously questioning past practices of paternalism and token participation. However, as with many aspects of consumerism there will be enhanced choice for many, but the trends outlined will also significantly diminish the choice of a proportion of people, especially those on the lowest of incomes and many of those in considerable housing need.

Ultimately the local housing authority could be reduced to the role, in terms of council housing provision, of a residuary welfare housing agency. It could be left to cope with the most difficult problems that other providers fail to resolve, e.g. the statutory duty to rehouse homeless families, letting to tenants evicted by other landlords. As the total stock decreases access to relets will increasingly be limited to homeless families. Many local authorities are already finding that their lettings are dominated by those who are homeless.

Council housing will increasingly be an aged shock 'more likely to be found in unfavourable locations with an increasing proportion of stock which is unsatisfactory and which increasingly will come to be used to house people of the lowest income groups.

Local authority housing in such a scenario is in danger of being transformed to a ghetto concept of housing which would lead to worsening social situations in such areas.'[21] Much will depend upon the extent to which assets from future sales and from higher rental incomes will be utilised to improve the quality of the existing stock. The housing finance legislation does not augur well in this direction with its emphasis on debt redemption.

There has already been a significant impact upon housing management and upon the urgency for improvement. The professional style is changing as are relations with tenants. Departmental structures continue to emphasise small-scale organisation through decentralisation of the service, including neighbourhood and estate based offices. Increasing pressures will emerge for greater local financial autonomy and control over repair and maintenance systems. Compulsory competitive tendering is already leading to client/contractor organisational realignments and to ensuring greater efficiency is demanded of central service departments of local authorities. Housing departments are likely to want firm service agreements with other departments (see Chapter 9).

In some cases, though probably in only a few by the early 1990s, local authority housing departments will be merged with existing housing associations, or will form and register their own associations. This is more likely to be the case in those districts with a relatively small housing stock.

The role of local authority housing departments will also shift, to one encouraging and enabling other providers to ensure adequate housing provision in a range of tenures and prices to match local needs. Its ability to supply new accommodation itself will be vastly reduced. The enabling role can only flow from an adequate appraisal of local housing needs and strategic thinking to anticipate future demands and needs.

Precise changes are difficult to predict. Housing markets are localised. National legislation and pressures will inevitably have impact in a differential way between localities. It has also been argued that the new legislation 'may lead to worse conditions for many black and ethnic minority people as well as to more direct and indirect discrimination against them in private and public housing.'[22]

Whether the Government will achieve its housing aims through this reform programme remains open to question. Most likely there will be a gradual rather than a revolutionary rate of change. Tenants are not likely to exercise the right to choose a new landlord on a significant scale if many of the opinion polls are correct. The outcome over the next five years or so depends on several factors. These include, first, the extent and speed with which new financial resources from the private sector will be drawn into the provision of housing for low income groups. Despite assured rents the past track record here does not suggest massive private investment waiting to come in. Second, the future pace of council house sales will be important to the local housing authority as it will reduce its capacity to cope with all but the most acute housing need cases, i.e. homelessness. The third factor is the rate at which tenants decide to opt for other landlords, which in turn will be related to the speed with which local authorities can deliver better services and keep rents within competitive levels, *vis-à-vis* rents of other social landlords. Fourth, the future pattern of house prices will have an effect, especially those towards the bottom end of the market for first-time buyers. A fifth factor will be the degree to which housing issues become of greater significance on the national agenda of political concern.

Obviously there is a degree of interplay between the various factors outlined. The future pattern of house prices in relation to income patterns, particularly as it affects first-time buyers, will provide a margin within which it will, or will not, be profitable for the private sector to provide assured tenancy rental units. Similarly construction costs and land prices, together with rates of return on capital from other competing investments, will accelerate or brake the private sector role in investment for low income housing. If private sector investment is not forthcoming then greater social housing through housing associations and local authorities will be needed. While if there is a breakdown of housing provision for certain groups of the population – e.g. new first-time buyers, the homeless, young people seeking hostel accommodation – then it is more likely that housing issues will once again rise within the political agenda creating wider debate about the future of social housing in Britain. Local authority tenants can keep open their right to opt for another landlord, thus there will be constant pressure to improve housing services for council tenants. Much will depend upon the degree of responsiveness by local authority housing staff and others.

Finally it is evident that much of the existing council housing stock will remain with local housing authorities well into the later 1990s. The local housing authority will thus retain a significant role where it is capable of developing its services to match new expectations and new demands. Much will depend on enhancing the management ingenuity and capacity of both local politicians and housing service professionals. Central government has challenged local housing authorities. Many have the capacity to respond effectively to that challenge and to steer themselves through the new complex legislation in the best interests of the housing needs of their local communities. Inevitably this will lead to greater diversification of organisational structures and modes of operation between local housing authorities. Perhaps that is a good sign for the future well-being of a responsive local housing authority and for local government more generally.

Notes and references

1. D. Donnison and C. Ungerson, *Housing Policy* (Harmondsworth, Penguin Books, 1982) p. 63.
2. J. B. Cullingworth, *Essays on Housing Policy: The British Scene* (London, Allen & Unwin, 1979) p. 8.
3. Ibid, p. 14.
4. Audit Commission, *Managing the Crisis in Council Housing* (London, HMSO, 1986).
5. Department of the Environment, D. MacLellan *et al*, *The Nature and Effectiveness of Housing Management in England* (London, HMSO, 1989).
6. H.M. Government, White Paper, *Housing: The Government's Proposals* (London, HMSO, 1987).
7. Ibid, para. 1.16.
8. D. Coleman, 'The New Housing Policy – A Critique', *Housing Studies*, vol. 4, no. 1 (1989) pp. 44–57.
9. Department of the Environment, *Tenants' Choice, the Government's Proposals for Legislation*, a consultation paper (London, DoE, 1987) para. 3.
10. Ibid, para. 5.
11. Association of District Councils, *ADC News*, 15 November 1988 (London, ADC).
12. Association of District Councils, *The Challenge of Tenants' Choice* (London, ADC, 1988).
13. C. Game, 'What's a Majority', *Public Service and Local Government*, January 1989, p. 38.

14. H. J. Davies, 'Local Government Under Seige', *Public Administration*, vol. 66, no. 1 (1988) pp. 91–101.
15. Department of the Environment, *Housing Action Trusts*, a consultation paper (London, DoE, 1987).
16. J. Salt, 'Labour Migration and Housing in the U.K.: An Overview', in C. Hamnett and J. Alden (eds), *Labour Markets and Housing* (London, Hutchinson, 1989).
17. Department of the Environment/Welsh Office, *New Financial Regime for Local Authority Housing in England and Wales*, a consultation paper (London and Cardiff, DoE/WO, 1988).
18. Institute of Housing, *Response to DoE/WO Consultation Papers*, New Financial regime for local authority housing in England and Wales, and Capital expenditure and finance (London, IoH, 1988).
19. Association of Metropolitan Authorities, *A New Financial Regime for Local Authority Housing in England and Wales. The AMA Response* (London, AMA, 1988).
20. P. McGurk, *The Future of Social Housing in the United Kingdom*, mimeo (London, Institute of Housing, 1987).
21. K. M. Spencer, 'The Role of Local Government in Low Income Housing Policy and Administration', paper to Anglo-German Foundation Conference on Housing for low income groups in Britain and West Germany: needs, provision and public support in the 1980s, Benn, Federal Republic of Germany, January 25–27, 1989.
22. Greater London Action Group for Race Equality, *Race Equality and the Housing Act* (London, GLARE, 1988).

6 Strengthening Local Democracy? The Government's Response to Widdicombe

Steve Leach

Introduction

The Government's proposed package of measures to 'maintain the proper working of local authorities in the years ahead'[1] is in one important sense quite untypical of the other legislative measures discussed in this book. It is untypical in that it is based on a considered response to a Committee of Inquiry (The Widdicombe Committee) which had been set up specifically to provide a basis of information, analysis and prescription in relation to the issue under consideration: the conduct of local authority business in the mid-1980s and, in particular, the changing role of local politics in this process.

The setting-up of an inquiry into the 'politicisation of local government' was first signalled at the 1984 Conservative Party Conference. This was in the face of a large number of resolutions expressing concern about the 'abuses' of political power which were (allegedly) increasingly taking place in (Labour-controlled) councils. The Widdicombe Committee reported in June 1986, its substantial (314 pages) volume of analysis and recommendations[2] being supplemented by four published volumes of research.[3] There followed a period of eighteen months when nothing was heard of the report beyond a cryptic commitment to 'implement

Widdicombe' in the Conservative Party's 1987 election manifest. Then in July 1988, over two years after the publication of the Widdicombe Report, a White Paper[4] outlining the Government's response was published. The proposals outlined in the White Paper formed (with a few important modifications) the basis of the legislative measures set out in Part I of the Local Government and Housing Act (1989).

In the process described above, there are two questions of particular interest to those seeking to understand the way in which the present Conservative Government (and its predecessor) have reached decisions on the introduction of major changes affecting local government. The first is why the 1983–7 Government went through the formalities of setting up a Committee of Inquiry in the first place, when they had not considered this to be necessary in relation to previous legislation of at least equivalent status constitutionally (e.g. the abolition of the GLC and the MCCs). The most likely explanation is that, given the weight of concern about 'political abuses' expressed at the 1984 Party Conference, the Conservative Government felt obliged to make some response, but because it had not thought through its position in any kind of detail, nor did it have at that stage the necessary knowledge on which to legislate (especially in relation to details of how widespread the so-called abuses were, and to what extent they involved *Conservative* as well as Labour-controlled councils), the 'departmental committee of inquiry' solution had attractions that it lacked in other situations where the Government's confidence about the nature of the problem and the required solutions were stronger. The requirement that the Committee of Inquiry should produce an *interim* report within a relatively short time-scale, on the highest-profile 'abuse' – 'political propaganda on the rates' – signalled to the party faithful that the Government meant business. The remaining issues could be viewed as less urgent.

The second question of interest is why there was such a long time-lag between the publication of the Committee's report, and the Government's response. The two-year hiatus demonstrates a period of reflection and preparation not always associated with the legislation of recent Conservative Governments!

It has to be recognised, in this connection, that the findings, recommendations and tone of the Widdicombe Report as a whole, including its sturdy defence of local government as an essential element in our democratic apparatus, were unlikely to have represented what the Government expected or hoped for. Nor was it likely that a recently appointed Secretary of State (Nicholas Ridley), faced with a long and detailed report which he had not personally commissioned, would want to make action on the basis of its recommendations a high priority, particularly when several of its messages seemed out of line with the prevailing Conservative view of local government. Hence there followed, it can be argued, the low-profile launch of the document, the period of consultation, and the subsequent long period of silence. The process that appears to have taken place during this last period is one in which the Widdicombe proposals have been selectively accepted, modified or rejected in line with increasingly explicit Government vision of the appropriate role of local government in a modern democracy.

The background to the Government's proposals

The Government's 'Response to the Report of the Widdicombe Committee of Inquiry' (Cm 433) is a substantial document, in terms both of its length (55 pages) and its content. In general, it upholds the standards of cogency and rational argument typically associated with White Papers (standards not always maintained by the Thatcher governments, as in the case, for example, of 'Streamlining the Cities'). The introduction to the White Paper includes an explicit and welcome commitment to the continued importance of local government in our political culture.

Local government has a very important role in the democratic life of this country. Local authorities provide or promote a wide range of public services that are best administered locally, under democratic control. They are able to so in a way that is responsive to local needs.

The reforms proposed are, it is argued, designed 'to ensure that local democracy and local accountability are substantially strengthened'.[5] The White Paper outlines a set of 'basic principles' which are subsequently used to provide a rationale for the Government's proposals. These principles are, first (and most

important), that local authorities should be clearly accountable to
their electors; second, that those who take decisions on behalf of
the council must reflect the decisions of the electorate; third, that
every councillor should be able to play a proper part in the
council's work; fourth, that those concerned in local authority
decisions should be free from any taint of suspicion that they are
favouring personal interests; fifth, that councils should be served
by an efficient, expert, politically impartial service, responsible to
the council as a whole; and sixth, that there should be effective
arrangements to ensure proper standards, and effective means of
redress for members of the public against 'unfair' council decisions.

Apart from the fifth principle which sidesteps a number of
genuine differences of view about the feasibility or desirability of
'political impartial' officers, it is hard to disagree with these
principles. Indeed many of them have an 'of course' flavour about
them. What is interesting is the way they are manipulated to
support the Government's proposals for reform.

In this chapter, emphasis is placed on those proposals which
impinge most directly on the political organisation and management of local authorities. Five areas of interest in the White Paper
are highlighted: the characteristics and composition of committees; the scope of co-option; the role of councillors; the political
activity of officers; and the division of internal management
responsibilities. In each case, although the main focus of attention
is the content of the White Paper, any differences between the
White Paper and the related measures in the 1989 Local Government and Housing Act are highlighted. An analysis of the underlying nature of the changes involved and their likely collective
impact is provided in the final section.

The characteristics and composition of committees

The Widdicombe Report draws an important distinction between
decision-taking committees and *deliberative* committees. The former term covers those committees or sub-committees which have
delegated powers to take decisions. The latter term covers committees (or sub-committees) which have no delegated powers to
take decisions in their own right. The Report recommended that

the principle of pro-rata membership as 'party balance' (in relation to the relative strengths of the different parties on the council) should be applied to the composition of decision-taking committees and that the openness of such meetings to the press and public under the terms of the 1985 (Access to Information) Act was entirely appropriate.[6] However, in the case of deliberative committees, Widdicombe's view was that the principles of party balance, openness of meetings to press and public, and the rights of all councillors and press and public to inspect documents need *not* apply.

The White Paper, however, specially rejects this recommendation. Whilst acknowledging that it is 'reasonable for leading members of a party group to meet from time to time to discuss policy co-ordination on sensitive issues'[7] – a form of words which implies a much more limited and infrequent concept of 'deliberation' than that which operates in most political authorities – it does not agree that such groups need to be given the special status of deliberative committees. An alternative, the White Paper proposes that such meetings should retain an informal status, with the provision of officer advice where appropriate, being secured through appropriate amendments to officers' terms and conditions of service (and/or published conventions), in respect of attendance of party group meetings. In other words the role currently played by deliberative committees will be replaced by extending the role of party group meetings to encompass the kind of informal and private member–officer discussions which had previously typically taken place in 'deliberative committees' of one kind or another.

This proposal conspicuously fails to appreciate the quite different climate and purpose of party group meetings and deliberative committees. Party group meetings are widely viewed by councillors as predominantly party political occasions. As the Widdicombe research showed, the attendance of officers at party groups is by no means as widespread as many would have forecast. In so far as chief officers *are* asked to attend party group meetings, it is usually to address the group on a specific item, to answer questions and then to depart, leaving the group to continue its private discussion. Any wider or more regular officer involvement in party group meetings was widely viewed by all political parties as 'inappropriate', given the purposes and traditions of party group meetings. Basically councillors do not want (with some specific or *ad hoc* exceptions) officers present on such occasions. To attempt to reconstitute deliberative committees as party group (or rather party sub-group) meetings is to misunderstand important features of local political culture. The facility which deliberative committees, at their best, provided was a basis for member/officer discussion on a more *equal* footing than would ever be possible in the setting of a group meeting. The 'what would happen if we did this' kind of discussion, the 'brainstorming session' and the interweaving of political purpose and professional knowledge and advice have all been facilitated by the use of deliberative forums. Such a format – unless there is more scope for informality and non-proportionality in the operation of working parties than seems apparent – will now become impossible.

What is likely to happen is that such deliberative 'working party' arrangements will be redefined as party group meetings, or more commonly party *sub*-group meetings, and will operate in much the same way as before. But it will be a 'redefinition of convenience', or necessity, which is incongruent with the traditions of party group operations within local authorities.

The second important element of the White Paper proposals on the composition of committees is the introduction of a principle of *pro rata* representation of political parties on all committees and sub-committees of a council. Given the scope for interpretation in relation to the principle of 'pro-rata' composition, the White Paper sets out four basic rules to secure the implementation of the principle. These rules are as follows:

Rule I: where a political group has a majority on the council, it is to have a majority on every committee; (this is to deal with the problem of narrow majorities on councils);
Rule II: if there is more than one political group on the council, then at least two political groups must have seats on every committee; (this is to ensure that at least one opposition group is guaranteed a seat on small committees);
Rule III: subject to rules I and II, the total number of seats for each political group on all the committees taken together should be, as nearly as possible, in proportion to the relative size of the group on the council: (this is to allow for minority parties not large enough to justify a seat on every committee);
Rule IV: subject to rules I, II and III, the number of seats for

each group on each committee should be, as nearly as possible, proportionate to the relative size of the group on the council (this is the basic rule).

It is clear that the government intend such principles to apply to *all* formally constituted council forums (including, it appears, non-decision-taking working parties) and to appointments of councillors to *outside* bodies (indeed, it is clearly the experience of the application of similar rules to the joint boards in the post-1986 metropolitan government system which forms the basis of the proposals). Area Committees whose areas contain less than 25 per cent of the authority's population will however be excepted and may consist of the local councillors *within* the identified area only. The intention is that the above principles should operate primarily as a 'fall-back' position, ultimately enforceable through the courts by way of judicial review, but not invokable if there were unanimous agreement with the arrangements actually made in a particular local authority.[8] Thus if a minority group wanted for some reason a less than pro-rata allocation of committee places, it would not be precluded from so doing.

The final provision of interest (co-option issues apart) relating to committee composition is the clear rejection of the Widdicombe Committee proposal that 'Chairman's Action' should be made lawful. The White Paper proposes instead the use of 'urgency committees' of say three members to deal with genuinely 'urgent' decisions of major significance, whilst 'less important' urgent decisions should (as is already the case in many councils) be delegated to officers.[9]

The scope of co-option

The Government's expressed concern in 1984 about the way in which some local councils were allegedly using their powers to co-opt non-council members on to committees to appoint some co-optees 'on the basis of sympathy with the majority party'[10] resulted in co-option being one of the key issues considered by Widdicombe. During the Widdicombe interview research, it became apparent that there was some substance for the Government's concern. The co-option of 'persons with experience in education' on to education committees was found to be increasingly influenced in both main parties by considerations of political support.

The Widdicombe Committee argued for an advisory role only for co-optees. Local authorities should, they recommended, continue to be permitted to invite such advisors to *attend* meetings of decision-taking committees, but advisors should *not* be allowed to vote. In terms of decision-responsibility and voting, decision-taking committees and sub-committees and sub-committees should consist *only* of councillors. More controversially, the Widdicombe Committee asked the Government to review the current statutory position of magistrates on police committees and church and teacher representatives on education committees, with a clear implication that practices in these committees should be brought in line with the above general principles.

These recommendations must have caused some difficulty for the Government. The principle of removing co-opters' voting rights on decision-taking committees and redefining them as 'advisors' would have certainly been welcomed as a sensible response to this area of potential abuse. The implied application of this principle to magistrates and church representatives would not! It was therefore a question of interest and speculation in the weeks before the White Paper's publication as to how the Government would deal with these apparently conflicting objectives.

The statement on page 2 of the White Paper of the principle that 'those who take decisions on behalf of the council must reflect the decisions of the electorate' clearly signalled the end of the voting powers of co-optees. Indeed the White Paper broadly accepted the diagnosis of the Widdicombe Committee and (up to a point) its recommendations. In general it argued that non-elected persons 'should not be appointed by the council as voting members of decision-taking committees and sub-committees'.[11]

The problem of the application of the principle to the role of magistrates on police committees is neatly side-stepped by the argument that magistrates are not really co-optees at all! 'The magistrate members are often referred to as co-opted, but this is a misuse of language . . . [they] are in effect *appointed* from outside the council . . . their presence reflects policy on the police service.'[12] Although this is probably correct in a narrow legal/ technical sense, there is likely to be a widespread view in local government circles that the underlying issues of the meaning of police accountability and the 'special status' of police committees *vis-à-vis* other council committees have been left unresolved and will continue to generate controversy.

In relation to the position of co-optees on education committees, the scope for arguing for 'exceptions' to the general principle is even more limited. The White Paper, whilst happy to redefine the role of teachers and other education professionals as advisory, and thus non-voting, is not prepared (following, one suspects, conflicts of view before the DoE and the DES) to reduce the influence of status of the church and voluntary school representatives in the same way. Thus 'the Government propose to make special provision to require councils to appoint representatives of those churches and any other organisations in the area who provide voluntary schools there, as members of education committees with full voting rights'.[13] In the Local Government and Housing Act it becomes clear that three such representatives are envisaged, and the authorities will also be required to appoint two teacher representatives as non-voting advisors. It is also made clear that in councils where one party has a *narrow* majority, the pro-rata Committee membership principles should be adjusted to ensure that the party has an overall majority on the education committee (i.e. the co-optees would not be allowed to hold the balance of power in such a situation).

The argument set out for making this one exception (police committees apart) to the general principle of discontinuing the practice of co-option with voting rights in local government is an ingenious one. The Government argue *that because the churches are substantially involved in the provision of education within the state systems*, their position is different from other Education Committee co-optees, and there is thereby a justification for continued voting status. The potential problem for the Government with this argument is the precedent that it sets for *other* areas of local government work. If 'substantial service providers' in education are to be located in this way, why not also in social services (e.g. a large voluntary organisation providing welfare services for the council) or in any other sphere of council activity?

The role of non-councillors on area or neighbourhood committees is left unresolved in the White Paper. On the one hand, the Government does not, it appears, 'wish to prevent non-councillors from taking part and having voting powers in what are essentially very local committees within council areas'.[14] At the time of writing it appears likely that the Government will permit co-optees with voting rights on neighbourhood-based committees, provided such committees cover less than 25 per cent of the authority's population.[15]

The role of councillors

The White Paper includes several provisions which will have a significant effect on the eligibility, time-availability and remuneration of councillors and the scope of their activities. In relation to the renumeration of councillors, the basic position adopted by the Government is that current membership should be based on the principle of voluntary public service to the community and that councillors should be neither worse off nor better off as a result of carrying out duties.[16] This position is out of line with the spirit of the Widdicombe analysis and recommendations on this topic in which it was acknowledged that the case for having full-time councillors (especially in large urban authorities) had become stronger and the numbers of such councillors who operated in this way had increased.

The White Paper does however take up the Widdicombe proposal that attendance allowance and financial loss allowances should be replaced by a basic flat rate allowance, payable to all councillors as an annual sum. But any expectation that this might imply realistic salaries for councillors is soon dispelled by the observation that 'the present (overall) level of allowances does not seem unreasonable'. Thus the Basic Flat Rate Allowance (BFRA) proposed is to be set at a level which involves *no increase* to the current overall level of expenditure on councillors' allowance. The status quo is, in this sense, to be maintained.

The replacement of the attendance allowance by the BFRA will, however, have some major effects. Any tendency for attendance allowances to 'encourage the proliferation of meeting'[17] will no longer operate. Indeed a whole set of choices involved in the attendance allowance systems – e.g. setting the level of the allowance (full or part) for different types or lengths of meeting, and the use (or otherwise) of such allowances for political meetings (such as those of a party group) – will no longer be necessary. The new system is certainly simpler. But is it fairer, or more congruent with the realities of local politics?

The attendance allowance system, for all its faults, certainly distinguished between the more active and the less active councillors. As the White Paper acknowledges, 'the main advantage of the current system is that it rewards the effort of those councillors who attent meetings'. The BFRA system will reward all councillors, in a given local authority, equally, irrespective of the level of activity involved (*and* in a given *type* of authority, irrespective of size). The Government's intention is that the level of BFRA should vary 'by type of local authority, but not by population'.[18] Details are currently being worked out with the local authority associations, but on the basis of the 'no overall-increase of expenditure' criterion, a figure, for a metropolitan district, of around £2000 would be implied, which is significantly less than the rate recommended by the Widdicombe Committee (£3000 at 1986 prices). The removal of the 'population banding within authority type' provision will also lead to some obvious anomalies, such as councillors in Teesdale (population 25 000) receiving the same BFRA as councillors in Bristol (population nearly 460 000).

To some extent, the continuation of Special Responsibility Allowance (SRA) will enable allowances for leading member to be 'topped up'. However, although the Government intends to 'review' the levels of SRA, the basic expenditure constraints under which the whole area of councillor remuneration will operate means that any significant increases on the current rates (authority maximum £25 000; individual councillor maximum £4570) look highly unlikely.

The overall impact of the introduction of the BFRA, therefore, means that the most a councillor '*qua* councillor' will be able to claim in the new system (expenses apart) will be around £7000, which is significantly less than is currently claimed by *some* councillors through attendance allowance and SRA. Most will not be able to claim more than £2500. Thus to be anything approaching a full-time councillor under the proposed new recommendation system will be markedly more difficult than it is now.

Nor is this proposed change the only provision which will affect in a fundamental way the time-availability of councillors. For those councillors who work for local authorities and who are not affected by the proposal regarding officers who are members of councils, commonly called 'twin-tracking' (see below), a new statutory upper limit of 26 days per year paid leave will be introduced (i.e. half a day per week) in respect of their responsibilities as councillors.[19] This proposal is in fact in line with a Widdicombe recommendation. Its effect will be to tighten up on the latitude allowed to *some* councillors by some employing authorities in relation to time off for council duties. This latitude enables a significant number of leading councillors – primarily but not wholly Labour councillors who work on other Labour-controlled authorities – to operate, if not as full-time councillors, certainly on the basis of considerably more than 26 days per year paid leave. Many authorities will be relatively unaffected by this provision, but in the metropolitan areas it will make up a significant impact. In one Northern authority, for example, the Leader, the Deputy Leader, and the Chair of the Finance Committee all work for neighbouring authorities, who have been up to now relatively generous in the provision of 'time off'. Under the new system their effective time-availability will be drastically reduced . . . unless, that is, they become mayor or chairmen of the council, in which case the statutory upper limit is waived!

Many thousands of existing and putative councillors will find their eligibility to stand directly affected by the proposals in the Act relating to twin-tracking. These proposals are discussed in detail in the next section. For now the point to make is that councillors who have what is judged as a politically sensitive post in another authority will have to choose between continuing to be a councillor and finding another job, or continuing in their current job and resigning as a councillor. Given the White Paper's position on councillor remuneration (see above) it would be a brave councillor who would put mortgage, family and career at risk by resigning his or her post, without the security of alternative employment of equivalent status.

There is a further twist in the tail of the White Paper's treatment of 'politically sensitive' posts, when it comes to consider councillor involvement in the appointment of staff. The increasing tendency for councillors to become involved in the 'management of a local authority, in a variety of different ways, was documented by the Widdicombe Report and the 'Political Organisation' research.[20] There was and is little concensus on the legitimacy of such involvement. Clearly one of the most explicit ways in which councillors can get involved in management issues is through staff selection processes. The Widdicombe research found that practices in this area varied considerably. In about 5 per cent of all authorities, councillors were formally responsible for the appointment of chief officers only; in about the same proportion of authorities they were responsible for *all* local authority employees.[21]

In the White Paper, a direct equivalence is drawn between the definition of 'politically sensitive' posts and the scope for councillors' involvement in staff appointments. Their powers in this field will cover chief officers and deputies *and* all the politically sensitive posts earmarked in the authority. Thus the more a council wishes to *extend* its scope for involvement in staff selection (through the creation of politically sensitive posts) the more it extends the number of members of staff who are barred from becoming (or remaining) councillors! In many authorities this dilemma will not necessarily cause significant problems. In the hothouse atmosphere of London borough government it is much more likely that it will.

There are many other provisions in the White Paper affecting the role of councillors. Their cumulative effect will be to constrain and formalise the role of councillors in majority party groups, whilst extending minority party rights. Thus the Government intends to take powers to enable a 'statutory core' of standing orders to be prescribed, if that should be judged desirable following discussions with the local authority associations. Amongst the topics which the Government consider should be included in such core standing orders are matters such as access to agendas for minority parties, and reference of matters from committee to full council by minority parties. Currently the content of standing orders is left to each local authority. The National Code of Local Government Conduct, which sets out standards of behaviour and conduct expected of councillors, is to be strengthened. There is to be a statutory register of councillors' pecuniary interests in each local authority. The scope of external Audit and the powers of the Ombudsman will be extended, significantly, but not spectacularly, in a variety of ways, although the extension of judicial review has been rejected. The net effect of these changes will be to circumscribe the way in which councils can operate and to formalise a number of practices which are currently left to the discretion of local councils. In fact the overall impact of the changes discussed in this section is likely to be to significantly reduce the motivation to stand (or continue) as a councillor.

The political activity of officers

The scope of the ban on twin-tracking has implications not only for councillor recruitment and involvement in staff selection but also of course for the activities of officers themselves. Indeed the White Paper's arguments on these matters are couched very much in terms of the problem caused by overt political activities of senior officers. Thus it is argued that 'senior officers who regularly advise members should be subject to restrictions on their public political activity'.[22] The nature of the restrictions is soon clarified. There is to be an application of the rules on political activity which apply to senior civil servants to the specified council posts. Thus in addition to the ban of such officers standing as councillors, political restrictions would also be enforced which would require them to 'abstain from holding office in a political party, speaking or writing publicly on matters of party political controversy (as opposed to matters that are of legitimate professional interest or concern) and canvassing at elections'.[23]

The scope of officer posts to be covered by such restrictions has clearly caused the Government some problems. The Widdicombe Committee recommended that *all* officers if principal officer grade and above should be prevented from standing (or continuing) as councillors. The position taken by the White Paper is that there is 'a strong case for regulating the activities of *some* officers outside the senior ranks (i.e. chief officer and deputy) who because of the particular nature of their work, should be seen as politically impartial'.[24] Officers falling into this category would be expected to include 'those whose duties involve, on a *regular* basis, offering advice to members, contact with the public, communicating with the media, as exercising a delegated discretion in the provision of services'.[25] Teachers (including heads) would be specifically excluded.

There will be real problems of interpretation of this 'politically sensitive' provision in the White Paper. Taken literally it could cover almost as many officers as would be covered by a 'principal officer' ban. In particular, the 'delegated discretion in the provision of services' clause will apply to increasing numbers of local authority staff, as the implications of compulsory competitive tendering begin to work their way through the organisation. Similarly 'contact with the public' will become a significant part of the work of many *junior* officers in the growing number of authorities which are committed to 'getting closer to the customer'! Thus the principle of 'political sensitivity' involves a minefield of definition and interpretation.

On this topic, however, there is a significant difference between the White Paper's proposals and the contents of the Act. Contrary to the White Paper proposal, the Act contains a clause which bans all council employees earning above a specified salary level (£13 500) from political activity (*including* the right to stand as a councillor). There will be an appeals procedure which will allow people to seek exemption from the ban, on the grounds that their job is *not* politically sensitive. An outside arbiter (probably a former local authority chief executive) is appointed to decide such cases. But the important point to stress is that the ban on political activity will apply to all posts at a salary level of £13 500 and above *unless* the occupant successfully applies for exemption. The reasons for this extension of the ban have not been made clear in subsequent ministerial statements.

A second Government proposal on political activity amongst officers has been equally vulnerable to change. The Widdicombe Committee, recognising the value of 'political advisors' in local authorities, and drawing on parallels with practices in central government to justify them, argued that local authorities should, subject to certain safeguards, be able, if they wish, to attach a limited number of officers to the party groups, or their leaders.[26] The White Paper explicitly rejects this recommendation, arguing that 'it is inappropriate for local authorities to employ at public expense staff whose purpose is to undertake political support duties for a particular party group or councillor, rather than to serve the council as a whole'.[27] A statutory ban is proposed for such appointments. The parallel with taxpayers' money and central government practices is ignored.

However, the Act retreats significantly from this position (without any subsequent exploration as to why 'political advisors on the rates' are now deemed to be permissible!). Councils are to be allowed to appoint up to three officers on maximum salaries of £13 500 to assist political groups. All groups will be restricted to one assistant. In councils where there are more than three groupings, the three largest groups will be allowed (if they wish it) such officer support. Thus U-turn, which followed lobbying from Conservative groups who appreciated the value of political advisors, is, however, more illusory than real. The salary level involved (not greater than £13 500 per annum) implies a limited research/progress-chasing assistance rather than anything approaching the status of the Whitehall equivalent. Furthermore the basis for distributing posts between political parties favours minority parties to a ludicrous extent. For example, in Labour-dominated Hull, the 55-strong Labour group will be entitled to one political advisor, as will the 3 Conservative councillors and the 2 Democrat councillors!

The government's concern to 'ensure that local democracy and local accountability are substantially strengthened'[28] apparently does not extend to the strengthening and facilitation of the governmental role of leading councillors in a local authority, to which the attachment of political advisors can make a major contribution. Here, as elsewhere when the central/local parallels break down, the White Paper offered nothing by way of explanation as to why the democratic control of (for example) the City of Birmingham does not require the kind of institutional support system enjoyed by a Minister of a small central government department.

The division of internal management responsibilities

The Widdicombe Committee's Report contained a number of recommendations designed to strengthen the role of the chief executive of a local authority. It recommended that 'local authorities should be statutorily required to appoint a chief executive, who should be the head of the authority's paid staff, with overall managerial responsibility for the discharge of functions by officers', and that 'all statutory functions relating to the propriety of council business ... should be vested in the chief executive rather than any other officer'.[29] These recommendations reflected the Committee's view that a strong chief executive, whose position would be equivalent to that of the managing director of a large private company was essential in relation *both* to the need for an efficient and effective local authority management system, *and* as the main channel through which the objectives of the ruling party group could be rationalised, directed and delivered.

The White Paper, however, moves very much in the opposite direction. It accepts none of the Widdicombe proposals for additional statutory functions for the chief executive. It does not even agree that it would be desirable to require all councils to appoint a chief executive. Instead the White Paper proposes that councils should be required to designate specific officers to hold responsibility for three specific functions: *financial probity* (i.e. reporting on prospective expenditure that would be unlawful under Part IX of the Local Government Finance Act 1988); *legal propriety* (i.e. responsibility for keeping under review the lawfulness and propriety of the council's actions and reporting on an action or inaction likely to result in illegality or maladministration); and *management co-ordination* (i.e. the co-ordination of the authority's functions, the organisation needed to discharge them, and the arrangements needed to ensure proper staffing of the structure).[30] In the Act, the legal propriety officer is redefined as the *monitoring* officer, and the management co-ordination officer as the *head of paid service*. Significantly, however, the post of the officer who is responsible for legal monitoring *cannot* be held by the person who has the formal responsibility for financial probity.

Thus the practice of combining chief executive/treasurer posts which has increased over the past few years, will not now be possible (*unless* the probity role is given to the council's solicitor). There will be a return to the pre-1974 situation when there was a ban on the posts of clerk and treasurer being held together. In the Government's view, this situation was (and will be) advantageous on a 'checks and balances' argument, and because of the 'additional responsibilities that have been given to the chief finance officer by the 1988 Local Government Finance Act'.[31] The chief finance officer and propriety officer should thus be complementary to each other, with any problems being capable of resolution through discussion and consultation (or, *in extremis*, through outside legal advice!).

The White Paper argument on this topic lacks coherence and conviction and one has to look beyond the White Paper for more plausible explanations for the change. It is a change which has aroused a great deal of critical comments not least among Widdicombe Committee members themselves. Sir Lawrence Boyle has commented, 'this virtually kills the chief executive role. In management terms it's an absolute nonsense to have policy aspects separate from management of the organisation. No managing director in the private sector would tolerate this'.[32] Even Audit Commission Controller Howard Davies has referred to the confusion inherent in the proposed new arrangements and argued that it will be some time before councils sort out appropriate structures.

There is little doubt that this proposal, seen widely as 'divide and rule' in nature, will not provide a framework for effective political and managerial direction of local authorities. It is possible that the Government's alarm about the activities of councils which they perceive as being 'extreme left-wing' in character has led them to favour a system where at least two powerful officers have formal responsibility for issuing warnings to councillors that they are transgressing the bounds of the permissible, rather than one ('all powerful') officer who may be subjected to informal political pressure (or may indeed be a 'political appointment', in the Government's terms). Whatever the motives, the proposal will not help local authorities develop a strategic direction, informed by local political priorities, to cope with the mass of new Government legislation which will radically change their role over the next few years.

Conclusions: the implications of the government's response

As has been demonstrated, there is a 'gap' or disparity in the Widdicombe process, between, on the one hand, the Widdicombe research findings and Widdicombe Committee report (which are broadly congruent, with some exceptions) and, on the other, the White Paper/legislative proposals. It is the reasons for this disparity which are of particular interest, and which merit further discussion in this concluding section.

As we have seen, the Widdicombe Report was the first 'official' Government-commissioned report not only to explicitly recognise the central role of party politics in local government, but also to argue strongly for the *legitimacy* of its role (if not of all its specific manifestations).

Indeed one of the professed aims of the Widdicombe Report (taking its brief seriously) was to try to strengthen local democracy, by ensuring that the constitutional framework for local decision-making was *supportive* of and *responsive* to political processes.

There are of course different conceptions of what local democracy means, and different aspects of it which might need strengthening. It was clearly the most familiar of these conceptions – representative democracy – which the Widdicombe Committee wished to strengthen. There are in principle two major ways in which local representative democracy can be strengthened: first by making it easier for local politicians (and in particular majority groups) to *govern effectively*; and second by trying to ensure that there are appropriate *safeguards* built into the local governmental process, such as proper representation of minority parties on committees, adequate channels for the redress of public grievances, etc. The first of these objectives is about facilitating a local equivalent of cabinet-type government: the second about ensuring adequate checks and balances to it. Both aims are legitimate. But they are of couse different. The Widdicombe Committee package involved a reasonably balanced mixture of the 'effective government' and 'checks and balances' types of proposal.

The task for those responsible for drafting the White Paper (and subsequently the legislation) was to produce a response which was *both* consistent with the Report's main arguments and recommendations *and* the Government's embryonic but fast-developing view of the role and scope of local government. For what has become apparent over the past two years is that the Government's emerging view of local democracy is *different* from the 'representative democracy' perspective which underpinned the Widdicombe proposals. Although the *outward form* of representative democracy has not (yet) been rejected, it is currently being transformed by a large injection of 'market democracy', which can be seen as an approach in which political activity is both tempered by market discipline *and* diminished by transferring more decisions into the market place (and/or transferring key functions to non-elected agencies).[33]

The new local authority management roles (see Chapter 9) involve contract-setting, monitoring, enabling, orchestration, and do not sit easily with the traditional machinery of representative democracy. In particular, it is highly unlikely that a large (80-member) council, composed of councillors concerned with details of service provision and management (and averaging nearly twenty hours a week input), would be viewed by the Government as compatible with their new vision. Is such a council really necessary to draft service provision contracts, monitor them, review them every four years, and otherwise co-ordinate the activities of an increasingly fragmented authority? One suspects not; a much smaller council, operating as a 'board of directors' would seem a much more compatible model! Indeed, such a vision of local government (including a predilection for local authorities of much smaller *population* size also) is set out in a recent Adam Smith Institute publication).[34]

This model represents, of course, a radical change in the concept of the role of both the local authority itself, and of the councillors represented on it. Because the vision was, in the spring of 1988, perhaps not yet clear enough in detail, *or* because the Government was not yet ready to make it explicit, the Widdicombe White Paper and the subsequent legislation have had to attempt to marry an explicit commitment to *strengthening* local (representative) democracy, with a *hidden* agenda of subsequently remodelling the role of representative democracy to incorporate a much stronger market/customer dimension. In these circumstances, the Government's retreat to a relatively apolitical position with regard to the role of local councils is at least consistent with the hidden agenda.

If this diagnosis is correct, the last thing you would expect the White Paper or legislation to do would be to accept the Widdicombe Committee proposals which involve strengthening 'effective government' at the local level. And sure enough, deliberative committees are not supported. Nor is increased remuneration for councillors. Nor is an enhanced general discretionary power. Nor was (until the last minute turnaround) the idea of political advisors. On the other hand the 'checks and balance' types of proposal for strengthening local democracy could be taken on board with very few problems of potential incompatibility with the Government's emerging vision; and indeed they have been. Hence the proposed ban on co-optees is endorsed, pro-rata membership of all committees and sub-committees is introduced, core standing orders supported, and so on.

Thus the reason why the legislation which has resulted from the Widdicombe process seems to amount to little more than piecemeal tinkering is that the Government has not yet fully worked through the implications of the restructured local authority for the role of councillors. The strengthening of the governmental aspect of the role of councillors in a representative democracy and its political nature has clearly been rejected (implicitly, if not explicitly). The appropriate alternative councillor role pattern is not yet clear. To that extent, the legislation is premature. For although the Government appear to think that their new vision of local government will require *less* input from councillors, there is an alternative view taken by John Stewart, that although the input demanded of councillors in the 'enabling council' will be different, it will be *equally demanding* (see Chapter 9).

What *is* clear is that the 'tidal force' of the politicisation of local government will receive a severe and possibly terminal setback from the legislative proposals. This process was in 1985 making the more politicised local authorities much more similar in their basic features to the Westminster/Whitehall model than they had been ten years previously. Cabinet government – albeit in a different guise – was a reality in many such authorities. Full-time councillors were becoming prevalent. Political advisors were on the increase. In relation to all these practices, and several others, the role of politics in local government has now become *distanced* from its role in central government. Local representatives' democracy is *not* going to be strengthened except in terms of 'checks and balances'. The arguably healthy level of political commitment in local government – and many if not all of its specific manifestations – identified by the Widdicombe research programme and endorsed by the Widdicombe Committee – are, it appears, not viewed as legitimate, or desirable by the centre.

Notes and references

1. Department of the Environment, *The Conduct of Local Authority*

Business: The Government Response to the Report of the Widdicombe Committee of Inquiry, Cmnd 433 (HMSO, 1988) p.v.

2. Department of the Environment, *The Report of the Committee of Inquiry into the Conduct of Local Authority Business (The Widdicombe Committee)*, Cmnd 997 (HMSO, 1986).
3. Research Volume I, *The Political Organisation of Local Authorities*, Cmnd 9798 (HMSO, June 1986); Research Volume II, *The Local Government Councillor*, Cmnd 9799 (HMSO, June 1986); Research Volume III, *The Local Government Elector*, Cmnd 9800 (HMSO, June 1986); Research Volume IV, *Aspects of Local Democracy*, Cmnd 9801 (HMSO, June 1986).
4. DoE (1988).
5. DoE (1988) p.v.
6. DoE (1986) Report p. 80.
7. DoE (1988) p. 6.
8. Ibid, p. 4.
9. Ibid, p. 7.
10. Patrick Jenkins, House of Commons statement, 6 February 1985.
11. DoE (1988) p. 5.
12. Ibid, p. 5.
13. Ibid, p. 6.
14. Ibid, p. 6.
15. Statement by DoE official at seminar at INLOGOV, 22 February 1989.
16. DoE (1988) p. 9.
17. Ibid, p. 10.
18. Ibid, p. 10.
19. Ibid, p. 20.
20. DoE (1986), Research vol. I, pp. 140–5.
21. Ibid, p. 132.
22. DoE (1988) p. 19.
23. Ibid, p. 19.
24. Ibid, p. 19.
25. Ibid, p. 19.
26. DoE (1986) Report pp. 151–2.
27. DoE (1988) p. 21.
28. Ibid, p.v.
29. DoE (1986) Report p. 144.
30. DoE (1988) p. 17.
31. Ibid, p. 18.
32. *Local Government Chronicle*, 12 August 1988, p. 22.
33. J. Gyford, S. Leach and C. Game, *The Changing Politics of Local Government* (Unwin Hyman, 1989) p. 338.
34. *Wiser Counsels, The Reform of Local Government* (The Adam Smith Institute, 1989).

7 Inner Cities, Economic Development and Social Services: The Government's Continuing Agenda

Gerry Stoker

One of the main characteristics of the Government's approach to local government from the mid-1980s onwards is the breadth and range of its concern. This chapter provides a 'round-up' of key changes not dealt with elsewhere in Part I of the book. Inner City Policy, Economic Development and Social Services are the main focus of attention.

Inner urban policy

The inner cities emerged again as a subject of political concern for the Government following the 1987 election. In a post-victory speech Mrs Thatcher identified the problems of the inner cities as a focus for attention and action. Whether by intention or otherwise she appeared to commit the Government to 'doing something' for the inner cities. There followed a period of intense ministerial and civil service discussion. There were rumours of a major white paper. What eventually emerged was a brochure called *Action for Cities*.[1]

At a press conference in March 1988 the Prime Minister, flanked by some half a dozen ministers, launched the brochure. It met a generally lukewarm reception. The absence of new big spending plans or major policy initiatives encouraged the verdict that the event was largely about public relations:

> So this was an obvious salespitch, a shameless hype, designed to remind the world that the famous inner cities . . . enjoy the attentions of six ministers as well as the Prime Minister herself.[2]

Indeed the concern with publicity has been a constant feature of the Government's post-1987 approach. In December 1988 the DoE published a glossy report on its achievements in 1987–8. A year after the launch of *Action for Cities* the Government held a further press conference to congratulate itself for creating 'a mood of optimism' in the inner cities. In addition the Government announced that it aimed to give its policies a 'little boost' by placing blue signs on those lands and buildings being redeveloped with central government support.[3]

It is misleading, however, to see the Government's inner urban policy simply as an exercise of shameless 'hype'. Behind the glossy brochures and press conferences the post-1987 repackaging on inner city policy has sought to provide a new coherence to a complex array of Government policies in this area. In addition it has introduced a number of new initiatives.

Four core themes now dominate inner city policy and give it a distinctive Thatcherite flavour. They echo key features of the post-1987 restructuring package directed towards local government outlined in Chapter 1. First, local government is no longer seen as the 'natural' agency for inner city regeneration as it was under Labour's 1977 White Paper. At worst local authorities are seen as causing inner city problems through their bureaucratic delays and failure to understand business requirements. At best they are only one among several agencies and institutions that the Government intends to use in order to implement its strategy.

Second, the Government is keen to ensure an increased accountability from local authorities to the centre in order to ensure that when acting in the inner city arena local authorities pursue the Government's priorities. Third, the private sector is seen as having the major role in leading the recovery of the inner city. Big business, in particular, is expected to draw on the spirit of

Victorian philanthropy to provide the leadership and some of the resources necessary to achieve success. Corporate social responsibility is to save the inner cities. Fourth, the programme is presented as requiring not only economic intervention but also the promotion of a new culture of enterprise and self-reliance among inner city residents. Below, the working-out of these themes in the complex of measures that make up the Government's inner city policy is briefly examined.

Urban Development Corporations (UDCs) are the flagships of the policy.[4] Building on the experience of the UDCs in London and Merseyside's docklands, declared in 1981, a second generation was established in 1987. Five UDCs were declared in the Black Country, Cardiff Bay, Teesside, Trafford Park and Tyne and Wear with each one having a budget of between £100–160m over five years. A third generation of mini-UDCs were launched in 1988 in Central Manchester and Leeds (each with a budget of £15m over 3/4 years), Sheffield (a budget of £50m for 7 years) and a further UDC has been proposed in Bristol. It seems likely that no more UDCs will be declared before the next general election.

UDCs are funded directly by central government and run by boards appointed by the Secretary of State for the Environment. The board is generally composed of local business and property interests, some local notables and with a minority representation from local authorities in the affected area. The boards are given the development control powers previously held by the local authority, and may also have vested to them the land holdings of the local authority and other public sector bodies in the area.

With the resources at their disposal, the power to give grants and undertake other appropriate activities, the UDCs are in a powerful position to stimulate the redevelopment of their areas. Their prime task is to create an environment and opportunities which attract private sector investment and development. UDCs do not see themselves as direct providers of industrial, shopping and housing facilities, rather they aim to act as catalysts for a private sector-led regeneration.

The London Docklands Development Corporation has had a strained and stormy relationship with the local authorities in its area,[5] and it was only after the 1987 general election that one of the authorities, the London Borough of Newham, concluded a 'social compact' in return for its co-operation over the redevelopment of the Royal Docks. The second and third generation UDCs have in contrast been met by a greater degree of co-operation from the affected local authorities. Councillors and officers in these authorities do resent the loss of control but there is a feeling that more will be achieved by working with the UDCs than by adopting a stance of outright opposition. Nevertheless there are plenty of signs of tension given the local authorities' concern with their communities and the UDCs' accountability to business interests and central government.

Other inner city initiatives also by-pass local authorities.[6] Six City Action Teams (CATs) were initiated in 1985, one for London and separate teams in Liverpool, Birmingham, Newcastle, Gateshead and Manchester/Salford. In 1988 two further CATs were established in Leeds and Nottingham. The CATs are composed of civil servants from the relevant departments and are intended to co-ordinate central government expenditure in the inner areas concerned as well as act as a contact point for private sector interest. Operating alongside CATs are Inner City Task Forces consisting of small teams of civil servants and private sector secondees. The Task Forces are more localised than CATs, dealing with immediate community and business difficulties such as local training and issues related to the problems of small businesses. By 1988 sixteen Task Forces had been established. In March 1989 it was announced that a further three were to be set up and three wound down having completed their programmes. Elsewhere in the book other 'inner city' by-pass initiatives are examined: in particular the establishment of City Technology Colleges (see Chapter 4) and Housing Action Trusts (see Chapter 5).

Local authorities retain a role in the Government's inner city policy through the Urban Programme. The funding provided by central government to local authorities under this programme has survived since the late 1960s. However, it should be noted that the total urban programme allocation for 1989–90 is £245m to be spread among 57 target authorities. This is a slight reduction on the previous year's allocation and contrasts with more than £250m spent by the ten established UDCs in 1988–9. Moreover throughout the 1980s the Government has sought to re-direct the priorities of the programme. Local Chambers of Commerce vet the local authorities' proposals. Tighter monitoring procedures by central government are also in operation. Government Ministers have insisted that in future half of Urban Programme funds should go on economic development, as opposed to the current 40 per cent.

The private sector rather than local authorities are seen as the main actors in inner city policy from the Government's perspective. The 'inner city breakfasts' hosted by Government Ministers which followed the launch of *Action for Cities* were aimed at business people, and indeed to the annoyance of some largely excluded local authority leaders. UDCs, HATs, CTCs, CATs and other government initiatives all look to the private sector. In addition in *Action for Cities* a new City Grant was announced replacing several other earlier measures. The new grant can be applied for directly by private sector developers and is given to support redevelopment projects in inner city areas. Local authorities are not involved in assessing the proposals. The setting-up of a new private sector-led development agency, British Urban Development, was also promoted at the launch of *Action for Cities*. The Confederation of British Industry have several inner city initiatives under way and in September 1988 published a report calling for further private sector-led regeneration, in direct response to the Prime Minister's call for action.

The *Action for Cities* document makes a great play of the new comprehensiveness of the Government measures. Thus reference is made to its broader education and housing policies. The safer-cities campaign aimed at bringing police, local residents and businesses together to combat crime is mentioned. A number of employment and training programmes are to be 'bent' to more directly meet inner city needs. The *Action for Cities* document announced six new inner city offices for the Small Firms Service, grants for inner city Local Enterprise Agencies, and other measures aimed at encouraging employment and small businesses in the inner cities. Inner city local authorities have been encouraged to declare Simplified Planning Zones (SPZs) under provisions which came into effect in November 1987. These zones will provide a partial replacement for the Enterprise Zone experiment which is now being run down. In an SPZ planning permission is given for a number of categories of development rather than on individual projects. The argument is that the decision-making process will thereby be speeded-up and attract greater private sector investment to such areas.

A final noteworthy feature of the post-1987 inner city package is the Government's insistence on the need for the people of inner city areas to commit themselves to enterprise and self-reliance. Government will play its part. Businessmen must invest. But the *Action for Cities* document comments: 'success will only happen if everyone plays their part – above all, the people who live in the cities themselves'.[7] Further it argues:

A fundamental change in attitudes has begun. The country is rediscovering enterprise and resourcefulness. There is a new national self-confidence. The gloomy view that a return to prosperity was impossible has been dispelled. Now is the time to dispel the gloom about Britain's inner cities.[8]

Whether the Government's programme will revive the inner cities remains to be seen, but there are good reasons for doubting its potential given the limited spending resources involved and the inadequate targeting of the benefits of that spending on the needs and problems of the majority of inner city residents.[9]

Economic development

Local authority activity in economic development has increased considerably since the mid-1970s. The range of activity is wide.[10] Local authorities have promoted their areas, provided industrial units and science parks for new enterprises, supported the establishment of small businesses and co-operatives, provided training centres for information technology, and sought to use their own purchasing and employment powers to underwrite their local economies. A few authorities have directly invested in companies through enterprise boards or other development companies.

Much of this economic development activity has been funded from the product of a 2p rate which local authorities can raise on a discretionary basis to meet the needs of their area. With the abolition of the rating system this power is brought into question. In addition provisions in the Local Government and Housing Act 1989 and proposals to transform employment training and small business advice raise severe doubts about the future role of local authorities in economic development.

The 1989 Local Government and Housing Act does give local authorities a new specific power to carry out economic development. But it also gives the Secretary of State for the Environment substantial reserve powers to prescribe the amount and the types of activity that can be undertaken. These powers will be capable of being applied to the activities of individual authorities. From the viewpoint of local authorities this new specific power resolves any lingering doubts about the legitimacy of local authority activity in this area. The doubts that it raise relate to exactly what economic development by local authorities the Government is going to deem as appropriate and supportable. A discretionary power to spend on activities other than economic development is also provided based not on the product of a 2p rate but rather calculated on the basis of adult population (£5 per head for single tier authorities and £2.50 per head for each authority in two-tier areas).

The changes in relation to employment training and small business advice are presented in two White Papers published in December 1988. One White Paper entitled *Employment for the 1990s* outlines provisions for training and providing advice for small businesses, and concludes:

> A key requirement is that the delivery of training, and its links with small firms and enterprise, must relate closely to the circumstances of each local area. The best way of achieving economic improvement differs from area to area. By tailoring approaches to their own circumstances, localities are more likely to find solutions that work. Moreover, it is at local level where individuals and institutions most directly share a sense of Community, and can best shape a common purpose.[11]

This seems like a classic argument for giving the responsibility for training and small business advice to elected local authorities. In fact the Government propose establishing a network of around 100 local Training and Enterprise Councils (TECs) 'to plan and deliver training and to promote and support the development of small businesses and self-employment within their area'.[12] In effect these agencies will be undertaking much of the work of the Manpower Services Commission (MSC). They will oversee national programmes such as the Youth Training Scheme (YTS) and Employment Training (ET). The administration of the MSC (renamed the Training Commission in 1988) will be disbanded to be replaced by a small Training Agency team operating inside the Department of Employment.

The second White Paper – *Scottish Enterprise* – deals with the situation north of the border. It too proposes a network of local agencies; but in addition suggests the amalgamation of the Training Agency in Scotland with the Scottish Development Agency.[13] The new agency Scottish Enterprise will have a Scotland-wide role for training, economic regeneration and attracting inward investment. The White Paper suggests the local agencies, as well as having the responsibilities of their English and Welsh counterparts, might also take on, in an evolutionary process, some of the SDAs former functions including property development, land reclamation and grant-aid to the private sector.

Two features of the TECs and Scotland's local agencies are worth emphasising. The first is that they are to be employer-led bodies, with two-thirds of their directors being private sector managers or businessmen. The remainder are to come from local authorities, trade unions and other bodies. The Government hopes to build on the network of private sector participants associated with the hundreds of local enterprise agencies which, with Government encouragement and the leadership of Business in the Community (BiC), have been established during the 1980s.[14] The Government, however, recognises the need to attract additional private sector 'leaders'. Indeed its campaign to attract such individuals was launched through a press conference in March 1989, headed by Margaret Thatcher, and with a television link to groups of business people around the country.

The second feature of the TECs and Scotland's local agencies is that they will operate on contract to the Government. Government schemes such as YTS, ET and the new Business Training Growth Scheme will form the bulk of their work. Each TEC will have an average annual budget of £20m of public money and will cover a population of about 250 000 people. About fifty staff from the former MSC will be seconded to each. In addition, however, TECs will have a local initiative fund, starting at about £250 000, to advance its own particular local objectives. For its main work the TEC must draw up a plan and specify targets. If these targets are exceeded then greater local financial freedom will be granted by central government.

How effective TECs and Scotland's local agencies will be in

training and small business advice is open to doubt. Opposition speakers and even some private sector voices doubt whether these private sector-led agencies will be able to deliver effective action in overcoming skills shortages. Worries have also been expressed about the diverting of money away from some of the support schemes for the long-term unemployed.[15]

The key issue, given the focus of this book, is the impact of these changes on the future role of local authorities in economic development. Here it is possible to present two scenarios. The first is that the regulation of local authority economic development implied by the 1989 Act is relatively light and that local authorities will continue to do most of the activities they have undertaken during the 1980s. The TECs and Scotland's local agencies will be run largely by the former MSC staff, seconded to them, and training and business advice activities will continue much as before but within a different administrative structure. The assumption here is that there will be major difficulties in the calibre and commitment of businessmen to run these agencies. Local authorities will be left to work with and alongside the former MSC staff much as they did during the 1980s.

A second scenario sees the provisions of the 1989 Act and the two White Papers as the beginning of the end of local authority economic development activity.[16] In Scotland the local agencies, assuming a considerable devolution of former SDA functions, are likely to dwarf the resources and powers available to any local authority economic development unit. In England and Wales the restrictions associated with the new economic development power will be progressively tightened, pushing local authorities out of areas where they are currently active and allowing TECs to expand their economic development activities. Indeed local authorities may ultimately end up as agents to the TECs, helping to implement policies formulated by these private sector-led agencies under guidance from central government.

Social services

Social services have not escaped the reforming eye of the Government. The 1989 Children's Act brings together a number of important provisions in relation to child care and introduces a number of changes in procedures and instruments.[17] But perhaps of greater significance, given the focus of this book, is the uncertainty about the future role of local authorities in community care following the publication of the Griffiths Report in March 1988.[18]

The Griffiths Report is widely viewed as a landmark review of community care. The report covered care provided by a range of agencies to elderly, handicapped and mentally ill people. It dealt with care in people's own homes, group homes, residential care homes, hostels and nursing homes but excluded care for children and hospital in-patients. The report followed a number of critical commentaries on the existing operation of community care services.[19] It was written to a brief which emphasised more effective management of existing funds rather than a commitment to examine the gap between need and levels of spending.

Griffith's analysis is, however, premised on a recognition of the scale of existing demand for community care and a realisation that demand is likely to grow in the future. It is estimated that current public spending in the field is about £6 billion. The report notes the increased proportion of elderly people in the population. It points out, for example, that the number of people aged over 85 is projected to rise from 459 000 in 1976 to 894 000 in 1996.[20]

Four elements of Griffiths' recommendations are highlighted below. First he proposes that local authorities' role as service providers should be reduced, whilst their role as managers of services and overseers of packages of care be increased. Local authorities should take the lead as arrangers and purchasers – not monopoly providers – of community care services. The report is clear that:

> Elected local authorities are best placed ... to assess local needs, set local priorities and monitor local performance.[21]

The report advocates, then, a key role for local authorities in the planning and management of community care.

A second element of the report is a commitment to the extension of a mixed economy of care. Families, the voluntary sector and the private sector are all seen as key service and support providers. A third point is that Griffiths advocates that people should be encouraged to pay for services, from the public, private and voluntary sectors if they have the ability to do so: 'what Griffiths is proposing is a greater reliance on means-testing for all community care services'.[22]

A fourth element of the Griffiths report is the strategic role given to central government. Local authorities would submit plans for community care in their area to the centre. Once plans were approved a new ring-fenced, specific central government grant would be made available to local authorities, covering 50 per cent of the cost of the plans. The centre would in the light of this proposal be able to agree targets and monitor performance.

In response to the report many local authority representatives welcomed the key role given to local councils. In November 1988 the Association of Directors of Social Services welcomed the main thrust of the report and the idea that local authorities should take on an enabling and overseeing role in the context of a mixed economy of provision.

Other voices[23] have been more critical, suggesting that Griffiths failed to address the case for more resources to be devoted to community care. Further, it is argued that Griffiths will give local authorities responsibility without the necessary resources; and thereby deliver to central government the control over spending it desires. Lister and Martin, for example, comment:

> Griffiths proposes new laws to impose obligations on councils for which insufficient funds will be available – enabling the government to make major reductions in spending while local authorities take the blame ... All the strings would be in the hands of central government ... the extended role for local government is as puppets.[24]

Others argue that local authorities will not be deemed fit to take on the new role proposed by Griffiths.[25] Rather the option might be to take responsibility out of local authority hands and pass it over to a new central government appointed authority run by directors and managers capable of operating in the environment of contract-letting and performance monitoring proposed in Griffiths' report. Such a model would parallel that suggested for the new district health authorities (DHAs) outlined in the 1989 White Paper *Working for Patients*. As part of a general reform of health service management DHA would operate an internal market for health services buying in services from a range of potential providers. In order to undertake this task effectively, however, the Government proposes that the membership of DHA should be reduced, dominated by appointees with relevant management skills and, in particular, that local authority representatives should be excluded.

The Government has waited more than a year before formally responding to Griffiths. At the time of writing no Government proposals have been made. Yet major changes in the role of local authorities in community care are undoubtedly destined in the future.

A continuing agenda

The Government's proposals in relation to inner cities, economic development and community care all imply a substantial shift in the role and responsibilities of local authorities. The changes in these areas follow the broad themes of the Government's programme identified in Chapter 1. So too do other changes in the offing. It is worth briefly noting these other areas of reform.

A White Paper on *The Future of Development Plans*,[26] published in January 1989, proposes a major restructuring of the land-use planning system. The White Paper suggests a substantial reduction in the planning role of county councils. County Structure Plans – which have played a key role in strategic planning control since 1968 – will be abolished. Instead county councils will set out their planning objectives in broad terms. But these statements will be purely advisory, unlike structure plans which have statutory backing. District councils, in contrast, will be obliged by law to prepare detailed local plans. At the moment only 20 per cent of district councils have formally adopted local plans. The White Paper suggests that if strategic issues need to be considered then the Secretary of State for the Environment will have a key role in specifying and determining such issues. But in addition district and county authorities could band together to form *ad hoc* regional groups modelled on the South East forum SERPLAN.

The aim of these planning proposals is to streamline the system; creating an environment of greater certainty for developers and with local plans providing an up-to-date indication of land available for development. Crucially the White Paper reserves powers to intervene in the process for the Secretary of State. Thus although the White Paper envisages a greater say for district councils this is likely to be about where development is located not on whether there should be development. The strategic powers are moved to the centre leaving district councils to produce detailed plans in tune with a centrally determined strategy. Such an approach would be in tune with Government measures in other policy areas.

Other environmental concerns have also provided a focus for Government attention. A consultation paper[27] launched in early 1989 sets out proposals in relation to waste management. Under current arrangements local authorities at different levels undertake directly the collection and disposal of waste and also regulate the disposal activities and sites of private sector operators. The Government argues with its new enthusiasm for 'green' issues that these arrangements do not adequately safeguard the environment, a charge which many local authorities regard as unfair. Under the new arrangements the activity of disposal (involving landfill sites, transfer stations and incinerators) is to be separated from the responsibility for overseeing such activity. The reform it is argued will improve efficiency and the process of regulation. In non-metropolitan areas county councils will retain a regulation function as Waste Regulation Authorities with an enhanced range of powers. But they will lose the ability to dispose of waste themselves; rather, their existing disposal operations will be formed into arms-length Local Authority Waste Disposal companies. The companies will be owned by the county councils but will have to compete for work with the private sector and be subject to the same system of licensing. In Wales and post-abolition London and metropolitan areas slightly different arrangements will apply but the principles of reform remain the same. So strong is the Governments' vision of a new model of local government that even in areas such as waste management a distinctively Thatcherite approach is observable.

Notes and references

1. HM Government, *Action for Cities* (HMSO, 1988).
2. H. Young, 'The shameless hype of inner-city policy is a way of saying thanks to the developers', *Guardian*, 8 March 1988.
3. Quoted in *Local Government Chronicle*, 3 March 1989.
4. For a fuller analysis, see G. Stoker, 'Urban Development Corporations: A Review', *Regional Studies*, vol. 23, no. 2 (1989).
5. For a case study, see T. Brindley, Y. Rydin and G. Stoker, *Remaking Planning* (Unwin Hyman, 1989) ch. 6.
6. Much of the analysis below draws on P. Lawless, 'British Inner Urban Policy: A Review', *Regional Studies*, vol. 22, no. 6 (1988).
7. HM Government, *Action for Cities*, p. 28.
8. Ibid, p. 3.
9. See Lawless, 'British Inner Urban Policy'; and T. Brindley and G. Stoker, 'Partnership in Inner City Urban Renewal – a critical analysis', *Local Government Policy Making*, vol. 15, no. 2 (1988) pp. 3–12.
10. For a general review, see J. Chandler and P. Lawless, *Local Authorities and the Creation of Employment* (Gower, 1986). It has been estimated that in the mid-1980s local authorities spent about £200m on such activities. See L. Mills and K. Young, 'Local Authorities and Economic Development', in V. Hausner (ed.), *Critical Issues in Urban Economic Development*, vol. 1 (Clarendon Press, 1986).
11. Department of Employment, *Employment for the 1990s*, CMS40 (HMSO, 1988) para. 5.1.
12. Ibid, para. 5.7.
13. For a discussion of the role of the SDA, see M. Keating and R. Boyle, *Remaking Urban Scotland* (Edinburgh University Press, 1986) ch. 5.
14. For a discussion of local enterprise agencies in Scotland, see ibid., ch. 7. For a full analysis, see S. Young, *Privatisation and Planning in Declining Areas* (Croom Helm, forthcoming).
15. For a preliminary assessment, see K. Hayton '"Employment for the 1990s" and "Scottish Enterprise": Their Impact Upon Local Economic Development', *Local Government Policy Making*, vol. 16, no. 1 (June 1989).
16. See ibid.
17. For a brief outline, see *Local Government Chronicle*, 16 December 1988, pp. 22–3.
18. R. Griffiths, *Community Care: An Agenda for Action* (HMSO, 1988).
19. House of Commons Social Services Committee, *Community Care Volume 1: Report*, HC 13–1, Session 1984–5 (HMSO, 1985); Audit Commission, *Making a Reality of Community Care* (HMSO, 1986).
20. For a fuller discussion of ageing trends, see E. Midwinter, 'Ageing Trends and Local Government', *Local Government Policy Making*, vol. 15, no. 3 (December 1988) pp. 9–14.

21. Griffiths, *Community Care*.
22. J. Russell and M. Brenton, 'Community Care and the Griffiths' Report', *Local Government Policy Making*, vol. 15, no. 3 (December 1988) p. 32.
23. Ibid.
24. J. Lister and G. Martin quoted in ibid, p. 32.
25. R. Jefferies, 'The Now Formidable Challenge of Community Care', *Local Government Chronicle*, 17 March 1989, p. 22.
26. Department of the Environment, *The Future of Development Plans*, Command S69 (HMSO, 1989).
27. Department of the Environment, *The Role and Functions of Waste Disposal Authority*, A Consultation Paper, 1989.

II WHAT FUTURE?

8 Creating a Local Government for a Post-Fordist Society: The Thatcherite Project?

Gerry Stoker

The post-1987 legislative programme of the Thatcher Government represents a profound attempt to change the role and functions of local government to make its activities, organisation and orientation compatible with the flexible economic structures, two-tier welfare system and enterprise culture which in the Thatcher vision constitute the key to a successful future for the UK.

The aim of this chapter is to explain the social and economic background to the Thatcherite model of local government using a model derived from the so-called 'regulationist' school of political economy.[1]

The regulationists distinguish three broad stages in the development of advanced capitalist societies. The first is a stage of 'competitive' regulation stretching from the mid-nineteenth century to the 1920s. The second phase is characterised by 'Fordist' regulation and runs from the 1930s to the early 1970s. A third phase is seen as beginning in the 1970s and is a period of transition from Fordism.

This chapter looks first at the regulationist account of Fordism and post-Fordism, its strengths and limitations. It proceeds to analyse the significance of the development of Fordism and its subsequent crisis for the nature of local government activity, organisation and functions, before presenting the case for regarding the Thatcher reforms as a programme to create a suitable form of local government for a post-Fordist society.

Farewell to Fordism?

Writers in the regulationist school argue that, from the early years of the twentieth century onwards, in capitalist societies a regime of competitive regulation progressively gave way to a new dominant set of rules, institutions and social relations. This period stretching from roughly the 1930s to 1970s they characterise as Fordist, a label derived from Ford Motor Company that exemplified the mass production techniques associated with the period. For regulationists, however, the concept of Fordism involves more than a particular form of manufacturing, it refers to the whole social organisation of a regime covering an interrelated set of production processes, wage regulations, consumption patterns, corporate management and structures, and state activities.

The account of Fordism which follows represents a very abbreviated and general summary drawn from the work of a range of regulationist writers and it is to these that the reader must look for a development of the arguments and supporting evidence[2] and for nationally specific accounts of different regimes of accumulation and the process of economic and social change.[3]

Fordism

The production process is a central concern for regulationists. The organisation of labour and technology necessary to produce physical or service products is at the core of capitalist economic activity. The Fordist regime is characterised by the development of mass production of key consumer goods including motor cars, electrical goods and other consumer durables. Those firms committed to mass production developed the use of assembly-line techniques, part standardisation, semi-automatic machinery and large-scale production runs. At the same time their labour input was reorganised around the use of unskilled or semi-skilled workers along with the routinisation of work, increased division of labour and a machine-paced work rate. These changes in the production process proved attractive in many sectors because of the economies of scale and increased productivity they could deliver.

Fordist production requires a mass workforce. It is also associated with the universalisation of the wage relation as the dominant means by which the workforce is provided for and rewarded. As the mass production methods yielded productivity gains so collective wage bargaining over wage rates and work-time developed. Through a process of struggle and conflict, trade unions organised and established themselves in the new mass production industries. Collective, and in some instances national pay bargaining, institutions were established. The tendency was for wage bargaining to be led by sectors such as the car industry, with wage settlements linked to increases in productivity plus rises in the cost of living. Parallel patterns of bargaining in other sectors and comparability mechanisms helped to ensure that wages in much of the rest of the economy were tied to those in the leading industrial sectors.

Crucial to the regulationist depiction of Fordism is the parallel rise of mass consumption alongside mass production. To claw back the high capital cost of purpose-built machinery and factories requires long production runs of standard products. Consumers must be willing and able to buy these standardised products. Thus, according to Aglietta:

> For the first time in history, Fordism created a norm of working-class consumption in which individual ownership of commodities governed the concrete practices of consumption. This involved a reversal of both traditional ways of life and of the initial experience of the working in an epoch of extreme poverty and total insecurity, which provided no basis for any stabilization of consumption habits.[4]

Fordism is therefore characterised by real standard of living increases which enable the widespread purchase of consumer goods such as cars, electrical goods and other consumer durables. In the Fordist stage, wages are no longer simply a cost, they are also an outlet for capitalist production. The process of mass consumption is further supported by advertising and by the availability of credit to underwrite private purchases.

Fordism is also associated with the rise of the large-scale business corporation. The risks associated with the high fixed costs and inflexible machinery of mass production encouraged the formation of large corporations capable of organising large-scale investment and dominating markets in order to ensure a combination of increased productivity and stable demand.

In addition the dominant private sector management culture reflects the division of labour between unskilled workers and the managers of the system characteristic of Fordist production. Management assumes a hierarchical, authoritarian character. It develops through centralised planning, systems analysis and programme budgeting. It is driven by the commitment to economies of scale, cost cutting and standardisation of product.

Regulationists see a distinctive role for the state in the Fordist period. State intervention in the economy to manage and sustain demand for, and provide the infrastructure necessary to, mass production is seen as essential. The state also takes an increased role through the collective provision of education, health, housing and income support. This increased role is seen as the product of several forces. In part it reflects working-class demands for better social conditions. Yet the welfare state is also essential to the Fordist regime of mass production and consumption. It enables the workforce to support and reproduce themselves and their dependents while at the same time operating the long working hours demanded by the economic system. It also helps to sustain the norm of consumption, providing the social stability and security in which mass consumption could flourish.

Fordism in crisis

Built into the Fordist regime of accumulation are several contradictory and destabilising tendencies. These provide the seeds for the breakdown of the regime in the long term. First, the commitment to mass production can lead to a crisis of over-production. As more and more firms gear up for mass production, so the ability to claw back the capital investment associated with this process becomes problematic as markets become saturated. A second tension within Fordism revolves around the position of the unskilled workers at the heart of the system. Assembly-line and machine-paced work offers the potential for productivity gains but it also opens the door to high absenteeism, labour turnover and disruptive localised strikes. A third tension reflects the inapplicability of Fordist labour processes to the organisation of some industrial sectors and in particular the service sector. This puts a general limitation on the productivity gains that Fordist techniques offer and in particular leads in state services to a spiralling of staffing and financial expenditure in comparison with the private sector. In this sense state services become an increasing burden in the economy.

These latent tensions according to the regulationists became increasingly manifest during the 1960s. They, combined with a general economic downturn, created an environment of uncertainty which further challenged the Fordist regime premised on mass production and consumption. The oil price shock and the stagnation of the early and mid-1970s contributed to the crisis. In Britain and elsewhere, the crisis led to a rapid process of de-industrialisation, factory closure and large-scale unemployment.

Fordism in transition

From the 1960s onwards, the availability of new technology began to open up the possibility of new forms of production and social organisation. Some writers refer to the development of 'neofordism' and argue that new technologies are being used to generate economic renewal within the general context of Fordist institutions and social relations.[5] Others go further and suggest the process of renewal is leading to the creation of a new 'post-Fordist' regime which will transcend the rules, social relations and institutional mechanisms of Fordism.[6] For the sake of establishing a stark comparison, the account below favours the argument of those who see the development of a new regime of accumulation. The details of production systems and relations that are emerging are still unclear. Experience varies from country to country, but a leading edge of change is observable.

In contrast to the mass production and consumption of Fordism, new post-Fordist sectors of the economy are increasingly developing the techniques of flexible production and segmented marketing. Using robotics, computer-aided automation and a whole range of applications offered by new information technology, leading companies have been developing their ability to engage in small-batch production and niche marketing.

Retailers such as Benetton, Sainsbury and Marks and Spencer

have led the way. The key to their method is rapid access to information from the market and flexible control over the process of production. For example, in the case of Benetton, computers provide daily, detailed information on product sales from its 2800 franchised European outlets. This feeds back into Benetton's head office in Northern Italy, and orders are then passed on to the small garment makers who operate on subcontract to Benetton. For Benetton an immediate response to expressed preferences in the market is made possible through the use of information technology and a system of subcontracting which ties multiple small-scale producers to serving its needs.

Parallel shifts have occurred in parts of manufacturing with increased flexibility in production. Computer-aided flexible auto-mation make small-batch runs economically viable. In the car industry, Toyota and other firms have developed their ability to produce small batches of production through machines which are not task-specific but which can produce a whole variety of products and through applying a 'just-in-time' system to their component suppliers (i.e. ordering on the basis of daily production plans and getting the components delivered right beside the line). As in retailing, the complex of processes, inside and outside the plant, are co-ordinated through computers.

The new system is also dependent to a much greater degree on marketing. The concern is with designing products for particular consumers rather than producing the standard product and then promoting it to the consumer through mass advertising. Market researchers break down market by age, household, locality and seek to link commodities with consumption patterns and 'life-styles'.

The economic transition is also associated with changes in corporate organisation. Small batch production systems encourage small and medium-sized business formation. Within the large corporations, there is a tendency to break up their organisations through creating decentralised units and by making more exten-sive use of franchising and sub-contracting. This in turn can lead to an increased polarisation of the labour force. Firms try to retain a core of full-time skilled workers through profit-sharing, high wage levels and other fringe benefits. They will, then, bring in specialist support as required and farm out low-skilled types of work to subcontractors. While core workers may be promised jobs for life, and receive high income and social benefits, those on the periphery may be faced with part-time, low-paid and highly controlled working environments.

More generally, post-Fordism is accompanied by much greater fluidity of local labour markets. This is reflected in extensive part-time and temporary work and the bringing into the labour market of increasingly high proportions of women, adolescents and marginal workers. In short, employers attempt to tune their payroll numbers as sensitively as possible to the demands of flexible production, while cultivating factions of the labour force whose potential for resistance in this process is likely to be low. The strength of trade unions and the dominance of collective wage-bargaining comes under threat.

This leading edge of change has in turn contributed to a shift in management culture and thinking epitomised by the popularity of texts such as *In Search of Excellence* and *A Passion for Excellence*.[7] Flexibility is the driving force behind production. Quality is emphasised in production and also in service to the customer. Within the organisation, control is not exercised through a rigid hierarchy but rather through the establishment of a corporate culture and control-systems using new technology. Senior management is asked to break from a focus on detail and concentrate on strategy and planning. Lower-level managers and workers are seen as having more immediate control of day-to-day decisions and greater devolved responsibility. They are subjected to control through targets and performance measures rather than through detailed, immediate supervision.

The role of the state in the transition to post-Fordism is not clear-cut.[8] The state is seen as having a key role in securing the economic and societal restructuring associated with post-Fordism, as well as managing the social costs of transition. Individual nation states are finding their own route to post-Fordism by a process of trial-and-error.

The scope and limitations of the Fordist/Post-Fordist paradigm

To refer to a society on the move from one epoch to another naturally calls forward the scepticism of any sensible reader (and writer for that matter!). No one schema can capture the full complexity of particular forms of society. Inevitably the Fordist/

Post-Fordist paradigm highlights some key features but neglects, perhaps, other important elements.[9] Moreover change does not occur in an abrupt or well-ordered way. The processes of political, economic and cultural change may well have different rhythms and time-scales. In particular, in the economic field it is not possible to demonstrate the dominance of Post-Fordism. In the UK, for example, some sectors such as clothing and furniture have seen the development of new production techniques. Retail and service industries have also developed new forms of organisation and production. Thus it is possible to talk of a leading edge of change but 'Fordist' production methods remain to a substantial degree in use.[10] Further, I do not see the regime as simply imposed on people but as the product of human struggle and conflict. Consequently it is the case that counter-tendencies may arise and social conflict may block or transform the pattern of change.

Despite these caveats it can nevertheless be argued that some attempt to relate the challenges facing local government to social and economic change is a valuable exercise. As regulationists point out, particular institutions help to sustain and determine historically specific regimes of accumulation. In this respect there can be no doubting the sheer scale of social and economic impact of modern local authorities. In 1986–7 local authorities spent approximately £40 billion. This accounted for about a quarter of all public expenditure and a tenth of the gross domestic product. Local authorities employ nearly three million people and in many areas they are the largest single local employer. These authorities are among the biggest landlords and landowners in the country. Plainly the scale and scope of modern local government makes it both a potentially crucial instrument of societal change and a prime object to be restructured if change is going to take its course.

Local government can therefore be seen as both conditioned by the social and economic context in which it operates and as a set of institutions with the potential to direct and intervene in that context. It is precisely because of this contradictory position that the restructuring of local government has become such a prominent issue under the reforming Thatcher Government.

Local government under Fordism

Local authorities in the Fordist era participated in the general expansion of state and activities associated with the period. In 1930 local authority current spending in England and Wales was £2161 million. By 1975 it had increased in real terms to £12 253 million. On the capital side, a fourfold increase in annual spending was achieved over the same period. The period of most rapid expansion was from the 1950s onward. Between 1952 and 1972 there was a 50 per cent increase in the number of full-time employees and an over 200 per cent increase in the number of part-time local authority workers.[11]

As Britain moved into the Fordist period, so it is also possible to see a substantial shift in the roles and responsibilities undertaken by local authorities beginning to take hold. Local government began to become less the handmaiden of developing industrial capitalism and more the midwife to the welfare state.[12] As Table 8.1 indicates, in 1910 trading utilities, basic infrastructure, poor relief and the police service constituted two-thirds of local authority spending. By 1935 these services took only just over half of local authority budgets, dropping to about 10 per cent by 1975. In contrast, education, housing and welfare spending had risen to take the lion's share of local authority expenditure by 1955, and by 1975 these three functions took two-thirds of the total local authority budget.

In the nineteenth and early twentieth centuries local authorities took responsibility for the highways, public cleansing, gas, water supply, electricity, tramways and omnibuses that were central to industrial expansion. In this way they supported the progress of capitalist production in the era of competitive regulation where technological advance occurred strongly in the production of goods sector, in those industries which provided the basic means of advanced industrial production. Police services and poor relief provided a response to the tensions and grinding poverty associated with the rapid growth in towns and cities in this period.

Under Fordism, local authorities increasingly refocused their activities and spending in order to become key instruments of the welfare state. Local authorities in this country lost responsibility for the trading utilities – such as gas, electricity, and later water – but were given new responsibilities for a range of services associ-

TABLE 8.1 Rank ordering of major local government services by spending level, 1885–1975 (selected years)

Year	Five highest ranking services	Percentage share of expenditure
1885	1. Basic infrastructure	17.1
	2. Poor relief	15.3
	3. Trading utilities	10.2
	4. Police	7.8
	5. Education	7.3
1910	1. Trading utilities	27.1
	2. Education	21.6
	3. Basic infrastructure	18.3
	4. Poor relief	9.7
	5. Police	5.2
1935	1. Trading utilities	24.5
	2. Education	18.9
	3. Basic infrastructure	15.7
	4. Housing	10.2
	5. Poor relief	7.8
1955	1. Education	30.9
	2. Housing	19.6
	3. Basic infrastructure	11.4
	4. Trading utilities	11.2
	5. Health and personal social services	6.3
1975	1. Education	29.5
	2. Housing	28.9
	3. Basic infrastructure	6.4
	4. Personal social services	5.1
	5. Police	4.3

Notes
1. Basic-infrastructure spending covers sewers, refuse, highways and lighting.
2. Trading utilities include water, gas, electricity, transport, harbours and docks.
3. Percentage expenditure figures calculated from current and capital accounts for England and Wales at 1975 prices.

Source: Calculations made from data in C. D. Foster, R. Jackman and M. Perlman, *Local Government Finance in a Unitary State* (Allen & Unwin, 1980) pp. 102–126.

ated with the welfare state. They provided key services such as housing and education directly. They planned future provision and established future need. They regulated the activities of citizens and businesses through land-use and environmental legislation. As such, local authorities helped to ensure an educated, housed and healthy workforce. At the same time the social stability and security necessary to sustain the norm of mass consumption was fostered. Through planning industrial sites and overseeing retail redevelopment (in town and suburban centres) local authorities provided a base on which mass production and consumption could flourish. Local authorities provided through their purchasing and the spending power of their employees considerable demand for the private sector. A jobs audit undertaken for Sheffield City Council, for example, reveals that 9843 jobs were directly dependent on the spending power of the City Council and its employees.[13]

During the Fordist era local authorities as well as expanding their welfare activities also took on some of the trappings of Fordist organisational principles and culture. Indeed, Geddes goes as far as identifying a 'Fordist state'. In doing so he is 'not merely referring to the functions undertaken by the state, but also to the organisation of production within the state ... according to methods and by labour processes derived from Fordist capital'.[14] According to Hoggett:

> The Keynesian welfare state has traditionally been concerned with the mass production of a few standardised products. Economies of scale have been constantly emphasised. Flexibility of production has been minimal.[15]

The Fordist character of local government organisation and management, however, should not be overstated. In the first place Fordist production methods developed in manufacturing industry – long production runs, assembly-line organisation, special-purpose machinery, task-specific labour input – were inadequate and inappropriate for the production of many services whether in the private or public sector. Local government, along with other service industries, was not in a position to adopt directly Fordist management and labour processes.

Nevertheless, in reviewing the functioning and management of local authorities from the 1930s to the earlier 1970s, Stewart[16] emphasises the dominance of three organising principles: *functionalism* (the division of the organisation around particular tasks and responsibilities); *uniformity* (the provision of services to a common standard and on a common pattern); and *hierarchy* (organisation through a large number of tiers, with accountability running from the field workers, to the chief officer and eventually to the committee) (see Chapter 9). So although Fordist production methods were not on the whole observable in local government, the organisational and management trappings of some elements of Fordism were present.

What can be argued, therefore, is that local government was influenced by the organisational and management style of leading Fordist private sector companies. Local authorities 'copied' the commitment of scale, centralised planning, hierarchical control and the production of a standard product. Further, when in Fordist industries the dangers of task-division and fragmentation were met with the development of corporate management and planning, so again local authorities were encouraged to follow. Benington[17] and Cockburn[18] explain how the techniques of programme budgeting, systems analysis and corporate management developed in private industry were transferred into local government management thinking in the 1960s and 1970s. That local authorities should look to the private sector for management lessons should not surprise us. It reflects the economic and cultural domination of private capital.[19]

Local government and the Fordist crisis

Elected local authorities were caught up in the Fordist crisis. In particular they were faced by the pressures to reduce public spending which emerged as a key element of the immediate response to economic difficulties.[20] Labour's Anthony Crosland told local authorities that 'the party was over'. The Wilson/ Callaghan Labour Government brought years of growth in local authority spending to a near standstill. This policy was vigorously continued with the election in 1979 of the Thatcher Government. Central government grants towards local authority spending were cut and a range of other measures including targets and penalties and rate-capping were introduced (Chapter 2). The Conservatives' programme was accompanied by much rhetoric about the need to eliminate waste and 'roll back the state'.

Paradoxically, despite the aggressive nature of the Conservatives' attack on local government, progress in reducing current expenditure up to the mid-1980s was modest. Capital spending was generally at historically low levels and staff growth was checked. But in no sense was local government pushed back into a minimalist role. Local government, like other areas of the welfare state, remained substantially intact.

The relative failure of the expenditure squeeze, in part, reflects the contradictory nature of such a demand for the Fordist system of social and economic organisation. Although public services are a burden they are also essential to the operation of a system of mass production and consumption. Moreover as King and Longstreth argue,[21] once the institutions of a particular regime are established, they have a considerable durability. The welfare state through its role as an employer and service provider has created substantial and powerful interests committed to its maintenance.

Alongside the battle over spending, the other major theme of this period is a growth of local authority innovation and experiment in response to new circumstances. The late 1970s onwards saw a growth in local authority experimentation in an effort to cope with economic changes that were occurring.[22] A major expansion of economic development activity took place, with by 1984 about half of all local authorities in England and Wales having an active policy and programme in the area. Most local economic initiatives in this period can be seen as aimed at restoring the conditions of Fordism. The provision of infrastructures, industrial units and grants were aimed largely at supporting the established manufacturing sector, preventing further closures and creating the conditions for expansion. Other initiatives such as unemployed centres sought to cope with the consequences of deindustrialisation. Geddes, however, does suggest that parts of the GLCs industrial strategy constituted a 'Left Post-Fordism', premised on the view that the transition from Fordism could 'offer significant opportunities for labour given selective and specific state interventions'[23] in sectors such as furniture, clothing and cultural industries. It is not clear how deeply engrained such thinking was in the actual intervention of the GLC. Moreover, with the abolition of the GLC 'Left Post-Fordism' lost its main champion.

Local authorities also began to face up to challenges posed by claims that their organisations suffered from 'Fordist' rigidities. The centralised, hierarchical organisation and the commitment to standard products, which followed Fordist principles, was criticised for its remoteness and lack of responsiveness through the rise of a whole range of community, user and single-issue pressure groups.[24] Left-Labour authorities experimented with decentralised service delivery, grants to the voluntary sector and specialist women's and race units in an effort to provide a greater degree of flexibility and diversity in their response to customers and citizens.[25]

Some 'New Right' Conservative authorities tried other routes to organisational change. The London Borough of Wandsworth, for example, contracted-out key services, launched a massive council house sales policy and generally pushed through efficiency and 'value for money' measures. The total of manual staff directly employed by the local authority fell from 3565 in 1978 to 1350 in 1987, with the officer side declining only slightly over the same time-period (3555 to 3464).[26] By not employing large numbers of manual staff directly, Wandsworth's political leaders claim the authority not only achieved substantial savings, but also gained greater control over service deliverers through the discipline of contracts and freed senior officers to concentrate on policy development.[27]

The Thatcher Government and Post-Fordism

In Britain it is the Thatcher Government which has provided the dominant strategic political response to the breakdown of Fordism. At first the Thatcher role was largely one of holding the ring during (or indeed facilitating) the process of deindustrialisation and economic recession that reached its peak in the early 1980s. The rhetoric emphasised the virtues of monetarism and a commitment to 'rolling back the state'. From the mid-1980s onwards, however, the Thatcher Government has placed a greater emphasis on actively creating the 'flexible economy' and establishing 'popular capitalism'.[28]

This process draws on the forces of economic and social change associated with the transition from Fordism. The programme builds on the trend towards flexible production systems and labour markets, the development of new patterns of consumption focused on distinctive 'lifestyles', the growth of small and medium-sized business formation, new patterns of corporate organisation, and new developments in management culture. It seeks to encourage such developments and give them a distinctive direction.

It is worth emphasising that Thatcher's strategy involves not so much a general rolling-back of the state as a shift in the pattern of institutions and rules at the state–market boundary. It requires new legislative and regulatory frameworks. It calls on substantial public sector subsidy and investment. It involves building on, in a selective way, certain economic changes and processes. The Thatcherite strategy involves an attempt to create new institutions, rules and social relations to support its vision of a Post-Fordist society.

The strategy operates on a broad front. There is a clear commitment to establishing Britain as a principal site for international financial institutions.[29] This builds on the longstanding strength of the financial sector but the process has been consolidated and opened up to foreign involvement through the abolition of exchange controls, deregulation of financial institutions and services and favourable tax treatment. The privatisation of major nationalised industries and corporations has also provided new opportunities for the financial sector, as well as providing a revenue-raising device for the government.[30]

On the industrial front, the more interventionist industrial reorganisation and regional policies of the 1960s and 70s have been replaced by a more market-focused concern with attracting inward investment and encouraging small businesses to grow. Gamble argues:

> For most sectors the government has not had an industrial strategy at all, but its overall accumulation strategy is clear enough. If the UK can offer the least regulated, least taxed and least unionised space in Europe, it will attract investment from transitional capital, which will ensure prosperity and employment, accelerate the internationalisation of the economy, and position Britain to take best advantage of the opportunities for investment and reorganisation of the economy created by the end of the Fordist era of mass production and mass consumption.[31]

For indigenous small businesses the government has offered

various tax breaks, investment schemes and a reduced degree of regulation.

A further feature of the Thatcherite strategy has been the sustained legislative attack on the position and strength of trade unions.[32] More generally efforts have been made to make labour markets more flexible in wages, hours and working conditions; a policy pursued through various industrial relations, employment and social security legislation.[33] The Manpower Services Commission (now the Training Agency) was given a key role not only in soaking up the unemployment associated with the process of restructuring but in promoting new skills and new attitudes to work.[34]

The welfare state is also attacked. A dual welfare system[35] is promoted through the encouragement of home ownership, private pensions, private medical insurance and private education, all underwritten by tax relief and other measures. In contrast, key welfare state services are deprived of resources and developed on a 'no-frills' basis.

Gamble emphasises that 'A key aspect of Thatcherism is that it promises not just an economic and a political revolution but a moral and cultural revolution as well. This has always been one of the sources of its strength and its appeal'.[36] An 'enterprise culture' is actively promoted. The state, bureaucracy, red-tape, the culture of dependency are attacked. People are encouraged to be self-reliant, active and to participate through markets and voluntary associations rather than to allow themselves to be represented through uncontrollable trade unions or local authorities.

The strategy of economic, social and ideological restructuring reaches its pinnacle in south-east regions of England. The growth of these regions has been greatly aided by public expenditure on roads, airports, defence contracts and the location of government offices and research establishments. The process is reinforced by the Government's active promotion of the Channel tunnel. There are, however, problems thrown up in this process. Not least in the objection of Government supporters in these prosperous regions to further congestion and growth. Further, there is the difficulty of the huge rigidity in the labour market introduced by the massive gap in house prices that has arisen between the North and South. Yet there are few signs of any serious attempt to break the dominance of the South East. 'It is not just that the outer south east votes for Mrs Thatcher; it is also being held up as the region which most conforms to her ideology.'[37] Its low level of unionisation, its active small business sector, its competitive labour markets, its hi-tech and service industries, its dual welfare system and its enterprise culture are promoted as the new model to which other regions should strive.

This section has sought to establish the breadth of the programme of restructuring associated with the Thatcher Government. It should be noted that the programme is to a degree flexible. Equally it has developed through a process of trial-and-error. Nevertheless, behind it all is a determination to radically shift the pattern of rules, institutions and social relations at the state–market boundary.

The restructuring of local government is a part of this broad programme of economic, social and ideological renewal. It is in this context that it becomes possible to understand the shift in the nature of Thatcher's challenge to local government from an emphasis on financial restraint in the early 1980s to the broad-ranging concern with its role, organisation, institutions and management which has emerged in the later part of the 1980s.

Creating a Post-Fordist local government

Under Fordism government took on the role of delivering welfare and other collective services. Central to this process were elected local authorities. They took most service delivery on directly, employing the staff and deploying the resources necessary to provide the services. In this way local authorities became major employers, landowners and resource allocators. In addition local authorities sought to plan and regulate the activities of others. The Government's post-1987 programme calls into question this tradition of direct service provision, planning and regulation through local authorities.

The role of a local authority will, in the words of the Secretary of State for the Environment, become a matter of 'enabling not providing'.[38] Responsibility for provision and the act of provision are to be separated to a much greater degree. Local authorities will retain responsibility for some services but they will not be expected to organise the provision of those services directly. Moreover local authorities are no longer to be the only or dominant agents of service delivery. The responsibility for services will be shared with other public and private sector organisations. To quote from Ridley again: 'I can foresee a much more diverse pattern of provision in the future by a variety of different agencies working alongside local authorities.'[39] And as for the regulatory role, 'the task is to find how to do this fairly, efficiently and swiftly without stifling initiative and enterprise'.[40]

The fragmentation of the institutions of local government and the confining of the responsibilities of elected local authorities is at the heart of the Government's programme. The compulsory competitive tendering legislation (CCT) opens areas such as refuse collection, leisure management and catering to private sector challenge. There is provision for the list of services subjected to CCT to be extended and from some New Right perspectives virtually all local authority services could be included within its ambit (see also Chapter 10).[41] Beyond the provisions of CCT, the legislative programme makes it plain that in many areas local authorities will be expected to withdraw almost wholly from direct provision to allow a host of other public, private or voluntary organisations to step into the vacuum. This is the Government's aim with respect to housing where the reform package envisages a residual role for local authorities concentrating 'on ensuring that those who are genuinely in need, and unable to get adequate housing on the open market, are properly catered for'. In education and social services direct provision by local authorities will continue to be widespread but a variety of different agencies will be encouraged to work alongside and in competition with local authorities.

The strategic planning and regulatory role of local authorities is under challenge in a number of areas. New agencies such as Urban Development Corporations and Training and Enterprise Councils by-pass local authorities. The strategic land-use planning responsibilities of county councils are threatened by the provisions of the 1988 White Paper on *The Future of Development Plans*. The Adam Smith Institute has identified building control and licensing, among other areas, where further relaxation of the regulatory regime of local authorities is required.[42]

The Government's programme, then, envisages a substantial shift in the pattern of institutions and responsibilities within the local government system. This process can be understood as an attempt to transform the production process, the pattern of consumption and the arrangements for political management associated with local government. In this way the interplay between the reform programme and the social and economic trends associated with a transition from Fordism can be explored. It is worth repeating, however, that I do not see the reform programme as rising automatically from the processes of social and economic change. Rather I see it as part of the Thatcher Government's strategic response to these processes. As such the programme bears the stamp of the political and ideological perspective of Thatcherism. The aim is to create a local government compatible with the flexible economic structures, two-tier welfare system and enterprise culture which in the Thatcher vision constitute the key to a successful future.

Transforming the production process

By the production process of local government, I refer to labour and technology which are necessary to produce services. Public services, along with many other service industries, are highly labour intensive. By opening up local authorities to competition and by fragmenting the responsibility for service delivery the Government's aim is to achieve a breakthrough to increased productivity in the public services. Davies, the controller of the Audit Commission, refers to 'the Government's attempts to inject into local authorities the impulse for increased productivity that has already been achieved in other parts of the economy'.[43]

It was noted earlier in the chapter that many services provided in the public or the private sector could not benefit directly from Fordist methods of production better suited to manufacturing. However, developments pioneered in the private sector open up the possibility of increased productivity in the service sector.[44] These developments, associated with the transition from Fordism, include the availability of new flexible machinery and information technology, an increased use of contracting-out, and more intensive techniques of labour management. John Banham, Davies' predecessor at the Audit Commission, sees the productivity drive in public services being driven by this private sector experience. The public sector is exhorted to learn from the private sector and at the same time make greater use of private sector contractors.[45]

In areas such as cleaning, catering and refuse disposal, private sector companies, it is argued, will be able to undercut the traditional local government providers. Their more capital-intensive way of organising, their use of new machinery and technology, and their more intensive management of labour will give them an advantage. Direct service providers in local author-ities, it is argued, will have to copy private sector techniques if they want to compete. This phenomenon is clearly emerging under the impact of compulsory competitive tendering for these services. And real 'productivity' gains appear to be in the offing. It has been estimated that of the 700 000 jobs in England and Wales directly affected by competitive tendering, between 10 000 and 200 000 may be lost.

More generally the availability of information technology in all its forms – data processing, communications and control, compu-ter-aided design, office automation – offers the possibility of recasting traditionally labour-intensive service activities. And one major use of such technology is to reduce the aggregate cost of a particular service and the employment within it.[46] In short there is scope for considerable productivity gains which could be achieved by the public sector restructuring itself or by allowing private firms to take over provision.

From the Government's perspective the virtues of this program-me are threefold. Firstly, it reduces the potential burden of public services on the economy. According to Banham:

> The scale of the value improvement opportunities in the public service is immense. In local government alone it is not unrealis-tic to think in terms of £3–4 billion a year.[47]

Second, new opportunities for private sector growth and activity are opened out. In areas of service provision which in the past were unattractive to the private sector opportunities for capital accumulation are now seen as beckoning.

Opening up a further range of local authority services to competitive tender obviously creates new opportunities for busi-ness interests. But in addition so does the fragmentation of provision in housing, education and social services and creation of single-purpose development agencies such as the UDCs. Mainte-nance contracts, financial services, old people's homes, consultan-cy, are some of the areas for private sector activity. By limiting its direct provision but instead seeking to support provision by others, the new local authorities will, according to Nicholas Ridley, not only achieve better value for money but also by 'the delegation of as much as possible for the private sector . . . help to promote local firms and jobs and entrepreneurs'.[48]

Third, the fragmented local government system will also underwrite the search for more flexibility in labour markets. Flexibility in labour organisation and markets in the public sector will complement that of the private sector. The power of large, unionised and organised local authority workers will be undermined as more and more providers find themselves operating in fragmented and competitive service units either as local authority direct service organisations, or for contractors, management buy-outs, housing associations, and opted-out schools. This in turn will encourage a break from the domination of national wage bargaining within the local government system. As Ridley notes:

> For many local government services our . . . legislation will exert a pressure on local authorities and unions to take more account of local market conditions when setting wage rates and working practices.[49]

The development of local bargaining, performance-related pay and 'retention and recruitment' packages for people with skills the local authority wants to keep or attract, may ultimately lead the local government system towards the sort of dual labour market system associated with Post-Fordist private corporations. The local authority of the future might seek to maintain a central core of highly skilled and high salaried employees and a peripheral range of part-time, low-paid employees moving in and out of employment as contracts demand.

The changing pattern of consumption

The universalistic welfare state expressed through local government is challenged in a number of ways by the Government's programme. As direct providers local authorities are no longer to be there to look after us from the 'cradle to the grave'. In some instances their role in direct provision will become residual. In others they will trade their services in competition with other service – public or private sector – providers. Among the consumers of welfare the divisions will increase between: those who can afford to take on 'private' solutions to housing, health care, transport or pension provision; those who have the skills (or good fortune) to get access to a high-quality public sector 'trading' provision such as CTCs, opted-out schools, housing associations and some local authority services; and those who have access to basic no-frills local authority provision.

Further, the Conservatives' programme promotes exchange through market forms as opposed to political, bureaucratic or professional mediation. Some goods and services will be returned to the private sector. For the remaining public services, market forms of conduct and exchange are to be ushered in to drive their production and distribution. The boundary-line between public services allocated on the basis of need and private services allocated according to ability to pay is to be made less sharp.

The language of reform emphasises the virtues of competition, choice and accountability in their market form. Competition between public sector agencies and with the private sector is seen as ensuring efficiency and responsiveness to the customer. The choice on offer takes the market form of an option of going elsewhere if a particular service is unsatisfactory. If you do not like your local authority's housing service then housing association or private landlord alternatives are to be made available. A further watchword of the reform programme is accountability, and what is offered is a particular form of market accountability premised on the view that there should be a close relation between paying and receiving. This is the rationale behind the introduction of community charge. It underlies the commitment to higher rent levels in housing provision and the charging provisions embodied within the 1989 Local Government and Housing Act.

These developments in turn contribute to a trend towards transforming the experience of public service consumption. Echoing the shift in private sector forms of consumption associated with the transition from Fordism the 'differentiated' consumer assumes a key role in the management thinking that is developing in local government. The 'Fordist' approach of providing a standard product for a captive user is no longer viable in an era of choice and competition. As noted earlier, during the 1980s many local authorities had already begun to experiment with less standardised and more responsive forms of service delivery. The Government's legislation simply makes such a customer orientation more essential.

The Audit Commission, again, has taken on and expanded the message about customer orientation. It transfers to the public sector Post-Fordist private management thinking about service delivery:

> Things have changed . . . councils' customers are more demanding and less grateful. They are also better informed, and better able to articulate their demands. People no longer accept that the council knows best . . . and quality is replacing quantity as the main target for local authorities.[50]

'No two customers have identical needs', the Audit Commission continues. 'It is therefore essential genuinely to understand customers, rather than simply to assume what their needs ought to be'. It concludes that the 'onset of competition makes understanding customers more urgent'. The penalty for failure becomes 'not simply poor service but loss of the customers to competitors that understand them better'.[51]

Interest in marketing is growing in local government.[52] School heads talk of the selling and packaging of their institutions because of the need to attract income-generating pupils. Housing departments talk of customer service quality and differentiated products. Leicester City Council's Director, for example, writes:

> Recognising the 'sub-market's and that every individual requires individual attention, we are now attempting to develop a range of services which can be marketed in return for added rent. We aim to offer a series of options such as insurance, internal redecoration, car alarms, gardening services and even cable TV.[53]

The strength and direction of some of these changes in the pattern of consumption is not clear-cut. The Government's reform package is, however, contributing to a process of profound restructuring. On the one hand, local government services seem to be following the Post-Fordist trend away from standardised products towards differentiated products aimed at different consumer groups. This process in turn is associated with a tendency for market allocation or quasi-market forms to determine the distribution of services rather than rationing through professional, bureaucratic or political decision. The aim, it would seem, is to make the system more responsive to those with the necessary money, knowledge or other resources to get access to more lifestyle-tailored, high-quality services. The whole process provides a stepping-stone towards a dual welfare system in which those that can afford it or who have the necessary skills acquire good-quality services in the private sector or in the market place of the public sector. Those without the necessary funds or skills are forced to rely on a basic no-frills state system.

New arrangements for political management

The Conservatives' programme encourages some substantial changes in the political management of the local government system. Several strands can be detected.

First, the arena and scope of local representative democracy appears to be more tightly constrained. Local accountability, even in a narrow financial sense, is unlikely to be enhanced by the introduction of community charge. Rather, because of the simultaneous removal of non-domestic rates from local control the dependence of local authorities on centrally determined grants is likely to be increased, with around three-quarters (as opposed to a previous half) of local authority income coming from the centre. As a result, expenditure of about 10 per cent above the average could well require the poll tax to be raised 40 per cent above the average.

> That is not genuine local accountability, but distorted accountability designed to produce the answer that the Government wants. Yet even then so little confidence does the Government have in local accountability that it has retained and even strengthened the power to cap local taxation.[54]

Legislation dealing with contracting-out, housing and education seeks to further constrain the room for manoeuvre held by local councillors. The post-Widdicombe legislation described in Chapter 6 seems likely to make the internal working of current machinery of representative democracy more problematic. Effective party government at the local level is challenged by the Government's failure to support appropriate renumeration for leading councillors and forums for party decision-making. Generally, it could be argued that the Government's plans envisage a considerably reduced role for councillors as local representatives. Further there appears to be a growing interest in reducing the number of councillors, turning them away from processes of local representation and party politics, and focusing attention on their role as 'business-like' managing directors of local authorities. One option floated by the Adam Smith Institute is for a small group of higher calibre and higher paid councillors to run the authority. 'The effect will be to produce more business-like councils and much more business-like councillors.'[55]

A second major development in the political management of the local government system is the creation of a variety of local decision-making bodies by-passing directly elected local authorities. Some such as Urban Development Corporations, Training and Enterprise Councils and Housing Action Trusts give business interests direct control over decisions and the allocation of public sector funds close to their interests, subject to central government influence. Business involvement in schools, colleges and polytechnics, and through City Technology Colleges, has also been enhanced as a result of the Government's programme.

Businesses are not the only sectional interest to have the option of increased control over services central to their interest or use. Parents and headteachers in both self-governing and opted-out schools are to be in a position to wield power and make decisions in areas that were previously the preserve of local authorities. In housing, too, the ring-fencing of the housing revenue account and the rise of competing social landlords potentially removes from the ambit of local councillors areas of decision-making and influence.

The institutional fragmentation of local government, then, brings with it a parallel fragmentation of the mechanisms of political representation and control. Collective control through an elected local authority is under challenge from a Conservative programme which hands over control of key services to sectional interests and more generally stresses the role of individual consumer participation in a market place of the public sector. The whole process is conditioned by limits and priorities determined by central government.

In embryonic form, some see the emergence of a new system of 'government by contract' (see also Chapter 11).[56] Central government will contract with executive agencies, quasi-governmental organisations, the private sector, voluntary associations and local authorities to achieve its policy objectives. It will be able to choose to which organisation to allocate resources and lay down performance targets and criteria. The sub-central government agencies including local authorities will in turn make greater use of subcontractors, management buy-outs and freestanding agencies to achieve service delivery to specified performance targets. Service users (individuals or companies) will be able to opt in or out of particular services and test the service they receive against the standard and quality for which they contracted. With only a little exaggeration, such a model turns the process of government into a dynamic paralleling that of a Post-Fordist Benetton!

Concluding remarks

This chapter has sought to examine the direction and consequences of the Conservative's programme for restructuring local government. I do not regard, however, the trends and developments I have identified as inevitable or irresistible. Indeed it is clear that the transformation in the role of local government envisaged in the Thatcherite strategy faces a number of obstacles. There is political resistance from both Conservative and opposition-controlled authorities. Organisational and institutional inertia will limit and distort change. The sheer complexity of some changes and the lack of appropriate technology to make them effective will also slow down progress. The next five years will see the complex mix of measure and counter-measure continue as both central government's strategies and concerns and the local government system's resistance and reaction adapt and develop.

Further, although the powers of elected local authorities are to a degree undermined by elements of the programme, these bodies remain organisations with a considerable range of resources and skills. In this sense I agree with Michael Clarke and John Stewart[57] that the potential remains for local authorities to mobilise their powers and, working with local community and user groups, develop initiatives and action in a direction not envisaged or necessarily favoured by the Thatcher Government.

For Clarke and Stewart the role of the enabling council is not restricted to the vision contained in Thatcherite thinking. For them an enabling council is one which takes a broad responsibility for the social and economic issues confronting its area and uses all the means at its disposal to meet the needs of those living in its area. This is the vision also offered in Stewart and Stoker's *From Local Administration to Community Government*,[58] in Robin Murray's *Breaking with Bureaucracy*,[59] and in the final chapter of this book. Plainly the odds in many respects favour the Ridley/ Thatcher vision! But the alternative vision is in many ways just as compatible with a transition for Fordism.

The future of local government whilst conditioned by social and economic changes is by no means predetermined by those changes. A political and ideological battleground surrounding local government remains.

Notes and references

Acknowledgements This chapter has benefited a great deal from comments provided on an earlier draft by John Benington, Desmond King and Kieron Walsh. Their telling criticisms of, and disagreements with, my initial analysis enabled me to revise my argument substantially. Indeed I still regard this chapter as very much work in progress. I will be glad if it stimulates further discussion and debate about what the future holds for local government and how best we can understand the major restructuring of local political institutions that is under way.

1. For an overview of the regulationist approach, see B. Jessop, 'Regulation Theory', Post-Fordism and the State', *Captial and Class*. no. 34 (1988) pp. 147–68; and B. Jessop, 'Regulation Theories in Retrospect and Prospect', Paper to the International Conference on Regulation, Barcelona, 16–18 June 1988. Both these papers provide an extensive bibliography of regulationist work.
2. In particular it draws extensively on M. Aglietta, *A Theory of Capitalist Regulation* (New Left Books, 1979); A. Lipietz, *Mirages and Miracles* (Verso, 1987); P. Blackburn, R. Coombs and K. Green, *Technology Economic Growth and the Labour Process* (Macmillan, 1989); B. Jessop, *Conservative Regimes and the Transition to Post-Fordism: The Cases of Britain and West Germany*, no. 47, Essex

Papers in Politics and Government, March 1988; M. de Vroey, 'A Regulation Approach Interpretation of the Contemporary Crisis', *Capital and Class*, no. 23 (1984).

3. See, for example, studies in Aglietta (USA), Lipietz (several countries) and Jessop (Britain and West Germany) cited in note 2. In addition, see M. Kenney and R. Florida, 'Beyond Mass Production: Production and the Labor Process in Japan', *Politics and Society*, vol. 16, no. 1 (March 1988) pp. 121–58.

4. Aglietta, *Theory of Capitalist Regulation*, p. 158.

5. Those that develop a neo-Fordist analysis include Aglietta, ibid, and Blackburn *et al.*, *Technology Economic Growth*.

6. The Post-Fordist analysis is presented in Jessop, *Conservative Regimes*. In addition it is presented in R. Murray, 'Life After Henry (Ford)', *Marxism Today*, October 1988, pp. 8–13.

7. T. Peters and R. Waterman, *In Search of Excellence* (Harper & Row, 1981); T. Peters and N. Austin, *A Passion for Excellence* (Random House, 1985).

8. On this point, see Jessop, *Conservative Regimes*.

9. For another related schema of social and economic change, see S. Lash and J. Urry, *The End of Organized Capitalism* (Polity, 1987).

10. This point I owe particularly to John Benington.

11. For a more detailed account, see G. Stoker, *The Politics of Local Government* (Macmillan, 1988) ch. 1.

12. This point is also made by R. Jackman, 'Local Government Finance', in M. Loughlin, M. D. Gelfrand and K. Young (eds), *Half a Century of Municipal Decline, 1935–1985* (Allen & Unwin, 1985) pp. 144–68.

13. Sheffield City Council, *Sheffield Jobs Audit*, 1985.

14. M. Geddes, 'The Capitalist State and the Local Economy', *Capital and Class*, no. 35 (Summer 1988) pp. 85–120.

15. P. Hoggett, 'A Farewell to Mass Production? Decentralisation as an Emergent Private and Public Sector Paradigm', in P. Hoggett and R. Hambleton (eds), *Decentralisation and Democracy*, Occasional Paper no. 28, School for Advanced Urban Studies, p. 233.

16. J. Stewart, 'The Function and Management of Local Authorities', in Louglin *et al.*, *Half a Century*, pp. 98–121.

17. J. Benington, *Local Government Becomes Big Business* (CDP, 1975).

18. C. Cockburn, *The Local State* (Pluto, 1977).

19. For an attempt to break the hold of private sector models on public sector management thinking, see J. Stewart and S. Ranson, *Management in the Public Domain* (LGTB, 1988); and S. Ranson and J. Stewart, 'Citizenship and Government: The Challenge for Management in the Public Domain', *Political Studies*, vol. 37, no. 1 (1989) pp. 5–25.

20. For a fuller discussion, see Stoker, *Politics of Local Government*, ch. 7.

21. D. King and F. Longstreth, 'The New Institutionalism: Structural Constraints and the Political Economy of State Policy', Paper presented at Annual Conference of the Political Studies Association,

Plymouth Polytechnic, 12–14 April 1988.
22. See J. Benington, 'Local Economic Strategies', *Local Economy*, vol. 1, no. 1 (1986) pp. 7–33; and J. Mawson and D. Miller, 'Interventionist Approaches to Local Employment and Economic Development', in V. A. Hausner (ed.), *Critical Issues in Urban Economic Development* (Oxford University Press, 1987).
23. Geddes, 'Capitalist State', pp. 94–5.
24. On the rise of community and user groups, see J. Gyford, 'Diversity, Secionalism and Local Democracy', in Committee of Inquiry into the Conduct of Local Authority Business (Chairman: D. Widdicombe), *Research Volume IV – Aspects of Local Democracy*, Cmnd 9805 (HMSO, 1986) pp. 106–31.
25. For a review, see Gyford, ibid, and Stoker, *Politics of Local Government*, ch. 9.
26. Figures taken from Annual Reports produced by Wandsworth in 1984–5 and 1986–7.
27. A point made strongly in P. Beresford, '*Good Council Guide: Wandsworth 1978–1987* (Centre for Policy Studies, 1987).
28. On this point, see Jessop, *Conservative Regimes*.
29. For a review which stresses the associated changes in rules and institutions, see M. Moran, 'Politics and Law in Financial Regulation', in C. Graham and T. Prosser (eds), *Waiving the Rules: The Constitution Under Thatcherism* (Open University Press, 1988) pp. 56–73.
30. Again for a review which focuses on the associated changes in rules and institution, see C. Graham and T. Prosser, 'Rolling Back the Frontiers? The Privatisation of State Enterprises', in Graham and Prosser, *Waiving the Rules*, pp. 73–95.
31. A. Gamble, 'On, And On, And On . . . ?', *Marxism Today*, November 1988, p. 14. For a fuller development, see A. Gamble, *The Free Economy and the Strong State* (Macmillan, 1988) pp. 224–31.
32. See K. Ewing, 'Trade Unions and the Constitution: The Impact of the New Conservatives', in Graham and Prosser, *Waiving the Rules*, pp. 135–53.
33. A. Brown and D. King, 'Economic Change and Labour Market Policy: Corporalist and Dualist Tendencies in Britain and Sweden; *West European Politics*, vol. 11, no. 3 (July 1988) pp. 75–91.
34. See the Annual Corporate Plans of the MSC. Also C. St John-Brooks, *Who Controls Training: The Rise of the MSC*, Fabian Tract 506 (1985).
35. See Jessop, *Conservative Regimes*, p. 24. For a more detailed discussion, N. Johnson, *The Welfare State in Transition* (Wheatsheaf, 1987); E. Papadakis and P. Taylor-Gooby, *The Private Provision of Public Welfare* (Wheatsheaf, 1987); and P. Alcock and P. Lee (eds), *Into the Third Term: Thatcherism and the Future of Welfare*, Social and Urban Policy Studies No. 1, Sheffield City Polytechnic.
36. Gamble, 'On, And On . . . , p. 13; and Gamble, *The Free Economy and Strong State*, ch. 6.

37. D. Massey, 'A New Class of Geography', *Marxism Today*, May 1988, pp. 12–17.
38. N. Ridley, *The Local Right: Enabling Not Providing* (Centre for Policy Studies, 1988).
39. Ibid, pp. 16–17.
40. Ibid, p. 29.
41. See, for example, Adam Smith Institute, *Wiser Counsels. The Reform of Local Government* (ASI, 1989).
42. Ibid, pp. 26–30.
43. Quoted in the *Guardian*, 27 February 1989, p. 3.
44. See Blackburn *et al.*, *Technology Economic Growth*, ch. 7.
45. J. Banham, *Redrawing the Frontiers of the Public Sector*, The 1988 Redcliffe Maud Memorial Lecture. Banham moved from the Audit Commission to become Director General of the Confederation of British Industry.
46. For a fuller discussion of the impact of IT, see Blackburn *et al. Technology Economic Growth*, and P. Blackburn and R. Sharpe (eds), *Britain's Industrial Renaissance?* (Routledge, 1988).
47. Banham, *Redrawing the Frontiers*, p. 10.
48. Ridley, *The Local Right*, p. 29.
49. Ibid, p. 28.
50. Audit Commission, *The Competitive Council*, Management Papers, no. 1, March 1988, para. 10.
51. Ibid, para. 27.
52. See K. Walsh, *Marketing in Local Government* (Longman, 1989).
53. T. Cantle, 'Leicester's Response to the Housing Act', *Local Government Policy Making*, vol. 15, no. 4 (March 1989) pp. 30–1.
54. J. Stewart and G. Stoker, *From Local Administration to Community Government*, Fabian Research Series 351 (1988) p. 3.
55. Adam Smith Institute, *Wiser Counsels*, p. 58. Indeed the Institute suggests that there should be an option for local communities to run their services through a community company rather than a local authority, pp. 50–4.
56. G. Mather, 'Government by Contract', Paper to RIPA Annual Conference, 1988.
57. M. Clarke and J. Stewart, *The Enabling Council* (LGTB, 1988).
58. Stewart and Stoker, *From Local Administration*.
59. R. Murray, *Breaking with Bureaucracy*, CLES Report, 1987.

9 The Changing Organisation and Management of Local Authorities

John Stewart

The Government's legislation challenges the role of local authorities but it is also challenging their way of working. Local authorities have come to define their role by the direct provision of services and their organisation and management have reflected that definition. The Government's legislation means that the role of local authorities can no longer be defined in those terms but must encompass contracting out the provision of services, enabling others to provide the service or regulating the provision. The new ways of working require changes in the management and organisation of local authorities.

Change was taking place even without the pressure of central government legislation. The certainties of an era of growth in which the need for established services went unchallenged had been replaced by an era of uncertainty in which local authorities faced a changing society. In such an era there is a need for local authorities to rediscover their role as local government, which is not defined by the direct provision of services, but by a concern for the problems and needs faced by a local community and by an emphasis on local choice on how those needs and problems are to be met (a concept developed under the phrase 'community government' in Chapter 12). In this chapter it is assumed that elected local authorities are justified by their role as local government rather than as agency for the delivery of services, and that their organisation and management should support that role.

The argument of this chapter is that management and organisation in local authorities have to change, not only to meet the requirements of the legislation but also to meet the challenge of local government. It will argue that the government legislation provides stimuli to the development of local authorities as local government, but also puts obstacles in the way. Those obstacles can be overcome if they use the important resources which they still have at their disposal not merely of finance, but of staff and their skill, of information, of land and property, of powers and duties, of influence and of the capacity to command attention. The need is to build the capacity to use those resources. For that a new management is required.

The chapter starts by describing past ways of working and the organisation and management that supported those ways of working. That is the starting-point for change.

The guiding organisational principles of the past

There has been a remarkable uniformity in the past organisation and management of local authorities. Although local authorities as local government are constituted for local choice, that choice has been limited by a set of organisational principles, which become embedded in their culture. Those principles supported and expressed their role as agencies for the delivery of a series of services, rather than as local government.

Local authorities have been organised for the direct provisions of services. That responsibility became so dominant in their working that many have come to see it as their only role. It was assumed almost without question that if they were given responsibility for a service they should provide that service directly. It was assumed too that they should themselves employ all the staff required to carry out the function.

Just how deeply these assumptions have been embedded can be seen in the arguments that surrounded local government reorganisation. The pervasive principle of the necessity of self-sufficiency drove the search for larger authorities. It led the Redcliffe Maud Report to assert that only an authority serving a population of some 250 000 or more will have at its disposal the range and the calibre of staff, and the technical and financial resources, necessary for effective provision of the whole group ... of education, housing and the personal services.[1]

If the direct provision of services is seen as an organisational necessity, then it is not surprising that the management of the local authority reflected that necessity. The local council organised service provision through a series of committees centring on the services provided. Inevitably much of the work of those committees focused on the running of services. The attention of councillors was turned away from wider concerns, focusing instead on the operational necessities of the services. It was as if councillors sought to control directly and immediately the operation of the services as their means of ensuring political direction. The committee cycle in which meeting follows meeting on a regular basis leads to agendas filled with the requirements of an ongoing process, that fails to separate direction from action or experience from review.

The service departments were organised for the delivery of services on a standard basis. Deep in their workings were:

the principle of uniformity, which meant that the departments were organised to provide a uniform service throughout the working of the authority
the principle of hierarchy which ensures the authority of the council and committee through tiers of control
the principle of functionalism which divides up the work of the authority according to the expertise required.

These principles ensure the reliable delivery of an established pattern of services on a continuing basis.

The central departments (Treasurer's, Personnel, Legal, etc.) have given support to the work of service departments, but have also enforced formal accountability of the departments and committees through detailed control of establishments and budgets. The principle of accountability has been interpreted more as adherence to rule and procedure, ensuring the formal responsibility of the council to the electorate, than on continuing accountability to the community or on management accountability for performance.

The culture of local authorities has been a professional culture. The senior positions in departments have been held by those drawn from the dominant professions in that department and professional boundaries have been the basis on which departmental territories have been defended. Professionalism has brought the strengths of expertise, commitment and accepted standards but it has meant that concerns of expertise and knowledge beyond the professions have lacked access or leverage.

Organisational assumptions based on these principles have been so deeply embedded that they have rarely been challenged – indeed they have been so much a part of the working practise that they have been seen not as assumptions but as facts of life in local government:

the assumption of self-sufficiency
the necessity of the traditional committee system
the departmental model based on the bureaucratic principle
the model of accountability enforced by detailed financial and personnel control
the dominance of the professional culture

In combination these organisational assumptions have defined the meaning of 'sound administration', even if they have not realised good management.

Strengths and weaknesses

These principles have brought great strengths to the working of local government. In the long years of growth between 1945 and 1975 there was a certainty about the tasks of local authorities, as they expanded their services to meet clear needs.

The working practices that these principles had sustained came under increasing attack as the era of growth turned into an era of constraint and as the certainties of past patterns of activities became the uncertainties of a changing society. The danger was that local authorities had become enclosed both from the community they governed and from the public they served, with the result that activities had become their own justification and the carrying-out of established procedures the measure of success.

If one considers local authorities as political institutions constituted both for local government and providing public service, the past ways of working can be and have been criticised for the

focus of council and committees on the operational requirements of services, rather than on the needs and problems of the community
the lack of a clear strategy in relation to those needs and problems
the failure to review both policy and performance
the barriers that limit both access for the public as customer and citizen and learning from the public about the experience of services
the lack of organisational space left by the operation of detailed controls for the effective development of management
the councillor as chair or member of a service committee tending to become more the representative of the producers than of the community.

Such criticisms were being made within local government as well as outside. As the politics of local government became more assertive under the challenge of change, left, right and centre in local politics made a similar analysis of the danger of 'professionalised bureaucracies' that determined what was needed by the public, without regard to what the public wanted. While diagnosis was shared, response was not shared – the left stressing the need to be responsive to the public as community and the right stressing the importance of responsiveness to the public in the market.

Change in management and organisation has come increasingly onto the agenda. There has been a new emphasis on the need to respond as local government to community problems, to focus on the public as customer and citizen, to develop strategies and to review performance.

The impact of government legislation – stimuli towards local government

Changes, then, were taking place before the government legislation, in part as awareness grew in local government of the need for change in the new era of uncertainty and in part under the stimulus of the Audit Commission, the Local Government Training Board and other organisations.[2]

One impact of central government legislation has been to stimulate local authorities to find new ways of working that encourage effective management as local government. Five results can be highlighted.

Clarification of policy

Compulsory competitive tendering means that local authorities have had to clarify their policies and to specify what they require from the services put out to contract. Too often in the past committee agendas have turned the attention of councillors away from what is needed from a service, towards how the service should be run. Yet it is the choice on what is needed that is at the heart of local government.

Monitoring of performance and quality

Where work is contracted out (or indeed contracted in) the local authority has to ensure that performance meets requirements. The emphasis is moved from direct provision to monitoring performance and to an emphasis on securing quality of service. Monitoring performance will also be needed of schools operating under local management schemes. Where the local authority is not involved in direct management it has to develop the means of monitoring performance with an emphasis on achievement and on quality.

The devolution of management responsibility

The contracting-out legislation and the legislation introducing local management of schools has led to the devolution of management responsibility. The separation of the contractor role from the client role and the requirements of the contract mean that there is a clear management responsibility to achieve the requirements of the council. As internal contracting extends within the council through service agreements between the central departments and other departments the same devolution of management responsibility is required throughout the working of the authority.

A focus on the public

The legislation providing for opting-out, whether in housing or in education, has reinforced the growing concern to provide services that are responsive to their customers.

The challenge to self-sufficiency

The government legislation challenges the assumption of self-sufficiency. It shows that where local authorities are given responsibility for a service they need not provide that service directly. The challenge to the principle of self-sufficiency could open up a wider enabling role. The enabling role may be seen merely as enabling other organisations to do the work of the authority, but it can mean enabling the community to meet the needs and problems they face in the most effective way possible, which may or may not be direct provision.[3]

The legislation can be seen as directly or indirectly, intentionally or unintentionally, leading local authorities to change in ways that support their role as local government focusing on community needs and problems, on what is required from a service, on public attitudes to the service, and on ensuring that performance is realised and quality achieved. These changes in ways of working can be welcomed by the advocate of local government, even though the reduction in responsibilities is opposed.

The impact of the legislation – the dangers to local government

There are however other consequences of the legislation that can weaken the role of local authorities as local government. These are the consequences not of particular parts of the legislation, but of its overall effect, along with other changes in our system of government. The effects which we shall highlight are:
the fragmentation of the system of local government between different agencies and organisations
the fragmentation of the organisation of local authorities themselves

each of which presents challenges for the management of local authorities, if a role as local government is to be sustained.

The fragmentation of the system of local government

Local authorities have never been all-purpose authorities, but in recent years the system of local government has become increasingly fragmented. In 1974 the powers of the county boroughs were divided between four authorities – county, district, health authorities and water authorities. Since 1979 and increasingly recently the process of fragmentation has proceeded apace. The abolition of the GLC and the metropolitan counties divided their functions between a wide variety of agencies. But beyond these specific changes we have seen the creation of a range of special-purpose agencies by-passing local authorities or hived off from them, such as the bus companies and airport companies established in the mid-1980s. The post-1987 legislation extends this process of fragmentation through, for example, the creation of Housing Action Trusts and the provision for grant-maintained schools.

Increasingly local authorities concerned as local government with the needs and problems of their areas have to work with and through other organisations. This requires from local authorities that seek such a role a new capacity for the management of influence rather than the management of action.

The management of influence has its own requirements.[4] Above all it requires an understanding that extends beyond organisational boundaries. Influence grows in organisational understanding. It requires too a capacity to realise and to use the many resources for influence. One simple example will make the point. Local authorities have representatives on many other organisations. They are resources often unused by local authorities. They may make no arrangements for briefing them or for receiving reports from them. Local authorities need to build an organisational focus for the enabling role required by the fragmented system.

The fragmentation within the local authority

The main change brought about by the legislation described in this book is fragmentation within local authorities. The direct and indirect effect of the legislation is to divide local authorities into a series of separate units whose relationships are increasingly conducted on a contractual or quasi-contractual basis.

Compulsory competitive tendering (CCT) means that certain of the work of the local authorities will be carried out by outside contractors whose relationship will be governed by the terms of the contract. But even where the contract is awarded internally it will be carried out by a Direct Services Organisation separated off from the client and other parts of the organisation and whose relationships will also be governed by the terms of the contract rather than by membership of the organisation or by hierarchical control. Beyond these direct effects, the pressures of CCT are leading local authorities to create semi-contractual relations within the organisation specifying the services to be given and the price to be paid.

The effect of other legislation reinforces this tendency. The arrangements for housing finance will lead to the ring-fencing of the housing revenue account. The provisions for the local management of schools make them semi-autonomous units responsible for delivering the national curriculum and such other requirements as the local authority can lay down for them.

Some of the effects of particular changes have already been discussed, but it is their overall effect in which danger lies.

The danger is that the local authority will become a series of separate units each with its own defined task, and that there will be no capacity to look beyond the units or to consider the interrelationship between them. Local government will be lost between the fragments and the responsibilities of those units will often be limited to the terms of contracts fixed for a defined period of time. The local authority could be in danger of

losing a community perspective
blocking its means of learning
lacking flexibility and adaptability
weakening public accountability
neglecting the public service ethic.

The weakening of the community perspective

The more the activities of units within local authorities are focused on the requirements of separate contracts, the greater the danger that they will not identify emerging problems or be able to deal with issues that concern more than one unit. The need is not sufficiently met by the client department which itself is in danger of focusing on the contract, rather than on the community it serves. There is a need for the authority to have the capacity to look beyond the separate contracts and to determine the relationship between them.

The barriers to learning

Learning will not easily flow across the boundaries of the fragmented authority, since the responsibilities of the separate units will be limited to their particular areas of concern. Departments have traditionally learnt, however imperfectly, through the hierarchy of accountability, from those who provide the service. Client is divided from contractor but still needs the understanding that comes from the direct provision of the service.

Learning is necessary, if local authorities are to be able to adjust their activities (and their contracts), in relation to the needs and problems of the areas they govern. They have to build into their organisation a capacity for the learning that could be lost in the newly fragmented structure.

The rigidity of contractual relations

A contract is not easily re-negotiated without a cost. A contract therefore tends to freeze the nature of a service for the period of the contract which may be up to five years or beyond. The more that work is subject to contract the greater the rigidity built into the structure. There is a reduction in the extent to which the local authority can adjust to changing circumstances. There is also a reduction in the flexibility of the authority in its day-to-day working because of its inability to move staff from one task to another or for staff to make day-to-day adjustments in their work in response to the immediate pressures they face.

The rigidity built into the contracts makes it important for the authority to consider the capacity for flexibility within them and also to consider how flexibility can be sustained and developed beyond the contracts.

Public accountability

Actions taken by local authorities are justified by public accountability. They exercise and will continue to exercise substantial power. For the exercise of such power accountability is required. Public accountability involves the right to know *of* and the right to voice *on* the activities of public authority and the power to hold to account.

In the developing pattern of local government, many of the activities for which local authorities are responsible will be carried out through other organisations, bound not by accountability to the public but by a contract of other form of agreement. Public accountability can be lost in misunderstanding. The local authority has to ensure that the requirements of public accountability are met through the forms in which contracts are managed.

The loss of the public service ethic

The dilemmas posed by many of these issues can be summed up as the danger to a public service ethic. Sir Robin Butler, the Head of the Civil Service, has made this point about developments in central government. He said:

> But I also believe that, in the course of that development, we must retain the unifying characteristics of the service which are not only its traditional strengths but its duties – the requirements of equity, accountability, impartiality and a wide view of the public interest. The unity of the Civil Service offers stability and a continuing corpus of tradition, knowledge and experience which is part of the infrastructure of a democratic society.

He believes:

> there need be no inconsistency between maintaining these long-established assets and virtues and the movement towards more individual responsibilities. Within the uniting framework provided by the special characteristics of Government work, it will be possible to achieve the flexibility which gives local managers the scope to provide effectively for the service they are delivering, the public they are serving and the local conditions they are faced with.[5]

The dilemmas can be resolved if they are faced. The issue is how the public service ethic can be maintained in a fragmented system. That places special requirements on the leadership of the authority.

Government legislation is changing the nature of management and organisation in local authorities as they seek to meet its requirements. My test of those changes is whether they help to make the local authority more effective as local government. Some of the changes do so, focusing the attention of councillors on what is required from a service more than on the organisation of the service, and defining their roles more by concern for the community and the customer than for the production process. Yet in the changes danger also lies. The local authority has to consider how

fragmentation can be balanced by an overall perspective
the loss of learning can be countered in new sources of learning
rigidity can be avoided in a capacity for flexibility
the confusion in public accountability can be countered by a re-focusing of accountability
the public service ethic be maintained in a fragmented structure

For if this is not achieved, local authorities cease to be local government, and without that they have no rationale.

A local authority that seeks to overcome those problems has to consider the organisation of the corporate capacity of the authority to ensure the overview to sustain the public interest, to seek out new sources of learning, to search out scope for flexibility, to sustain public accountability and to maintain the public service ethic. What is needed is central organisation, not to control, but to enhance organisational capacity. A fragmented system creates a need for system management, for without that, there can be no local government.

One of the changes brought about by the impact of the government legislation is, therefore, a reconsideration of the role of the central capacity of the authority. It will be important for the chief executive to focus on these issues and to have organisational support in those tasks. We could see the emergence of a chief executive's department as the department of local government sustaining community strategy, policy direction, organisational review and organisational values and working with a councillor forum that can give expression to those requirements. Perhaps both chief executive and Policy and Resources Committees can gain new meanings in expressing and supporting local government.

In conclusion – a new management

The challenge for local authorities is to meet the requirements of the legislation and yet to sustain the values of local government in a changed and changing environment. Clearly traditional patterns of organisation and management have to change also. A new management is needed that

will be grounded in political purpose and political direction
will focus on the needs and problems faced by the community, but will not see the responsibilities of the authority as limited to direct provision.
will be close to the public as customer and as citizen
will develop an enabling role in using the resources of the authority to meet community needs
will sustain and develop a capacity for learning that will not be limited to contractual requirements
will set directions for the authority and clarify policy requirements
will develop pluralism in ways of working, building a capacity for indirect as well as direct management or for the management of influence and the management of contracts as well as the management of action
will devolve management responsibility both within contracts and outside them as a basis for action and accountability
will review performance and develop quality monitoring
will express a public service ethic in organisational values
will develop active staff management to develop, to motivate and to learn
will build an organisation that can realise the potential within, removing the barriers to the development of staff
will break out of the limitation of past organisational forms to meet new requirements, reforming committee cycles, and modifying bureaucratic working
will redefine the role of the centre of the local authority as the

expression of the values and purposes of local government by system management

will support the many roles of the councillor beyond the traditional committee role

will build a capacity for general management beyond the professional career.

For the tasks now required of management are many and various and both the organisation and processes of local authorities have to face not merely the continuing necessities of direct provision, but of new modes of working. That will require a new management that realises the potential of local government in difficult times.

Notes and references

1. *Report, Royal Commission on Local Government in England 1966–1969*, Cmnd 4040 (HMSO, 1987) para. 257.
2. Cf The Audit Commission, *The Competitive Council* 1988; Michael Clarke and John Stewart *Managing Tomorrow* (The Local Government Training Board, 1988).
3. Michael Clarke and John Stewart, *The Enabling Authority* (Local Government Training Board, 1988).
4. John Stewart, *Understanding the Management of Local Government* (Longman, 1988) pp. 32–43.
5. Sir Robin Butler, *Government and Good Management – are they compatible?* (Institute of Personnel Management).

10 The New Right, the New Left and Local Government

Desmond S. King

Introduction

As the other chapters in this volume document, major changes are occurring to British local government. These changes are significant ones which challenge conventional conceptions about the purposes of local government and the political values which should be represented in the political institutions of local authorities. This chapter reviews the political values commonly imputed by the left and the right to local government institutions and assesses how these values have fared in national and local policy during the 1980s.[1] The chapter is therefore concerned primarily with normative arguments and not simply with describing government policy. It is not assumed that there is any direct relationship between political values and public policy but it is assumed that political principles constitute relevant criteria with which to discuss public policy.[2]

The chapter draws a broad distinction between theories of the new right of which the Conservatives are taken as representative and theories of the left based upon the policies and writings of local and national Labour party politicians. With regard to these two political groupings the liberal and social democratic political values influencing their respective theories of local government are examined.[3] The main contention is that both the left and the right confront a problem over local government.

For the left the core issue is: how are meaningful powers of local choice to be combined with a commitment to the achievement of social democratic objectives such as the social rights of citizenship?[4] This issue is a pressing one because with the dominance of national politics by the Conservative Party during the 1980s the left has regenerated its interest in local democracy. It is not a new problem in that devising a theory about the division of power by area has always been difficult for social democrats: the imperative of increasing equality has implied national redistributive policies which have eroded local discretionary powers.[5] But since the late 1970s the most creative work of local left politicians has involved formulating distinct local economic interventionist strategies focused on particular authorities only, independently of national policy. The objective of reducing inequality through national policy has been compromised in the politics of local activists.

The political right has a rigorous theory of local government. The right (and especially the 1980s' 'new right'[6]) is committed, for political and economic reasons, to the maximisation of local choice, accountability and fiscal management, and welcomes variation between local authorities in service provision and standards. The problem here is that national policy fails dramatically, through its centralising tendency, to realise these principles.

The chapter is divided into two parts, the first reviewing the political values for local government inherited from the liberal and social democratic traditions. The second part develops a typology of left and right theories of local government, relates them to the earlier values, and discusses them critically in the light of sample policies. The concluding section restates the problem of local government facing the left and the right.

Two preliminary points should be noted. The first is that political theorists addressing the design of government institutions tend to adopt a national focus.[7] What theorising there is about local government has been undertaken by scholars elsewhere, notably Americans such as Harvey, Peterson and Tiebout.[8] The neglect of theory is regrettable. All political institutions, and all treatises for local government, are premised on political values, whether or not they are made explicit.

The second point concerns the weak constitutional position of local government in Britain. If the British constitution is ambiguous about central government it is almost silent about local authorities with the exception of the overarching *ultra vires* doctrine. This doctrine holds that sub-national authorities may undertake no activities not expressly empowered to them by Parliament. Parliamentary sovereignty is absolute and structures the institutions and activities of local government, enabling the national government to modify the 'rules of the game' underlying central–local relations and local institutions when and as it sees fit.[9] There are no constitutional constraints upon such modifications, a position restated in the Widdicombe Committee Report:

> The position of local government in our political system is . . . governed by constitutional convention as well as by the simple fact that it derives its existence and its powers from Parliament. It would, however, be wrong to assume that such constitutional convention amounts to or derives from any natural right for local government to exist. It is a convention based on, and subject to, the contribution which local government can bring to good government.[10]

There are political cultural constraints upon government control but they are hardly decisive and rarely defined by national politicians beyond a general but flexible belief in the 'importance' of local government. Both the postwar professionalisation of local government and emphasis upon administrative duties have weakened the ties between local communities and local authorities as a political and participatory institution expressive of local community concerns, thereby weakening the position of local government in the community. The Widdicombe Report did however report considerable support for the retention of local government institutions in its opinion surveys.[11]

The problem of local government

Within these constitutional and cultural limits what political values ought to inform local government and for what activities should it be responsible? The standard liberal answer is that national government sets policy parameters within which local authorities administer services but varying them to meet best local needs. This argument implies that certain activities have consequences for residents of the local community *only* and these should be decided upon locally. This position is the distinct 'liberal' defence of local government, in the tradition of John Stuart Mill.[12] By implication local authorities should have substantial discretion in the discharge of their local responsibilities. Local authorities provide a mechanism through which conflicts about local issues – that is, issues which do not affect those living outside the local jurisdiction – can be resolved thereby enhancing personal liberty and local control.

The difficulty with the conventional liberal position is how few activities it includes and how activities which initially may seem to have no implications outside the locality do so subsequently. It is very difficult to draw a distinction between first-order issues which should be resolved by the national government and second-order issues which can be devolved to local authorities and in respect of which they should hold discretionary enabling powers. For example, take gender rights and welfare state institutions. Through service provision local authorities exercise a key role in implementing the welfare state. Increasingly, feminists have criticised the gender bias of welfare state institutions. What appears to be a second-order problem – the administration of specified services – raises first-order questions – in this case what gender assumptions should underpin welfare state institutions. Drawing distinctions between appropriate spheres of government activity and allocating functions on that basis is difficult. It requires assumptions about political cultural values, definitions of problems and solutions, and political needs which may not be valid, or may cease to be generally accepted over time.

Social democrats confront a problem of distinguishing between national and local government too. The postwar social democratic commitment to reducing inequality and to facilitating equality of opportunity produced a concern with interpersonal inequalities. That is, in order to reduce historical inequalities in education, health, employment and welfare opportunities social democrats constructed national welfare state institutions. A corollary of this strategy was to reduce the discretionary powers of local authorities to ensure that their decisions would not compromise the pursuit of national objectives. The national commitment to interpersonal equality required a commitment to territorial equity which was inconsistent with substantial local powers. In reality, the picture is more complicated. Since the national pursuit of equality was concerned with equality of opportunity rather than of outcome, some role was left to local authorities in responding to the circumstances of their area. But the general principle is clear: a concern with national standards and equities – even if not rigidly conceived – compromises by definition the scope for local autonomy. However, since the late 1970s the activities of local Labour activists indicate a shift away from their previous commitment to national policies for reducing inequality toward an acceptance of a role for local authorities. These issues can be illustrated further by a consideration of the political values imputed by liberals and social democrats to local government.

Political values for local government

The core liberal values: liberty, participation and efficiency

In the liberal tradition of writing about local government the dominant intellectual influence is Mill, who valued politics as a means of achieving freedom, nourishing the self-development of the individual and satisfying the imperatives of allocative efficiency.[13] Local government is claimed to enhance *liberty* by forming a bulwark against the power of the state. More recently, scholars argue that local government diffuses power in the political system.[14] Instead of concentrating all political power centrally, local government and the division of power it implies, renders the polity pluralistic. In Britain the diffusion argument is important as a political objective in a highly unitary state but its realisation is weakened by the constitutional supremacy of Parliament. Local government allows power to be spread to some extent but since local institutions are constituted and reconstituted at central discretion this attribute is relative. Without constitutional changes it is difficult to see how the argument could be sustained.

For the 'new right', freedom is defined by the 'power to choose', and exercising individual choice through local government is a further dimension of the political value of freedom. This objective has its most rigorous formulation in public choice theory of which the 'Tiebout hypothesis' is representative.[15] Tiebout argues that for each unit of local government there is a natural 'optimum community size' based on the mixture of taxes levied and services provided toward which all local governments should strive. This 'optimum community size' will be achieved as a consequence of individual consumers' 'searching around' to find that community which suits their needs best. Individual choice determines how local authorities act. If taxes rise intolerably or desired services are not provided then consumers will respond through either 'voice', articulating their discontent, or 'exit', departing from the jurisdiction. A local authority concerned about its fiscal buoyancy must respond to such consumer dissatisfaction. Those consumers unable to exercise these options or convinced of the rightness of the changes will maintain 'loyalty'.[16]

Political participation is a value also imputed to local government. The central claim is that citizens can participate in the running of those affairs which affect them directly and can hold accountable their elected representatives. Participation is at the core of Western ideas about political democracy and a number of claims about its value can be distinguished. First, participation can be advocated as the basis for self-development, a key part of Mill's theory. However, while self-growth is now universally praised it is seldom invoked for its own sake. Second, participation is the necessary basis for the exercise of individual choice by voters. This argument links with the third claim of realising policy objectives and ensuring that certain principles and criteria (for example, non-discrimination and allocative efficiency) are met in local policy.

Fourth, participation can be tied to ideas about community-maintenance and respect for historical traditions. One of the reasons for local government is to allow those citizens who feel part of a particular community to govern themselves and to make decisions about those issues affecting them directly. Political participation is the necessary basis for such local self-government since it enables citizens to express themselves and their concerns about their community. The great difficulty with this argument is how to define community. Is it a sociological phenomenon, a geographical area or a psychological feeling, or all three? Furthermore, the changes in local government boundaries and rapid growth of cities in the twentieth century have eroded the direct link between sociological communities and administrative units. Fifth, Jones and Stewart stress 'localism' in local government, which again requires participation.[17] The claim here is that 'local government is local' and therefore best able to address the needs of local voters, who reside in a particular area and hold opinions about its governance. People require a local political institution through which to address their local needs and to express their desires for that community. Local government can undertake this role more effectively than central government because it is closer to people, has greater contact with them and can respond to changing needs. It is a position opposed directly, therefore, to one based upon national minimum standards. Finally, participation might be pursued for socialist reasons. Participation and control of local government could provide the means for pursuing policies which, for example, aim to transform the local economy and its relationship to the community.

The third core liberal political value for local government is allocative *efficiency*. Local government can allocate public goods and services in the most economically efficient way, a point noted by Mill. Local authorities can address the particular requirements of their jurisdiction and can equalise service provision across the system of local government – though the liberal theory of local government presumes diversity and differences in the system. Within national parameters local authorities should have the discretion to allocate services according to local needs. However, if the premises of the Tiebout hypothesis are operating – the maximisation of individual choice – and local governments have discretionary powers then inter-regional inequalities are more likely to result than equalities because authorities have quite different fiscal bases with which to fund local services.

Some observations about the core liberal values

The three core liberal values each reflect the liberal principle that people should be able to engage in any activity which does not have consequences for others, a claim about which some remarks can be advanced. First, the apparently harmless idea that local authorities know best the needs of their locality and should therefore exercise control over service allocation hides a deeper question: how are local powers of policymaking to be reconciled with national standards? This question is an important one if there are certain political principles and objectives considered important by the national political community – for example, that discrimination by gender or race should not be tolerated or that certain rights should be available to all members of the community irrespective of in which local authority's jurisdiction they reside. There are a number of answers to this quandary. One empirical response holds that discussion of national standards neglects how these are established through local practice:

> national minimum standards, in statutes or statutory instruments, are in fact rare. Most mandatory obligations laid on local authorities are general, empowering local authorities to perform certain functions, giving them duties and laying down procedures, while leaving local authorities discretion about the level and extent of the service provided, its frequency and intensity. The standards which have emerged are not nationally determined. Such standards are in effect standards achieved through local choice.[18]

This judicious response arises from the pivotal role of local authorities, through implementation, in shaping policy. Elsewhere, Jones has elaborated upon the practical difficulties of determining national minimum standards and the difficulties of enforcing them through various performance indicators. He concludes that 'the consequence of the standards approach will be an increase in central civil servants, situated in regional offices so that they can inspect local authorities, to ensure that they conform to the minimum, and can check their claims about the costs of standards ... Thus the minimum standards solution is highly centralist.'[19] This argument can be criticised for exaggerating the problems of a minimum standards approach and for neglecting the potentially undesirable results of expanding local powers: the difficulty of devising input measures is hardly insurmountable for ensuring that political objectives agreed upon nationally are being enforced in a non-discriminatory fashion.

A second response is to determine that national and universal parameters are drawn for policy within which local authorities must modify their policies as they see best for their local needs. It is this second response which seems the more cogent but here the difficulty is ensuring that the powers accruing to local authorities are significant.

The difficulty with both these responses is determining how local choice can be both faithful to national priorities and ensure consequential local power. Can either be achieved without compromising the other? Furthermore, achieving the appropriate balance is difficult enough when there is national agreement about specific priorities, but when that agreement itself is eroded – as it has been during the 1980s – then reconciling local choice and national standards is even more complex. If local choice is granted under these circumstances there are dangers of local abuses of power, the pursuit of discriminatory policies – think of the American South before 1965 – and the growth of significant inequalities between different regions of the country. Central government cannot be viewed as a panacea to all problems of inequality, discrimination and inter-regional variations – a point repeatedly made by local government advocates. But national government can set certain standards, derived from national consensus, with which to guide policy. These standards may compromise the capacity of local authorities to enjoy considerable powers of local choice. If local government is given substantial local powers they may wish, for instance, to expand the role of the market in meeting their statutory obligations. Historical experience suggests that market processes generate inequalities and discrimination, which is why the welfare state was instituted.[20] Having reduced the role of the market at the national level it seems strange to allow its reintroduction at the local level, yet such a development must be tolerated if local powers are to be real. If left-wing politicians want to devolve power they should acknowledge the likely consequences of such actions: while one authority pursues policies they approve of, another will behave quite differently.

This outcome leads to a related issue: the tension often ascribed to the relationship between allocative efficiency and political participation. Both are important political values but facilitating wide participation may produce policy mixes which do not maximise the efficient allocation of local services. This tension has been recognised in a series of government commissions on local government. For instance, it is commonly argued that certain economies of scale can be realised in particular local government boundaries and not in others, an argument which may be used to oppose the construction of small authorities based on particular communities.

Social democratic values: redistribution and autonomy

Social democrats do not dispute the importance of liberty, participation and efficiency as foundational values of political institutions. However, they add a fourth value, that of redistribution, contending that the pursuit of allocative efficiency should be tempered by a concern for economic redistribution. Indeed, such redistribution may be a necessary basis for the effective achievement of liberty and participation. In practice, redistribution has meant introducing a progressive tax system which levies tax proportionate to income and uses these revenues to fund public institutions – such as schools, hospitals, housing and universities – which establish equality of opportunity and advance equality of outcome. But these social democratic objectives have been considered the appropriate business of national not local government. Local authorities have lacked the requisite resources and interventionist powers to make binding policy and, for the same principles valued by Tiebout, they cannot coerce citizens into remaining within their tax regime. Accordingly, the national arena is designated as the one through which redistributive social aims are best pursued.[21]

A fifth value imputed to local government by some socialists – at least by implication – and other theorists is that of autonomy. The idea here is that local governments require a minimum of independence if they are to be able to pursue their own policies. Autonomy refers to both fiscal independence and political powers. In the British political system both attributes of autonomy are weak: the doctrine of *ultra vires* undercuts local political power while the reluctance of the central government to grant fiscal control to local authorities reduces the scope for financial independence. The issue of local finances runs through numerous government commissions, with the principal conclusion that the absence of significant revenue powers – a revenue base independent of central government interference and influence – makes the achievement of local autonomy extremely difficult.[22] Advocates of local government recognise this problem and promote a local income or other tax which local authorities can control and direct as they wish. The main practical constraint with this proposal is the link between local and national tax systems and the consistent unwillingness of governments to leave local finance to local authorities. For instance, the new community charge is intended allegedly to increase local financial accountability but its rate will be subject to national limits.

Just as national political institutions embody political values and normative positions so do local institutions; the substance of these values must be analysed by scholars of local government. That there are difficulties in realising the political principles implied by these values will be apparent in the next part of the chapter which identifies five different theories of local government based on current policies and debates.

Theories of local government: a left–right typology

The distinction drawn between the new right and the left can be further sub-divided into two and three perspectives respectively. The new right embraces both liberal and conservative variants, each implying a different role for local government. The left covers three distinct groupings. First the old statist Labour Party tradition, much criticised now, which was responsible for removing functions from the local to the national level in the post-1945 period thereby devaluing local authorities. Second, the recent Labour activist phenomenon commonly referred to as the 'new urban left', in many ways a reaction to the statist tradition. And third, the movement toward community control or 'enabling' not necessarily linked to the Labour Party though enjoying support within certain parts of it. The five approaches are discussed below.

The right and local government

The liberal new right

The Conservatives have traditionally supported local government and, theoretically, decentralised local government has a significant position within right-wing arguments. The liberal right is committed to maximising individual freedom and to limiting government. Both aims imply decentralisation and considerable powers of local government. The post-1979 Conservative administration has, however, drawn not only upon a liberal political and economic tradition but also upon a conservative, authoritarian one which contradicts, many commentators suggest, the liberal precepts.[23]

Representative of the liberal theory is the 'Tiebout hypothesis' discussed above. Tiebout argued that there was an 'optimum community size, toward which local governments could strive. Optimality pertains to the efficient allocation of municipal services, defined 'in terms of the number of residents for which this bundle of services can be produced at the lowest average cost'.[24] Such efficiency will increase individual freedom and choice since citizens will calculate the cost–benefit ratio of service provision (that is, costs in taxes paid and benefits in standard and appropriateness of the services provided) in other jurisdictions before deciding upon a particular residence. Such rational behaviour forces local government to be cost-efficient in its provision of services and to maintain a prosperous economy.

The 'Tiebout hypothesis' is reflected in the community charge legislation and in the pressure to expand compulsory competitive tendering by local authorities, a strategy which reflects other new right criticisms of the inefficiency of the public sector.[25] The community charge is supposed to link directly the consumption of local services with their cost. Accountability is being defined in fiscal terms. This legislation, therefore, embodies specific political values – principally accountability narrowly conceived – about local political institutions. Such an interpretation is supported in the arguments marshalled by the minister introducing the changes when he emphasises how the community charge is intended to allow voters to compare the policies of different local authorities: 'there will therefore be a direct relationship between each authority's spending level and the Community Charge which it has to levy. And the electorate will be able to make direct comparisons between different authorities on the standards of service they provide and the level of charge they levy.'[26] If the Tieboutian principles were being adhered to fully, local authorities would retain complete control over the level of the new charge.

The inconsistences of the community charge can be joined with flaws inherent in the Tieboutian logic. For example, there is little evidence that local residents are able either to calculate their cost–benefit function or to choose to live where they can afford to. Most people live where they do because there is employment there, and while some may be able to pick and choose jobs in different areas many people cannot. In addition, feelings of community and belonging may also discourage residents from 'exiting' an unfavourable tax zone; 'voice' or sullen quietism may be a more likely response.

Politically, the Tiebout hypothesis is appealing to the new right for another reason. One empirical consequence of this theory is the promotion of inter-regional inequality and the weakening of any redistributive role for local government. Power given to local authorities about how to set their local taxes and to allocate their local public goods will produce inequalities because some communities have a wealthier fiscal base than others with which to finance local services. There are also conflicts between groups within the one locality based on different income positions, the resolution of which may require the imposition of national controls. This outcome is problematic only if policymakers are committed to certain national standards and the new right is intent upon the erosion of such standards. The Tieboutian logic imposes costs on local authorities which do pursue redistributive policies; the emphasis is upon the allocation of local public goods only, a point noted by Peterson:

> efficiency in local government promotes city interests. [T]he closer any locality moves toward this ideal match between taxes and services, the more attractive its land becomes. It is thus in the interest of local governments to operate as efficiently as possible. Operating efficiently hardly means operating so as to enhance equality.[27]

For the liberal new right, welfare consists in the maximisation of collective good regardless of how this aggregation is distributed across individuals or, in the case of local government, spatially, an approach which ultimately equates social justice and efficiency. The liberal political value of allocative efficiency overrides any concern with redistribution for social justice.

The Conservative new right

In a recent pamphlet the minister responsible for local government, Nicholas Ridley, provided a major statement of Conservative Government policy toward local authorities.[28] The author proclaims Conservative commitment to local government and to encouraging local diversity and innovation. Yet throughout the pamphlet it is the new right values of conservatism, not liberalism, which predominate. The value of allocative efficiency preempts those of liberty and participation.

Parliamentary sovereignty is paramount: 'Parliament must continue to play a role in determining the essential framework in which local authorities operate.'[29] The central government should specify local functions, the constitutional position of local authorities, their taxation levels, 'standards of provision for services of a national character',[30] and ensure allocative efficiency in local service provision. The author is clear about public expectations too: 'what the general public wants of local government is that it should provide good services as efficiently as possible',[31] an objective which requires a commitment to competition, personal responsibility, and increased use of the private sector.

There is an ambivalence in Ridley's position regarding local authority service provision. The Conservatives seem to want to grant considerable powers to local authorities but fear the fiscal consequences of so doing. In other words, the Conservatives are keen on local government as long as these local authorities satisfy central criteria and aims, as the following passage indicates:

> what is clear . . . is that the more effectively and efficiently local authorities operate in providing services in an accountable way, responsive to needs of their local communities and competing effectively with other providers where that is relevant, the less need there is likely to be for central government and detailed control . . . Conversely, where local responsibility breaks down there is inevitably stronger pressure for central intervention.[32]

Absent from this position is a willingness to grant greater local freedom *per se*; rather there is a reliance upon the conservative, 'strong state', strand of new right theory. This centralist position is supported by the constitutional position of Parliament and it is revealing that the Conservatives are unwilling to query this status.

The Conservatives emphasise accountability defined fiscally as a 'more direct relationship between payment for local services through local taxation and the services being provided'.[33] The community charge will force financial prudence upon authorities and stimulate greater participation by voters acting as consumers with precise fiscal objectives and worries: 'the level of the Community Charge and the costs of services provided by different councils will be compared and questioned'.[34] But there are major areas of Conservative local policy which are not subject to the imperatives of accountability and participation. For instance, the financially large urban development corporations have been established without significant local representation. These corporations are administering large budgets and implementing policies with fundamental implications for the development of the local communities, yet these latter are denied effective representation and cannot therefore hold the corporations accountable, however this value is defined.[35]

In sum, the new right liberal strand has a philosophy of local government based on the principle that local communities should control taxing and spending policies which satisfies best their voters. The key political values are those of liberty and accountability, defined fiscally, and allocative efficiency with a constant attention to the scope of reducing government and expanding private sector responsibilities. These are the values and aims which have been promoted by the new right think-tanks such as the Institute of Economic Affairs, the Adam Smith Institute and the Centre for Policy Studies. But government policy has reflected these principles in part only. The community charge, and drive to competitive tendering, both stem from the accountability and efficiency priorities, but the Government has neither implemented these as fully as they might nor questioned the fundamental Parliamentary sovereignty and central government dominance which a proper reading of their liberal principles would dictate. To explain this pattern, it is necessary to turn to the second conservative strand of new right theory manifested in policies such as the urban development corporations as well as in the half-hearted devolution of fiscal power to local authorities. The liberal precepts are compromised by central dominated policies. What approximates a robust liberal theory of local government is precluded from becoming a robust liberal practice of local government.

The left and local government

The postwar statist tradition

Like the Conservatives, the Labour Party have long paid lip-service to the importance of local government but concentrated upon national policy. The postwar welfare state initiative was a national policy, though many of the policies were administered locally within national parameters – for example, the introduction of comprehensive education at the secondary level. Between 1945 and the mid-1970s, the Labour Party's dominant policy focus was upon nationalisation policies and the pursuit of equality of opportunity through national redistributive policies.

This statist tradition, the reliance upon national planning, signalled, to some extent, the decline of local government as an independent entity, since political priorities, such as those associated with the welfare state, were judged national responsibilities to be pursued in universal public policies. Local government was, as a consequence, reduced increasingly to an administrative position, a conception strengthened by the new professionals increasingly dominating local authorities in the post-1945 decades. Regional and urban policies were nationally formulated with the objective of eliminating inter-regional and inter-urban inequalities. Such egalitarian aims were judged to be national, not local, responsibilities. The commitment to national standards of equality of opportunity implied that the freedom of local authorities to pursue their own policies should be limited, except in those areas where local initiatives did not contravene national objectives.

The neglect of local government by the Labour Party informs David Blunkett and Keith Jackson's recent book. They criticise the postwar Labour administration's welfare state policies for neglecting the potential of local authorities, pursuing instead the statist and nationalisation model – characterised as 'Labour's great mistake'.[36] The statist tradition is now repudiated by Labour Party members nationally and locally. Like the Conservatives, Labour stress now the rights and needs of the consumers of state services. Gone is the automatic commitment to the nationalisation of large industries and the public ownership of the means of production. Statist Labour activists remain committed to a national policy for pursuing citizenship and reducing inequalities, however, and this commitment implies a more modest evaluation of local government's potential. At the local level, the themes of decentralisation, greater participation and consumer control have been developed by the 'new urban left'.

Local government for redistribution: the urban left

By the mid-1970s the statist tradition was questioned not only over national policy but for local government too. This questioning attained its fullest local expression in a phenomenon daubed the 'new urban left'. This loose political grouping was concentrated in the larger metropolitan authorities and London. Even as a loose category the term is problematic. Scholars now draw two clear divisions – between Liverpool and other cities, querying the inclusion of the policies of the former within the urban left; and between the remaining metropolitan counties and London, the latter holding the most 'radical' conception of the transformative potential of local government.

The new urban left encouraged the establishment of new committees dealing with race relations, women's issues and police accountability among other topics. New urban left activists were committed to local government as an arena for change and radicalism and not simply as a forum from which to stage a career into Parliament. The most ambitious initiative for producing significant change was economic. The new urban left were responsible for the founding of local enterprise boards which attempted to give local authorities the capacity to intervene in their local economies, but to intervene in a socially positive sense. An important division lies here between the Greater London Enterprise Board (GLEB) and the Boards of the other authorities, since the former's investment and employment strategies are generally interpreted as the most socialist.[37]

The development of local economic strategies marked a break with the postwar statist which because of the commitment to eroding inequality on a national basis did not encourage local authority redistributive initiatives.[38] For various reasons, principally the dominance of the Conservatives nationally, the urban left pursued the possibilities for redistributive socialist policies at the local level.

The urban left's political values were social democratic, the reduction of inequality, combined with a commitment to greater

participation in local government and an attentiveness to allocative efficiency. Change was to be brought about at the local level
with the active participation of those citizens affected directly. It
was in this sense a very localist strategy and one which could have
different results in different areas, intensifying inter-regional
inequalities – a paradoxical outcome for socialists. The urban left
assumed the maintenance of national welfare state standards but
wanted to advance socialist economic and political objectives by
direct, local investment policies.

The new urban left illustrates the potential for local government. Local politics can be the location of new political developments in ideas and movements, as has been illustrated historically
by municipal socialism and the ratepayers' movement among
others. The commitment to redefining socialism, to establishing
local institutions of democracy and to undertaking local initiatives
suggest the resilience of local politics. Undoubtedly, the unfavourable national arena influenced this development significantly as did
the debates within the Labour Party about their objectives. But
the new urban left indicates also the sharp limitation to local
politics in Britain. Ultimate power rests with Westminster and its
exercise is relatively easy, as demonstrated by the abolition of the
GLC and MCCs in 1986 – all loci of political opposition to the
national administration. It should be noted that if the political
party roles were reversed and it was a 'new local right' opposing a
Labour Government there is little grounds for thinking that it
would not exercise the same constitutional powers to impose its
will which the Tories have used in the 1980s. At the core of the
dilemma is the lack of a normative theory of local government
which specifies clearly what powers are available to local authorities and what initiatives they can pursue within this framework.
Such a theory might be less agreeable to the new urban left than to
the local right, since real powers of local initiative could be
expected to compromise national standards to which the Labour
Party has been committed historically.

Communitarian local government: enabling local government

There is a third strand to current left, or quasi-left, theories of
local government whose practitioners want to grant local government 'enabling' powers to bring the community into decision-

making as fully as possible. For Blunkett and Jackson local politics is defined as a means by which 'people can run their own affairs, adopting an increasingly broad perspective as confidence in democracy grows'.[39] In contrast to the new right, Blunkett and Jackson have a much richer notion of how communities underpin local political institutions and provide the basis for self-government. Their central focus is the erosion of local government powers in the 1980s and they conclude rightly that the 'conflict between central and local government has been fought not over economic or technical issues but over different views of the world'.[40]

Unlike the new right, Blunkett and Jackson recognise that reform requires a change in the position of Parliament, though they do not advocate ending *ultra vires*, but rather legislating specific local powers.[41] First, local authorities must have the power to initiate policy in areas which affect their jurisdiction, a classic liberal objective; second, the power to set their own taxation levels and thus to have local revenue autonomy, a prerequisite for effective local participation and policymaking; third, the ending of capital borrowing restrictions; and, fourth, the removal of legal restraints on trading. There is also a call for a 'new relationship' between central and local government in economic policy. These proposals are sensible and build on political values like participation, representation, allocative efficiency and redistribution. However, Blunkett and Jackson do not consider accountability and efficiency in the exclusively fiscal scene adduced to the new right above. Rather, these values arise from the shared sense of community – though this term is not well defined – and the desire for self-government to formulate collective responses to specific needs which this community sense induces.

Absent from this analysis is any discussion of the consequence of greater local autonomy for equality and inequality. Local government is not idealised – there are many criticisms of existing practices and attitudes in local government. But there is no evaluation of the problems resulting from inter-regional inequality, they are very keen on the progressive initiatives undertaken by Sheffield city council but have nothing to say about 'unprogressive' local initiatives – a likely consequence of granting greater initiatory powers to all local authorities. Blunkett and Jackson continue to subscribe to the social democratic welfare state model with some decentralisation thrown in. There is insufficient acknow-

ledgement of the divisions about the purposes of local government
and how these are to be resolved. Blunkett and Jackson developing normative theory of local government authorities assumes that
local authorities will be 'progressive' they do not make clear their
attitude to 'regressive' ones.

Table 10.1 summarises the five theories of local government and
indicates their respective implications for the role of local government and likely policy outcomes. The table indicates also a policy
illustrative of the five theories. The community charge with its
liberal pretension of devolving power and maximising individual
choice seems to represent that strand of new right theory. The
urban development corporations with their accountability to the
centre reflect the centralist thrust of new right conservatism. The
centrally determined introduction of comprehensive schools is an
example of the old statist Labour Party tradition: the centre
decides upon the appropriate policy and standards and leaves
implementation to subnational authorities. The new urban left's
keenness upon local redistributive experiments is well represented
by the policies of local enterprise boards, while the enabling aims
of community theorists suggests the introduction of a local income
tax with which fiscal base local authorities can pursue whatever
policies the community supports. The statist left tradition mini-
mises variation (to minimise inter-personal and inter-regional
inequality) between authorities, a power which the authoritarian
new right theory potentially holds too. The liberal new right and
the community theories both imply significant differences between
local authorities as determined by their respective constituents.
The new urban left also implies inter-personal and inter-regional
inequality across localities, though this outcome is less favourably
embraced by them than by the liberal right or community left.
These differences reflect the different conceptions of the appropriate role of local government: either as central agent or local
representative body.

The two most coherent positions are the liberal right and statist
left. The former declares: devolve power and accept the consequent inequality and variation across districts. The statist left
pursues the elimination of inequality and, on that basis, constructs
national priorities and criteria to be satisfied in local policies.
While this latter stance looks rather dated in relation to the
Morrisonian nationalisation tradition it still seems valuable as

TABLE 10.1   Five theories of local government

| | | Ideological level | | | |
		New Right		Left	
Variants	liberal new right	conservative new right	urban left	communitarian	statist
Values	liberty participation efficiency	central authority/ efficiency	redistribution/ participation	liberty participation redistribution	social citizenship
The role of local government	serves community	central agent	serves community	serves community	central agent
Illustrative policy	community charge	urban corporations	enterprise boards	local income tax	comprehensive education
Policy outcome	promotes variation and inequality	central pattern of services within efficiency criteria	inter-personal and -regional variation in services	inter-personal and-regional variation in service delivery	central pattern to reduce inequality

promoting social rights of citizenship.[42] The five theories produce two sorts of outcomes: inter-personal and inter-regional variation and inequality in local policy or the satisfaction of some national standard determined by the centre. The most recent theory and practice of local government represents a commitment to the first position, certainly by the left.

There will always be variation between policy delivery in different local authorities and such variation need not correspond with inequality of service delivery either between persons or areas. In this chapter the term 'variation' is used to refer to those outcomes which do promote inequality between persons or jurisdictions. However, a commitment to equality of opportunity, imputed here to the postwar statist tradition to local government, will normally imply a commitment to diminishing variations in service outcomes within and between local authorities.

Conclusion

This chapter has reviewed the approaches of the left and right to the central theoretical problem of local government: in a unitary state, how are powers and responsibilities to be divided between the national and local tiers of government? If a political community is committed to national objectives and standards then the scope for local government autonomy will be necessarily constrained. Certainly, some local discretionary powers can be retained to address local circumstances but the criteria by which this discretion is exercised will be national ones. Broadly, this was the practice of the three postwar decades in Britain when both the left and right shared a commitment to the expansion of welfare state institutions thereby according local authorities an increasingly administrative role. This practice was coupled with a continued rhetorical commitment to the importance of local government and of local political participation but an actual weakening of these local institutions.

The new right

During the 1980s two significant developments occurred which altered fundamentally this conventional view of local government and revived the problem of dividing power by area within the British polity. The first was the propagation of new right theories whose advocates attacked the institutions of the welfare state – and the public sector in general – as inefficient and promoted greater consumer control of state activities. As noted above, new right thought covers two strands – liberal and conservative. For the liberal (and indeed Conservative) new right, inequality is a necessary feature of the political order and pursuing national policies toward territorial or inter-personal equity is misguided. The irony for new right advocates is that the Conservative Government influenced by their ideas is not prepared to implement them fully. Thus, the community charge will cover less than one third of local government finances when the logic of this policy implies that much more control should be developed to the local authority.

The new right pressure groups still have much persuading to do if their schemes for local government are to be realised. National policies such as the urban development corporations and the current version of the community charge distort rather than implement the core liberal values which these new right pressure groups have been promoting. In the short term, however, the policies of councils such as those in Bradford and Wandsworth indicate a significant and growing local new right in local government whose aims the government may have to acknowledge in national policy.

The urban left

The second development concerns the left's approach to local government. The statist Labour Party tradition sought inter-personal equality of opportunity regardless of where citizens lived. This objective dictated a national policy which did not end local government but certainly diminished its policymaking role considerably. The failure of this centralised strategy – inequality was still a serious problem by the 1970s[43] – and the electoral success of the Conservatives contributed to the growth of an active municipal left in British cities. One of the most important manifestations of this renewed local strategy was economic. Local enterprise boards were established to pursue the political values of participation and redistribution at the local level. This latter concern marked a significant break with previous social democratic because the absence of a local income tax and the freedom of movement between local authorities, as well as their constitutional weakness, amounted to serious limitations upon local governments' capacity to undertake policies for social change. The so-called new urban left broke with this traditional stance and undertook intervention-ist economic policies. The cost of such policies, however, creates problems or social democrats: by holding power and intervening in some jurisdictions only, the new urban left was contributing to inter-regional variation of policy outcomes and the possible wide-ning of inter-personal inequalities of outcome.

These outcomes have two important implications. First, they imply that the urban left seeks greater local autonomy as a political base for policymaking. But, second, the granting of such local autonomy enhances the potential for inter-regional inequality because in those local authorities where the new right triumphs electorally liberal policies will be implemented. This outcome is the great dilemma for a social democratic theory of local government and the principal reason why their policies to reduce inequality have been undertaken nationally. The economic policies of the new urban left and the cells for greater local autonomy by local Labour politicians both suggest that there has been an acceptance of this implication.[44]

Whether or not this conclusion is accepted, creative left theorists need to think about the constitutional position of local government. What ought to be the 'rules of the game' for local government and how should they be represented in political institutions? The rules agreed could be broad enough to design institutions without affecting outcomes – that is, specify certain requirements such as a local income tax and constitutionally guaranteed powers[45] – a neo-Rawlsian position. Or they could extend to a general welfare principle such as that the least well off be consistently advantaged. Or finally a restatement and strengthening of the postwar consensus position – that national policy sets fairly tight universal standards within which local authorities vary implementation to meet local needs. This last option is attractive because it addresses best the problem of reconciling national standards and local choice. It is this problem which is critical for the left for two reasons. First, the new right has an answer to this question – encourage variation – based on a liberal new right theory of the necessity of inequality of outcome; the left has no such theory. Second, the changes in national politics and in local government are eroding any previously accepted objectives – most notably be weakening welfare state institutions – and it is far from clear that the left wishes to contribute to the process of their dissolution. Addressing inequality and variation at the local level, rather than accepting them as ineluctable developments, is a necessary response to these changes.

Notes and references

The author wishes to thank Michael Goldsmith, Robert Goodin, George Jones, Rod Rhodes, John Stewart, and Gerry Stoker for helpful comments on an earlier draft of this chapter though none of them bear any responsibility for the final version.

1. The material in this chapter is drawn from Desmond S. King, *The Cities: Political Values and City Politics* (Routledge, forthcoming).
2. On the importance of political principles and values, see Brian Barry, *Political Argument* (Harvester, 1965).
3. In this chapter the terms 'socialist' and 'social democratic' are used interchangeably.

4. See Robert E. Goodin, *Reasons for Welfare* (Princeton University Press, 1988); and Desmond S. King and Jeremy Waldron, 'Citizenship, Social Citizenship and the Defence of Welfare Provision', *British Journal of Political Science*, vol. 18, no. 4 (1988) pp. 415–45.
5. For a discussion of this issue, see Brian Barry, 'Morality and Geography', Paper presented to the Annual Meeting of the American Society for Political and Legal Philosophy, 1980; David Heald, *Public Expenditure* (Martin Robertson, 1983); and King, *The Cities*.
6. See Desmond S. King, *The New Right: Politics, Markets and Citizenship* (Macmillan and Dorsey Press, 1987).
7. See John Rawls, *A Theory of Justice* (Oxford University Press, 1971); and Roberto M. Unger, *Politics* (Cambridge University Press, 1988).
8. See David Harvey, *Social Justice and the City* (Johns Hopkins University Press, 1973); Paul E. Peterson, *City Limits* (University of Chicago Press, 1981); and Charles Tiebout, 'A Pure Theory of Local Expenditures', *Journal of Political Economy*, vol. 64, pp. 16–24.
9. The phrase 'rules of the game' is taken from R. A. W. Rhodes, *Beyond Westminster and Whitehall* (Unwin Hyman, 1988).
10. David Widdicombe, *The Conduct of Local Authority Business*, Report of the Committee of Inquiry into the conduct of Local Authority Business (Chairman: David Widdicombe) Cmnd 9797 (London, HMSO, 1986) p. 46.
11. Widdicombe, *Conduct of Local Authority Business*.
12. John Stuart Mill, *Considerations on Representative Government* (Dent, 1972).
13. Mill, *Considerations*; L. J. Sharpe, 'Theories and Values of Local Government', *Political Studies*, vol. 18 (1970) pp. 153–74; and Dilys Hill, *Democratic Theory and Local Government* (Allen & Unwin, 1976).
14. George Jones and John Stewart, *The Case for Local Government* (Allen & Unwin, 2nd edn 1985); and Widdicombe, *Conduct of Local Authority*.
15. Tiebout, 'Pure Theory of Local Expenditures'.
16. Albert Hirschman, *Exit, Voice and Loyalty* (Princeton University Press, 1970).
17. Jones and Stewart, *Case for Local Government*.
18. Ibid, pp. 81–2.
19. George Jones, *Responsibility and Government*, Inaugural Lecture, London School of Economics and Political Science, 1977.
20. See Goodwin, *Reasons for Welfare*; and Raymond Plant, *Equality, Markets and the New Right* (Fabian Society, 1984).
21. Harvey, *Social Justice and the City*; Heald, *Public Expenditure*; and Peterson, *City Limits*.
22. F. Layfield (Chairman), *Local Government Finance*. Report of the Committee of Inquiry, Cmnd 6453 (London, HMSO, 1976).
23. See King, *The New Right*; Kenneth Hoover and Raymond Plant, *Conservative Capitalism* (Routledge, 1988); and Andrew Gamble,

The Strong State and the Free Economy (Macmillan, 1988).

24. Tiebout, 'Pure Theory of Local Expenditures', p. 419.
25. Competitive tendering also reflects the criticisms of William Niskanen, *Bureaucracy: Servant or Master?* (Institute of Economic Affairs, 1971).
26. Nicholas Ridley, *The Local Right* (Centre for Policy Studies, 1988); and see parliamentary debates during the third reading of the Local Government Finance Act 1988, Hansard, especially 18 April 1988, vol. 131, columns 569–642.
27. Peterson, *City Limits*, p. 37.
28. Ridley, *Local Right*.
29. Ibid, p. 10.
30. Ibid, p. 11.
31. Ibid, p. 28.
32. Ibid, p. 13.
33. Ibid, p. 8.
34. Ibid, p. 33.
35. See King, *The Cities*.
36. David Blunkett and Keith Jackson, *Democracy in Crisis* (Hogarth, 1987) p. 64.
37. John Gyford, *The Politics of Local Socialism* (Allen & Unwin, 1986); Hugh Morrison, *The Regeneration of Local Economies* (Oxford University Press, 1987); and King, *The Cities*.
38. There are historical precedents on the left, however: see Andrew Sancton, 'British Socialist Theories in the Division of Power by Area', *Political Studies*, vol. 24, no. 2 (1976) pp. 158–70.
    The GLEB drew up a series of investment strategies for the London economy and provided capital to small firms which satisfied specific criteria such as being co-operatives, involving trades unions, employing minorities or women. According to the *London Industrial Strategy* (GLC, 1985) produced by the GLEB, their main emphasis was to be upon production and the character of that production: the stress is upon 'socially useful production' which 'takes as its starting point not the priorities of the balance sheet, but the provision of work for all who wish it in jobs that are geared to meeting social needs' (p. 18). Commercial viability is not ignored but social objectives are given priority in GLEB grant allocations. The GLEB stressed active intervention – that is, the formulation of projects either from the beginning or according to specific criteria – and produced a series of detailed studies of the main sectors of the London economy together with proposals for their development.
39. Blunkett and Jackson, *Democracy in Crisis*, p. 5; see also Jones and Stewart, *Case for Local Government*.
40. Blunkett and Jackson, *Democracy in Crisis*, p. 189.
41. Ibid, pp. 204–6.
42. Goodin, *Reasons for Welfare*.
43. See Julian LeGrand, *The Strategy of Equality* (Allen & Unwin, 1982); and Robert E. Goodin and Julian LeGrand (eds), *Not Only the Poor* (Allen & Unwin, 1987).

44. See King, *The Cities*, where reports of interviews with activists on this question are recorded.
45. See Jones and Stewart, *Case for Local Government*, for one version of such a theory.

11 Thatcherism and Local Government: An Evaluation

Graham Mather

Has there been a Thatcherite blueprint for the emasculation, transformation or replacement of local government in Britain? And what will determine the development of local government in the next decade?

It is easy to enumerate and categorise developments in central/ local government relationships since 1979 against a model of consistent central attacks on local autonomy, and as part of a coherent plan to stamp out political opposition. Yet this thesis is beset by internal contradictions, tensions, and unfinished business; the end product is unconvincing. We must look elsewhere than to a pre-established and inexorable master plan for the keys to a proper evaluation of the last ten years for local government, and the factors which are already shaping the next.

Supporters of local government can make a strong case that it has been cash controlled, constrained, supervised, bypassed and generally downtrodden during the Thatcher years. It has certainly not basked in a warm glow of central government admiration. There can also be little doubt that these largely centralising pressures sit oddly with the perceived or claimed advantages of local government. Local government has much to offer Thatcherism:[1] it can respond more flexibly than the centre to the varying wishes and requirements of local residents; it promotes competition and experimentation in the way public services are provided; it can act as a brake, check or balance to central power;

it provides a comparator to test the efficiency of government; it is more open than central government, lacking the apparatus of official secrecy; its decisions can be challenged more readily through courts and tribunals; it is more accountable, especially in the way that financial matters are supervised and audited, than many central government institutions.

That the relationship has, in practice, turned out to be unhappy therefore needs some explaining. One approach is to assert that the Thatcher government perceived local government as financially reckless, managerially inefficient and politically non-supportive. On this model, many local authorities were seen as at odds with the policies of the centre, on a scale ranging from inert and passive (most traditional authorities of whatever colour) to threateningly and aggressively hostile (the GLC, Merseyside, the Met Counties and a large number of hard left local authorities stretching from inner London via Clay Cross to Scotland).

Yet to suggest that the impact of Thatcherism is confined to measures to deal with such political problems is unconvincing. I will argue that many Thatcherite innovations in local government practice have achieved a permanence that would not apply to a series of measures motivated by pure political advantage. They have faced little intellectual challenge and have bedded down more quickly than might have been anticipated, amounting to a culture change which has continuing and self-perpetuating effects.

The development of the relationship between the Thatcher Government and local government is more effectively assessed by taking bearings from some particular known fixed points. One is the Thatcherite commitment to 'better value for money'. It is a straightforward concept, based on the underlying premise that monopoly services provided free at the point of consumption and untested by competitive forces are unlikely to be efficient in the medium and long term; that they are likely to perpetuate restrictive practices and producer-led service delivery; and that they entangle the interests of those specifying the services (the authority) with those providing them (the direct employees of the authority, who are also policy advisors and quality controllers). This premise, once understood, explains much dissatisfaction with local government practices and policies.

The second fixed point is the introduction, across government generally, of tougher and more extensive central government financial systems and controls. These have provided the means of resolving particular issues between central and local government, and strengthening pressures for efficiency, but are probably now becoming a major contributor to the continuing stresses and tensions between local authorities and the centre. This chapter looks particularly at the problems which result from local government being largely financed by cash raised by or reallocated from the centre.

Accompanying and underlying these specific issues is the relative strength of ideology demonstrated by the Thatcher Government. This, as displayed in the area of local government, is not an all-pervasive systemisation of politics, but simply a reluctance to allow the policy agenda to be determined elsewhere. It was against this rock that the dynamic political entrepreneurism of the Greater London council and the metropolitan county councils foundered. Especially because it sees itself as paying for local policy choices, the Thatcher Government has been vigilant to police the borders of what it sees as acceptable local policy innovation. In the absence of radical change to the financing structure, this pattern of intervention is unlikely to change.

Finally, Thatcherism is relating to local government has been reluctant to expend political energy on thoroughgoing reforms of institutional structures. This same institutional conservatism has been notable in its treatment of the central government machine.[2] When it has innovated, it has tended to initiate radical change through existing machinery. It is in this respect that it has proved most sharply distinct from the Heath government. Perhaps this is one reason why it has proved so difficult for those in local government to understand. A government less conservative in terms of local government structures might have been more familiar and predictable and, ironically, easier for those in local government to come to terms with and to influence.

In considering the impact of the Thatcher years it is probably local government's role in the provision of services that provides the most fertile area for assessment, especially insofar as policy change has been designed to introduce value for money, competition and modern management techniques. The financial structure of local government, and its constitutional position, rank second and third. Together these three areas contain the key to the future development of policy.

There is no doubt that, even if it is accepted that the Thatcher Government did not come to power with, nor has it developed, a grand plan for a systematic assault on local government, its impact has been as dramatic as if it had such a *schema*.

Local government's weak position

It would be unwise to underestimate the scale of the challenge which faces local government in Britain today. After ten years of Thatcherism it is weak and unstable, constrained, bypassed and destabilised by a series of central government policy decisions. Its spending decisions are second-guessed by central government and third-guessed by district auditors and the Audit Commission. Its structure has been modified, regionalised, de-regionalised, revised and curtailed in a patchwork of policy change over the past two decades. The frequency of the changes testify to a fundamental uncertainty of role.

Local authority financing has become an incomprehensible science. Rate support grant formulae are far beyond the comprehension of educated laymen. They conceal, none too well, a crude annual political battle of interests, local against central and one authority and group of authority against another.

National pay bargaining systems, to which local authorities are tied, have gone out of fashion and some authorities have already raised the prospect of moving outside national agreements. At the other end of the spectrum, creative accountancy to escape central government cash controls has arguably gone beyond levels which regulatory agencies like the Audit Commission will tolerate.

Against this background, politicians in national government have discovered during the Thatcher years that local government on traditional lines is dispensable. The model of the development corporation is as significant in its recognition that the local franchise may be abrogated as for its challenge to the supporting apparatus of planning controls, zoning and licensing. It raises the prospect of a continuing shift of significant local functions from elected to appointed organisations, which may operate in partnership with new types of business groups.

Local government is the test bed for a new type of tax which is flat and broad and of which the primary purpose – to what extent attainable in practice is discussed later – is to re-establish a direct link between taxation and representation.

So far as service provision is concerned, local government during most of the Thatcher years has failed to measure up to the expectations of national politicians, expectations which are increasingly informed by comparison with the modern management techniques of business. In the Audit Commission, central government has set up an agency to tell local government how to function. The process, however, shows signs of having moved already and from emulation of business techniques to direct involvement of business itself.

Contracting-out threatens not only to revolutionise the practical business of service delivery by local authorities, but to transform the very nature of local government itself. It now seems clear that local government is changing its nature as it withdraws from the provision of services to a much more modest role as specifier, purchaser and regulator of community services.

The opting-out of entire schools from local authority provision, and of entire authorities from joint provision, will spend up that process of change.

Are the changes reversible?

The analysis set out above, and the assessment of a series of continuing changes developed in part I of this volume, appear to show a clear weakening of local government against other institutions. For local government officers and numbers alike it is undoubtedly a sobering picture. So the first question must be: can the trends that I have sought to describe be put into reverse? The evidence suggests not.

The problems confronting local government do not seem to be the result of temporary aberration in Whitehall. They cannot be dismissed as the mere result of ideological excess. It was the President of the Society of Local Authority Chief Executives, Mr Michael Rush, who said that if councils did not accept the customer-first model of service provision by becoming more responsive to their local communities they would face increasing moves by the Government to strip away their key functions, such as running schools. He said that authorities should accept the introduction of competitive tender legislation and plans to allow council housing tenants to opt out of local authority control.[3]

The message that confrontation and resistance would not prove effective was echoed in the response of local authority organisations to the community charge, where after an initial reluctance to accept that the change was here to stay Scottish authorities are now buckling down to the details of implementation.[4]

Nor are the proposals for competitive tendering out of line with observable trends elsewhere. Similar requirements have been introduced by circular, affecting district health authorities, and the first results are beginning to be subjected to academic analysis. A study by Robin Milne of Glasgow University[5] examined six contracts put to tender in three hotel-type services within one regional health authority. Apart from one contract where costs saved were marginal, the cost savings achieved ranged from between 33 per cent to 65 per cent. In health authorities, as in local government, the need to specify contract services may provide many former administrators with the first opportunity actively to manage their service delivery, by taking decisions about means of provision and type and standard of service delivery free from the continuum which tends to assume that, once a service is provided, it should continue indefinitely along broadly similar lines. Competitive tenders may have provided a shock of discontinuity which has given back to local authority officials their power to manage.

It is significant that, to a degree, the same process is underway in central government. The Treasury has issued guidelines about the use of competitive tender processes in central government: 'Departments should establish a rolling programme for reviewing their activities with a view to identifying areas to be tested by competition. They should set targets for a proportion of their activities to be reviewed each year'.[6]

This approach suggests that, in theory at least, there is virtually no limit to the range of functions, currently provided in-house by central government, that will eventually fall within the scope of scrutiny for eventual contracting-out. In central government, local government, the National Health Service, all the indications are that contracting-out will by the end of the century have transformed the way in which services are provided to the public. It remains to be seen, however, how quickly central government will feel able to subject itself to the disciplines which it has enforced upon local authorities and make the tender procedure statutory rather than discretionary.

Thatcherism has assumed that the provision of services is at the heart of the function of modern local government. It has taken the view that testing the services customers of local government require against the various competing options and means by which they can be provided leads to a discovery process which will arrive at the core or residual role of local government. By examining this process in operation it is possible to assess the nature of the crisis which today confronts local government in Britain, and to estimate what future local government may have. Local government went wrong in the service provision area by failing to appreciate that it lagged behind private sector management techniques which, themselves, were to be abruptly sharpened and refined as a consequence of the 1980/81 recession. John Banham, Director general of the CBI, came to prominence as the Controller of the Audit Commission who began the process of introducing local government to modern management, and he has recently set out some of the problems:

> No-one should be surprised that managing in the public sector is particularly difficult. The lack of clear structure and accountability, rapid changes in leadership (and thus priorities), centralised pay bargaining and control over conditions of service, . . . all add up to a formidable list of competitive handicaps.
>
> There is more. The management style and traditions of the public service are simply not compatible with the demands of a competitive market place. The hallmarks of the public service seem to me to include: concern for equity rather than results, process rather than outcome, language rather than analysis, economy rather than value for money, avoidance of risks rather than reward, appearance rather than reality, consensus rather than competition, short rather than longer term.[7]

The Audit Commission has calculated that implementation of the present Government's manifesto commitments could cut council spending by 30 per cent over the lifetime of the present Parliament, falling from £30bn last year to under £21bn, on the assumption that one-half of education spending becomes 'opted out' and one-quarter of local authority services go to private provision after competitive tender.

Its chief executive has suggested that trench warfare will not be a success and that the alternative to total surrender requires local authorities to take the initiative in moving to decentralised housing management, co-operation with inner city task forces and charging systems for council services.

When approached in this way, the core roles necessarily fulfilled by direct employees of local government are extremely limited. Once public sector managers see the opportunities of greater independence, less politicisation, new financial rewards comparable with those in the private sector, opportunities for management buy-outs, equity investment and all the challenges of a career which combines business efficiency with public service, there is likely to be a powerful demand from managers to adopt the new structures.

Without a clear contract-based relationship, the consequences would be much less satisfactory. Lines of accountability would be confused and it would prove impossible to disentangle political from executive or administrative decisions. The resulting half-way house would prove attractive neither to local government officers nor outside high-flyers who could otherwise be brought in. The ability to adopt private sector management techniques, especially concerning remuneration, would be severely constrained.

The same tensions are now recognised in the United States. The 1988 US Presidential Commission on Privatization reported:

> Government managers face obstacles to efficiency rarely encountered in the private sector. Government managers lack a baseline for comparisons, have no imperative to make a profit, and are not challenged by competitors who might capture their business if they fail to deliver in the most efficient manner. Although government managers can be encumbered by legislative and fiscal restrictions that force them to operate inefficiently, competition can identify the managerial changes necessary to effect savings within a government organization, or provide for transfer to more efficient providers in the private sector.[8]

The most blatant challenge to local authority autonomy and power, the establishment of development corporations, has met not with public outrage, but overall with enthusiasm. In Docklands and in the new mini development corporations it appears that a sufficiently wide range of political views are represented on development corporation boards to secure their long-term presence as alternative means of tackling particularly acute problems of local economic underperformance. This is not to say that they are necessarily an ideal model. It is interesting that, in a recent IEA study on problems of inner city vacant land, the authors say:

> Given the extreme degree of decay and neglect that had occurred in the dockland areas of [London and Liverpool], the establishment of development corporations was certainly justified. Similarly, the extension of the concept elsewhere is almost certainly correct. That democratic local government is abrogated is symptomatic of the desperate situation which years of neglect had allowed to develop. However appropriate this mechanism may be for coping with crisis situations, it cannot be advocated as the general solution . . . put another way, how can we ensure that normal planning, development and re-development processes never again give rise to the necessity to set up an urban development corporation?[9]

It remains the case, however, that a direct challenge to key local authority roles and functions has been carried into effect with little difficulty and only muted protest. This reality presents those who would defend a traditional model of local government with a critical task. They must face the possibility that, at the same time that local government is bringing itself up to date in terms of streamlined management and private sector techniques exercised through an elective framework, central government is moving a step further: and that its new creations have a key difference, that they are unelected.

Councillors and officers may find that a new contest opens up, between elected bodies which seem cumbersome, disputatious, prone to capture by political extremists, excessively responsive to the 'vote motive', and in the sway of powerful local interests. At best, it may seem, they represent a bureaucratised parody of an early model of local government and civic responsibility, slowing down new development and presenting a thousand niggling obstacles to reform; at worst, they frustrate adaptation, deter business investment, embark on dubious financing, enjoy gesture politics and offer a constant political and economic challenge to the central government.

Given that local authorities are ultimately controlled by statute and lack constitutional protection, such a tension seems to offer a one-way bet in favour of the centre, which on this model has every incentive to make opportunistic transfers of power to unelected bodies. Whilst one or two commentators from local government have begun to recognise the problem, across the generality of local government there is little sign that the problem is appreciated or that a real defence of the elected authority, or proposals to meet the challenge of its competitors, are in prospect.

Longer term the same picture

Short term there does not seem to be much prospect of reversing the trends which have been identified. What is the longer-term prospect? Again, I would like to develop the argument from the starting-point of service provision. Of the range of services provided by local government it is difficult to establish a formula which will settle a neat dividing line between core and ancillary functions, between roles which can be filled only by local government and functions which can be discontinued left to market provision, contracted-out, franchised, or be the subject of management buy-outs by officers.

It is certainly the case that there is a long list of services which may be subjected to one or more of these approaches, as a recent study by the Adam Smith Institute suggested:

Architects, surveyors and valuers
Catering
Cemeteries and crematoria
Cleaning
Cesspool emptying
Data processing
Gritting and snow clearance
Highway maintenance
Holding and delivery stores
Laundry services

Legal services
Maintenance
Management
Meal provision and delivery
Parks and garden maintenance
Payroll administration, revenue collection, cash in transit
Pest control
Printing
Provision of residential homes and day centres
Refuse collection and disposal
Rent collection
Sale of council houses
School meals
School transport
Security and caretaking
Street cleaning
Transport
Vehicle maintenance[10]

The list is long enough to show that a substantial proportion of local authority functions could change their nature. What will this mean in practice? It suggests that local government will be transformed out of recognition. As the delivery of local government services is increasingly provided by contractors, or others not on local authority payrolls, there will be an entirely new type of local government officer. Instead of managing or administering in-house staff, he will need to be skilled in the arts of contract specification, purchasing and supply, and quality control.

Chairmen of committees will no longer preside over pyramids of employees, requiring fortnightly or monthly meetings, going on until late in the evening, clocking up the attendance allowances. Their business could be despatched in one, two or three meetings a year. Their staff need comprise only a handful of skilled professional purchasers, contract settlers, and quality control supervisors. Departments could be amalgamated and functions combined. No longer would there be a need for narrow specialisation. As modern authorities are already beginning to find, multi-function environmental teams can bring together the work of planning, environmental health and cleansing functions in a way which makes a more user-friendly and more approachable service for customers. Multi-function inspectors can achieve economies of scale by operating on behalf of several regulatory functions in an authority which, traditionally, would each have had their own officers. One-stop services in town halls, with staff trained to assist members of the public through the bewildering complexities of local government structure, can help to deliver more efficient service and cut out waiting time, redirection of telephone calls and confused and overlapping responses to customer requirements.

Social services – charitable support

The contracting-out process need not be confined to front-line services of a technical nature, or ancillary or support functions alone. Caring and personal social services will experience a growth in the provision of services by charities working alongside local authorities. It is already the case that many services for the old or housebound are supplied by charitable agencies with grants from, or as agents for, local authorities.

Charity funding from fundraising and donations in the UK increased in cash terms by 116 per cent between 1980 and 1985, whilst grants from statutory bodies went up by 138 per cent over the period. There can be little doubt that this process will develop new forms of relationship between local government and specialist charities. Charities have an expertise in caring services which can match or exceed the best in local government. Modern large charities have a scale of operation which can usefully complement the activity of local authorities. Charities have a much easier means of harnessing voluntary support than public authorities. They have ease of access to business funding: a significant benefit when government cash is in less ready supply. These relationships will create particularly testing challenges as the voluntary sector seeks to fulfil a number of functions in its relations with the state, from wholly independent provision, to a catalytic and exhortatory role, through structured partnerships to direct provision on behalf of the state.

It is all the more encouraging, therefore, that a recent NCVO/ RIPA study attached particular importance to the role of contracts. Its comments point to the future:

Public authorities and voluntary organisations need to get together to define good practice in the related fields of accountability, value for money review, and evaluation. Clear contracts, with both sides understanding what was to be expected, were for some participants the best safeguard. While voluntary organisations are often accused of vagueness and can be rather precious about their objectives, it is often the public authority which is hazy as to why it is funding a particular organization. Clarity about the nature of a contract and where it begins and ends should . . . allow voluntary organisations to own their own souls, even if parts of their bodies were for hire.[11]

The education model

If, therefore, all the indications are that charitable involvement in social services will grow, what is the future for the other main area of local authority activity, education? Again, it should be considered from the standpoint of service supply. All the trends in education policy today highlight parental choice of service provision. New departures in state education – City Technology Colleges, once again bypassing local government – mark another significant step, the development of per capita funding techniques which allow parents to reallocate expenditure from the public sector to schools which will to a large extent be independent of public authority control.

How far will this process go? It will depend upon parent preference: whether they wish to exercise greater influence over the type of education which their children receive. It is frequently asserted that this wish to choose is not widely shared: that only a handful of parents would wish to have a wider range of options. This argument may well be true insofar as parents may not be eager to become closely involved in the running of schools or as parent governors or part of a parents collective taking a detailed interest in the administration of schools. There is evidence, however, that parents would welcome a greater ability to allocate the amount of spending which local government currently disposes on their behalf.

If this is a guide, it may well be the case that the role of local authorities in the direct provision of education services will be reduced dramatically by the end of the century. It is possible to contemplate the possibility that their role will largely be to administer a credit system by which per capita sums are made available to parents, and a quality control system insofar as this is not provided by central government. This vision has been adopted by King,[12] who has suggested that the opting-out scheme for schools is likely to be a halfway house towards an education credit scheme:

> In effect, all state schools in an area will be given an equivalent amount of money per pupil – the amount being fixed by the local authority – and parents can choose between opted-out schools and others. The opted-out schools will be given all the money due to them directly from the central government; in turn, the centre will pay correspondingly less in grant to the collection funds in the areas concerned because the counties there will no longer be financing all the schools themselves. If, in time, all schools opted out then the main difference from a voucher scheme would be that parents might have limited access to schools in other areas or private schools.

Local government as regulator

Critical to the changing role of local government is its regulatory function. As it moves from being a larger employer of direct service providers to a specifier, purchaser and facilitator this regulatory role looms large. It is a potential opportunity for local government growth: just as, at the centre, government *ownership* of large parts of the economy has been replaced by *regulation* of privatised industries, broadcasting, corporate mergers and so on.

This regulatory function can overlap into a planning role, and the pattern of local government partnership with statutory agencies, development corporations and the private sector will be significant in shaping the balance of local authority functions over the next decade. It is sufficient here to note two considerations. It is already clear that local authorities cannot expect, in a Thatcherite government, to be the dominant partners in such joint ventures. There is, however, a preparedness to see some formalisation of the local authority function of business facilitator, promoter of commercial and industrial development and, to an extent, equity or loan partner in local economic activity.

The second consideration is that local authorities must expect some eventual tightening of control on these regulatory and development functions. Such control will not necessarily be direct from the centre: as in attempts to define the scope of local authority economic policy activities. It may have a market slant, and be introduced by economic techniques of pricing or costing. There is a strengthening desire to assess the costs and benefits of governmental activity at all levels, to 'price' legislative and regulatory action by assessing its direct and compliance costs on those affected. This deregulatory thrust has begun in Whitehall, through the establishment of an Enterprise and Deregulation Unit. It can also be seen, for example, in current attempts to trim back the regulatory structures introduced into the City by the Financial Services Act. Customers of privatised telephone, electricity and water industries will have rights to direct penalty payments for failure to meet pre-set service standards. These processes have owed much to complaints by regulatees and customers, complaints which have been bolstered by analysis of unanticipated heavy costs and adverse economic effects of the regulatory mechanism. It is likely to spread into other regulatory bodies, including local authorities. They too may find that the costs of compliance with particular environmental, highway, planning or other measures will be made explicit: or that failure to achieve a particular standard of service in, for example, repair of housing stock or quality of cleansing service will expose them to penalties.

In the same way, the operation of local government's most prominent regulatory structure, the town and country planning system, is already a matter of acute economic controversy. Because the value of planning consent hugely outstrips land values themselves, authorities have already begun to 'price' this value, and to part with planning permission only in return for value on the part of the developer. As they are generally precluded (by central government) from seeking cash itself, substitutes have emerged in the mechanism of planning gain: infrastructure improvements, environmental landscaping, new libraries or community centres provided 'free' by the developer.

Local authorities may discover that economics will force itself further into this structure. If planning permission is valuable and developers continue to be prepared to pay a price for it, their bids will gradually inform councillors of the way in which their regulatory decisions have profound financial effects. These pressures may lead to something much closer to a 'market' in planning consent in which it is seen as acceptable to 'sell' consents to developers for cash payable to the authority itself, and to use some of the proceeds to compensate local residents directly whose interests may be damaged by development and who currently have no cash remedy.[13]

Local government finance

I have argued that an analysis developed from local service provision restricts the likely future role of local government. The same is true if local government finance is considered. If local government is to have functions independent of central government, those functions would, in logic, be expected to lend themselves to local financing. The wishes and preferences of particular communities, as manifested through local elections, have no moral claim on the cash of communities elsewhere.

Yet Britain's system of local government finance operates on precisely the opposite basis. It has come to rely upon an elaborate system of roundtripping of cash from residents of one community to another, collected locally, reallocated centrally, dependent upon the political clout of Area A against Area B, coupled with an arbitrary assessment of 'need' of one area against another determined by a third set of public officials.

An authority may be a recipient of Rate Support Grant or it may receive nothing. It may contribute to the London Rate Equalisation Scheme or draw from it. It is an unstable system because it imposes annual political tensions as the interests fight it out to determine their allocation or contribution. That instability will worsen as the community charge makes the disparities more obvious, and the consequences of the annual fixing of local authority finance more apparent.

Changing the system is being achieved with the help of 'safety nets'. These add another layer of redistribution of local finance, by which authorities which would otherwise gain from the new arrangements will transfer money to those which would otherwise lose. As a consequence an authority like Camden would, according to estimates by CIPFA, see its much publicised putative poll tax rate of £732 reduced to £382.

As CIPFA commented, 'Unless the degree of safety netting can be reduced before the community charge system is implemented . . . it is likely that any safety nets established around 1990 could continue well into the 21st century if inflation rates remain low. So long as safety nets remain in place they would prevent the new system working as it is intended to and would also obscure the relationship between local spending and local taxation decisions.'[14]

The reality is that attempts to control local authority spending centrally may work in the short term but are in the long term doomed to failure. The combination of overall cash limits, local spending targets, needs grants, standard grants and uniform business rate reallocations condemns central government to detailed annual intervention in the financing of every local authority. The process cannot keep up with changing local requirements, population changes or changes in patterns of spending policy. A crude rate cap may be achieved; but local accountability is sacrificed.

If there is to be an effective link between local spending and local taxation the reallocative functions of central government must be superseded. One way of securing this is, as has been discussed from time to time, to remove education finance from the local authority system. It may be thought that this is a timely move, consonant with changes in the way in which education services are being provided. Two arguments are raised against it.

The first is that the money must still be found and, if removed from local taxation, would have to be met by an increase in income tax. This, it is felt, might be misunderstood. The second is that the removal of the redistributive system of local government finance would cause insuperable difficulties for 'losing' authorities. Neither argument is convincing.

The effect of transferring education finance to the centre would be neutral in overall tax revenue, provided that local authorities financed local expenditure from local taxes. What would the consequences of this be? It is clear that there would be a 'big bang', with lots of winners and losers. Some local authorities would face formidable problems as they attempted to achieve an income base strong enough to finance their remaining activities, some of which would undoubtedly be discontinued, others made subject to charge, others contracted-out or franchised. Yet these consequences are of the same kind as those which seem likely to occur anyway.

The unstable nature of the local government finance system has direct policy consequences for local authorities. One perceptive expert, Noel Hepworth, has highlighted the likely impact of increasing community charge costs, forcing local authorities to reduce spending, to look for increased central government grants, to campaign for more rebates or to see the removal of some services from local government altogether.[15] The outcome may, as he suggests, be a combination of measures; these would involve the extension of charging for services, in a competitive market with the authority's role limited to that of catalyst or facilitator; new partnerships with the centre, tied to grant aid specifically linked to particular objectives; together with the eventual replacement of the community charge with a 'capped' local income tax.

A more comprehensive, but no less radical, vision of future local government finance comes from King. He has suggested that it would take little modification to the post-1990 system of local government finance to reduce dramatically the amount of grant passing from the centre. In his model, this would be achieved by moving to a centralised education voucher system and to financing roads from user charges. At this stage local authorities would no longer receive reallocated business rates and would still stand in need of some central grant: but it is envisaged that this need could be reduced by creating further local tax powers, affecting businesses, and also possibly by the introduction of a local income tax, and offsetting these increased taxes by grant reductions.[16]

Local government's constitutional settlement

In retrospect, the abolition of the GLC and metropolitan county councils was not a typical manifestation of the Thatcher approach to local government, but rather a final expedient, reluctantly undertaken and perceived to carry a high political price. To some degree it was prompted by the belief that these authorities were consciously attempting to usurp functions considered by ministers to be the province of national government. There was particular concern that local authorities seemed to be prepared to embark on policies which would establish economic policies of municipal ownership of local businesses through enterprise boards, with heavy subsidisation of favoured interest groups and political allies, resulting in entrenched, aggressive and confrontational local fiefdoms presenting a powerful political and even economic challenge to central government. Beneath the jokes about the 'Peoples Republic of South Yorkshire' and the exasperation with the administrative and presentational skills of the GLC leaders, lay real concerns. To that degree there was a constitutional motivation in the decision; it is also possible to argue that if the benefits of local government lie to large extent in its closeness to local residents, the abolished authorities were demonstrably too large.

With the benefit of hindsight it is probable that the political sound and fury over GLC and metropolitan county abolition was overdone. The authorities were forgotten almost as soon as abolition had taken place. Dire warnings of insuperable administrative obstacles for effective service provision by successor bodies proved misplaced. The techniques of service provision by joint boards proved generally painless; staff and assets of the authorities were redeployed with little fuss. The outcome may be anticipated to suggest that, however strong the reluctance to restructure local government may seem to be, abolition of authorities can be achieved without difficulty or regret.

So will the county councils be next? There were few cries of outrage when the Association of District Councils published a report commissioned from the School of Advanced Urban Studies at Bristol University which suggested, on the basis of a pilot study in Cheshire, that district councils would be able and willing to take over many county functions, individually or in groups, including education, social services, fire, police and highways. Whilst it would be unwise to build a large superstructure on the slender foundations of this one study, and whilst it is clear that institutional conservatism is unlikely to be quickly displaced from Thatcherite thinking, I would be reluctant to rule out moves in this direction in the medium-term future.

Repeated suggestions from a number of sources and policy perspectives have pointed to the potential benefits from the transfer of certain local authority functions to national financing;

intellectual debate on these issues has not yet been joined, but rather deferred, primarily on the grounds that it is not the time to look at large structural reforms. The same argument, together with an understandable political reluctance to disturb a system operated by large numbers of local political supporters, and with powerful historical and emotional undertones, may account in large measure for the caution displayed towards handing over county council powers.

Yet these issues cannot be postponed for ever, not least because, on the foregoing analysis, the instability of local government finance will ensure that problems of central/local government relationships will reappear annually on ministers' desks as central grants are fought over, and redistributive patterns decided. If, as seems likely, the policy review of the Labour Party leads to proposals for some new regional structure of government, that too may help to break the policy blockage. It would be a confident prophet who would rule out a new Green Paper on local government finance, and a new Green Paper on local government structure, if Mrs Thatcher's Government were to be re-elected in the early 1990s.

Conclusion

Local government faces, therefore, a simple issue. Is its future best secured by linkage to central government control, or to policies generated locally and financed at local level?

The issue cannot be fudged. Central government will not grant or redistribute finance without accountability. Parliamentary sovereignty makes it difficult to imagine a new constitutional settlement which could grant to local government a guaranteed role for the future. Left with its remaining administrative functions, it will be national legislation which sets the scene unless by breaking out of national financing it re-establishes the breathing space to reflect local requirements in local policies, to compete more vigorously for investment, skills and population, to reinforce local characteristics.

A new look at local government finance is unlikely to be long delayed. In the meantime, as local authorities become more businesslike the contribution of business itself is likely to increase.

Business can be expected to strengthen its contribution across a range of fronts: as contractor for the direct provision of services, influencing their nature and delivery through its bids, prices and performance standards; as model for the organisation and management of services remaining in direct provision by the public sector, through management consultancy, emulation and example; through the secondment of staff and a developing interchange between the public sector, business and the academic world, inter-relationships which are still noticeably underdeveloped in Britain by comparison with competitor economies; through formal structures of consultation; and through new agencies, whether development corporations and agencies, charitable bodies or specific enterprise trusts like Business in the Community.

As local government becomes more businesslike, business will undoubtedly consider that the business of local government is its business, too. Such an involvement will require a strengthened determination by business to involve itself in both policy and delivery mechanisms, as part of a general contribution to social well-being as well as directly as a contractor. It will also necessitate careful consideration by government of its use of consultative structures. Experience with Business Ratepayer Consultative Committees does suggest that they proved useful in bringing together councillors and businessmen who might, otherwise, have had little contact, and that they helped to establish dialogue and clarity over local authority budget and finance plans. At national level, it is not clear that the two way flow between business and Whitehall is so strong that institutions like NEDC can be swept aside, although a broadening of its business base to cover the wider range of representative business bodies might be timely.

The integration of local government operations with those of business is understood more easily if local government is recognised to be shifting from a continuum, a time-hallowed way of doing things through a fixed administrative system, to a series of contracts: (a) Contracts with central government, by which local government receives grant support in return for ever more tightly defined provision of services and functions. These contracts are competitive: the centre can choose to spend the money elsewhere, as with UDCs. They may be implied, but increasingly they are *explicit*: just as, for example, the new Training Enterprise Councils (TECs) have an explicitly contractual relationship with the Training Agency.[17] (b) Contracts with outside, private sector service providers. (c) Contracts, also, with authority officers, increasingly appointed on fixed term, performance-related agreements. And (d) contracts with customers, who will have strengthened rights to redress for unsatisfactory service – plus, increasingly, the right to go elsewhere.

This contract model separates the political process of determination of objectives and specification of services from their delivery, removing conflict of interest which occurs when those specifying a service are also its deliverers. It reduces the public choice phenomenon of lobbying for bureaucratic expansion by introducing built-in competitive pressures. It facilitates review of policy objectives by requiring regular reassessment and respecification within a democratic framework. It strengthens opportunities for quality control and concentration of resources on supervision and compliance. It regularises relationships between central government and local authorities and competing agencies. It is a force for transparency of funding. It is compatible with earmarking of finance to measurable service delivery, developing the model of the community charge. It is compatible with specific remedies and new enforcement powers for individuals who have suffered loss by reason of government failure, or the failure of agencies granted monopoly or other enhanced powers by the state.

The future of local government should be seen in this sense of a series of contracts: with central government for the 'purchase' of particular grant-supported services; with contractors for the operation of execution of functions and services; with residents through more closely defined charging mechanisms, including the community charge; and with partners, including the voluntary sector and the business community. The strengths and adaptability of local government have been seen in full measure over the past decade. The signs are that it is already adapting quickly to this new pattern, and that it will not be long before it is Whitehall, rather than Town Halls, which is overdue for a dose of Thatcherite radicalism.

The affinities between Thatcherite theology and its relationships with local authorities will then become more apparent, as the apparently centralising, transitional stage gives way to a network of contractual arrangements which inexorably promote competition and choice by the operation of the contract mechanisms of specification, tender, monitoring and review. This model may seem to leave the elected status of local government somewhat behind. Yet that, too, fits into a radical framework – and not because of any antipathy to voting and elections, but rather because practice has caught up with theory. It is more clearly understood that the politician's vote motive, its appeals to interest groups, its trade-offs and opportunities for 'deals', its short-termism and organisational rigidities, the incentives it provides for building up alliances built on dependency, have together proved an ineffective means of delivering local services to local customers. In the 1990s, the onus will be on the elected politicians to show that they are necessary to this service provision, rather than upon business to show that it has a role: and that change reflects the cumulative effect of Thatcherism on local government.

Notes and references

1. See, for example, Dr David King and Professor Peter Jackson, *Economic Affairs*, vol. 9, no. 1 (October/November 1988).
2. See, e.g., Peter Hennessy, *Whitehall* (Sidgwick & Jackson, 1989).
3. *Financial Times*, 9 July 1987.
4. Cipfa Services Ltd has established a special Community Charge Unit with detailed step-by-step guidance on implementation of community charge systems.
5. *Public Administration*, vol. 65 (Summer 1987).
6. *Using Private Enterprise in Government*, Report of a multi-departmental review of competitive tendering and contracting for services in Government Departments (HMSO, 1986).
7. John Banham, *Redrawing the Frontiers of the Welfare State*, 1988 Redcliffe-Maud Memorial Lecture.
8. US Govt Printing Office, Washington, 1988.
9. Michael Chisholm and Philip Kivell, *Inner City Waste Land*, Hobart Paper 108 (IEA, 1987).
10. *Omega File* (Adam Smith Institute, London, 1985).
11. *Into the 1990s: Voluntary Organisations and the Public Sector* (Royal Institute of Public Administration, 1988).
12. David King, 'The Next Green Paper on Local Government Finance Economic Affairs, vol. 9, no. 1 (October/November, 1988).
13. See, e.g., Alan Evans, *No Room! No Room!* (IEA, 1988).
14. *Paying for Local Government*, Update August 1987 (CIPFA, London).
15. Noel Hepworth, *What Future for Local Government?*, IEA *Inquiry*, August 1988.

16. David King, op cit.
17. *Training and Enterprise Councils: a prospectus for the 1990s*, Employment Department Group, March 1989.

12   A Future for Local Authorities as Community Government

John Stewart

This book has recorded a series of changes in the nature of local government brought about by legislation introduced by the Conservative Government. Few in local government see the present changes as representing the completion of the Government's legislative programme. Further change is expected – certainly if the Government is elected for a fourth term. Graham Mather's chapter has set out one scenario for the future of local government, based on a further development of present policies. This chapter sets out an alternative scenario.

The limitations of structural change

Too often consideration of the future for local government has concentrated on issues of structure. Discussion has focused on how the functions of local government should be divided between tiers, whether a tier should be abolished or whether a regional tier of government should be created. Yet if an alternative to the Government's programme for the future of local government is to be developed, it will not be found in the advocacy of structural change.

To discuss structural change is to evade the real challenge of the Government's legislation, which is to the nature of local government: its role and way of working. To focus on structure is to assume either that these issues have all been resolved by the

236

Government's programme or that all that is required is to restore local authorities to their previous position. Neither is an adequate response. The Government's programme is incomplete – further change is inevitable. The slogans 'Defend Jobs and Services' and 'Defend Local Democracy' aroused but little response because they assumed too readily that all was well in local government.

The consideration of structure is a distraction from – as it has so often been in the past – the real issue of the role and way of working of local authorities. It is only when we know the nature of local government sought that it is meaningful to discuss such issues as structures, tiers and boundaries. The challenge of the Government's programme is not met by proposals for a new structure. If a development of that programme is not to be the only future discussed, an alternative programme has to be developed for local government.

The lessons of the experience of Western Europe

To develop an alternative future it is necessary to break out of the constraints on thinking imposed by past experience. We assume too readily that local government has to be the local government that we have known – yet it is that assumption that the Government's programme challenges. The value of European experience – or indeed of comparative experience generally – is that it challenges our past concepts of the nature of local government.

The experience of increasing control over local authorities in the UK differs from the recent trend in Europe and in other countries. While in this country the effect of the Government's actions over a period of ten years has been to weaken local government and to extend the powers of central government, the trend elsewhere has been the reverse. Writing about North-Western continental Europe, Norton concluded 'there has been almost everywhere a serious attempt to decentralise power from state government to local government, with major reforms in practice in Scandinavia and in France and some modest achievement in Germany.'[1] There is a realisation in those European countries that there is only a limited capacity in central government to meet the challenges of a changing society and that there is a need for central government to focus on the issues which it alone can deal with and to strengthen local government to increase the overall capacity of the governmental system.

The European pattern reflects a different concept of the role of local government from that dominant in this country. It has been customary to regard the UK as having a strong system of local government, since local authorities have a wide range of responsibilities. Those responsibilities derived from the many statutes that gave powers to and laid duties upon them. Many of those statutes were broadly drawn, giving considerable discretion. This apparent strength concealed a weakness in the concept of local government. Local authorities came to be seen as first and foremost agencies for the provision of a series of separate services required by national legislation. The focus was on the services and not upon the community.

While European local authorites have duties laid upon them, which in some cases will be greater or less than in the UK, those duties do not define their role. In most Western European countries, local authorities are given the power of general competence: that is, the right to take any action on behalf of its local community, that is not specifically barred to it. The starting-point is not a set of defined powers and duties, but a wide-ranging power to which is added national duties. In practice, of course, the bulk of their activities are the provision of national services in accordance with those duties. The importance of the power of general competence lies less in the activities that it makes possible, than in the concept of local government to which it gives expression.

It is often argued that to give local authorities in the UK a power of general competence would make little practical difference, and that they had until recently only made limited use of their power to spend the 2p rate (about to be changed to an amount per adult) on 'expenditure which in their opinion is in the interests of their area or any part of it or all or some of its inhabitants' (Local Government Act 1982, S 137 (i)). That is to misunderstand the significance of a power of general competence.

The power of general competence should be seen as an expression of a concept of local government as the community government itself. As Alan Norton has argued:

The commune or municipality in European law is the general body of the inhabitants of an administrative area. The citizens of the commune or of other local territorial authority areas are in law conceived as governing themselves through an elected council as their sole agent. The word 'communal' (and the German equivalent 'Gemeinde') carry meanings of community and common ownership.[2]

As the community governing itself, the local authority is entitled to take actions that are sought by that community. It need not search for specific powers, because the powers derive from the concept of local government itself. Because the local authority is the community governing itself, it is or can be concerned with any needs or problems faced in the community, and not merely the services it provides directly. The identity of the authority does not derive from the services provided, but from the community.

Because it is the community governing itself it recognises the readiness to work with and through others. Joint action with other authorities or working through another organisation is readily undertaken.

Syndicates or consortia of local authorities which appoint their own officers or are served by officers of participating authorities are widely employed in France, Italy, and Germany to carry out tasks which can most effectively be performed on a combined scale and have specific legal forms. Similarly joint authorities are set up in Scandinavia for transport and other purposes.[3]

In the UK it has been assumed that a local authority should not merely provide the service directly but should employ all the staff involved in the provision of the service. It was almost as if the size of an authority should be determined by the specialist skills required. Stated like that, it shows the absurdity of the approach, but that result derived from the concept of local government as an agency for the delivery of services. It has led to local authorities being far larger than in other countries in the world as Table 12.1 shows.[4] The size of local authorities in other countries is smaller because their role is not defined by the services provided, but by the community they serve.

The value of the experience of other countries is that it shows that there are many forms of local government and the present form taken in the UK is not the only one. Indeed one can find

TABLE 12.1 Average population size of local authorities

England Wales	122 740
Sweden	29 527
Denmark	17 963
Australia	14 125
USA	12 000
Norway	8 891
New Zealand	7 980
Italy	6 717
Canada	5 011
West Germany	2 694
France	1 320

Source: Goldsmith and Newton (see note 4).

other traditions of local government in this country. The strength of urban government in the latter part of the nineteenth century was an expression of the community governing itself. Local authorities used private bill legislation to extend their powers to meet the problems of their areas. Tramways, water supply, gas and eventually electricity undertakings were created by municipal enterprise in response to the needs of urban areas. That tradition was lost as local authorities came to see their main role as the delivery of services specified in national legislation and accepted the stimulus of central government grant and circular as the main spur to action. Past traditions were lost to a much greater extent in this country than elsewhere.

A concept of community government

If one abandons the assumption that the primary role of local authorities is to act as agencies for the administration of a series of separate services, then a new basis for the future of local government can be explored. Because the phrase 'local government' is associated with that assumption the phrase 'community government' will be used to mark the new role.

As community government, local authorities' primary role is concern for the problems and issues faced by local communities. They are the means by which communities confront and resolve those problems and issues that are beyond the scope of individuals or of other modes of social action.

The concept of community government is not based on an idealistic picture of local communities. It recognises within communities many differing interests and values. Conflicts exist as well as shared purposes. Community government is achieved through political processes that express different interests and values and seek their resolution in political action. A local authority is a political institution for the authoritative determination of community values.

Implicit in this concept of the role of local authorities is a requirement for new ways of working as an enabling authority, a responsive authority and an accountable authority. The enabling authority is concerned with the problem and issues faced by local communities. Its aim is to secure that those problems and issues are met in the most effective way. That may or may not require direct provision of a service. In a pluralistic society, there can and should be many modes of social action. As community government, local authorities in the enabling role can sustain those many modes.

The responsive authority seeks to provide services not *to* the public, but *for* the public and *with* the public. The barriers that surround the local authority have to be challenged. The responsive local authority looks outward to the community it serves rather than looking inward to the organisation. The responsive authority develops new forms of working that depart from past organisational forms. It works not merely through traditional departments, but in decentralised offices and with user organisations, community groups and tenants' co-operatives.

The accountable authority recognises that it is responsible to and accountable to the community. That requires the recognition of a governing relationship in which the local authority governs and is governed by the local community. Community government is achieved through citizenship. An electoral process in which only a minority vote is not a sufficient basis of accountability.

Community government challenges past organisational assumptions. The traditional committee system build around services cannot adequately express the wider requirements of community government. Departments built upon the bureaucratic principles of uniformity, hierarchy and functionalism cannot realise the potential of the responsive authority. Existing processes for accountability are too limited to promote citizenship.

The concept of community government suggests roles and ways of working that are very different from those suggested by the Government's programme. Community government is based on the needs and problems faced by local communities. The Government's programmes, while challenging the need for a local authority to provide services directly, still defines their role by their responsibilities for a series of services, and if one of the results of the Government's programme is to reduce those responsibilities then the future of local government inevitably appears uncertain.

The differences are reflected in different concepts of an enabling authority. The Government's view is restricted to the present responsibilities of local authorities and their role will be about enabling others to act on its behalf in carrying out those responsibilities. It is summed up in the sub-title of Nicholas Ridley's pamphlet – 'enabling not providing'.[5] The viewpoint put forward here is much broader. The local authority will use the most effective means at its disposal to meet the needs of those who live within its area. That need not include direct provision, but does not rule it out. It is as foolish to rule out direct provision as it is to insist on its necessity in every instance. Whereas the Government's approach is based on the assumed superiority of the competitive relationships of the market, the enabling authority based on community government recognises value in different modes of social action.

Individual choice in the market provides the model for the Government's programme for extending choice in education and housing. Their approach is, however, a limited approach because they have had to recognise implicitly if not explicitly the limitations of market models and the necessity of collective choice. Thus in education, while apparently extending parental choice, that choice has been limited by the introduction of a national curriculum. The Government recognise in the national curriculum the need for collective choice – at the national level.

Community government recognises the role of collective choice at the level of the community as well as nationally. A responsive authority based on community government would explore the scope for extending individual choice, but also see a role for local collective choice.

Differences are also shown in the broad basis of local accountability required by community government, compared with the

Government who have argued that local accountability will be achieved through the introduction of the community charge.

> Local accountability depends crucially on the relationship be-
> tween paying for local services and voting in local elections.[6]

That is, however, to limit accountability to requirements for financial payment – accountability being achieved when payment is made by all – whereas community government stresses the basis of accountability in citizenship.

Although the Government's programme is based on the assumed superiority of the market, the Government recognises the necessity of collective action. Problems are created by the market as well as being resolved by it. The growing hazards of the environment are at least in part the product of market forces. Many of the issues faced by society are beyond the capacity of the market to deal with unaided. Thus, the growth in private provision of the elderly has been produced by social security. The reality is that our society is structured by governmental action and the market itself depends upon that structure. The reality is recognised by the present Government. Its period of office has been marked often by change in the form of government than by its extent. Even where industries have been privatised, regulation has replaced direct ownership where the result has been to create private monopolies or where wider social interests are recognised. There can be debate about the extent of government's role but the market cannot replace that role, for the market itself depends upon government.

The Government accepts the necessity of governmental action, but because it assumes that the market is the means of providing choice in society, it does not recognise that collective choice is itself a means of extending choice and that local collective choice can extend choice further. Community government is based on the assumption that local authorities can be the means for extending choice to local communities. Local authorities have the capacity to give expression to values that cannot be realised in the market whilst allowing diversity in society. Once the need for collective choice is accepted, the case for community government is the case for diversity through local collective choice.

The case for community government

The case for community government has to be grounded in present society – not its past. It is grounded in the needs of government in an uncertain society. Society is changing rapidly and on many dimensions:

economic re-structuring not as a once-for-all change, but as a continuing process
changing patterns of work and employment
demographic change altering balances within society
changing social norms challenging many past assumptions
growing threats to the environment
the increasing vulnerability of society
the recognition of a multi-cultural society
growing awareness of the discriminations within society.

The significance lies less in the particular changes – for everybody can make their own list and give their own emphasis – than in the extent of change and in the many dimensions on which the change is taking place. Uncertainty lies in the interaction between these changes, for in interaction the simplicities of trend analysis disappear.

There is a deeper uncertainty felt at the level of the local community. It is an uncertainty as to the right solution to many of the problems and issues faced. In the long years of growth, services grew in certainty, in response to perceived need and in accordance with the accepted professional solution. There was a 'right solution' to most of the problems perceived in our towns and countryside – pursued by central government and by local authorities alike. Now there is no certainty in the solutions. There are ideas about approaches to be adopted to the inner cities and their problems, but no assurance that they will necessarily resolve them, any more than there is certainty in the response to the changing nature of our countryside or to the scale of environmental problems. There was always uncertainty; what has happened is that it is now increasingly recognised.

Public uncertainty has grown as the 'certain' solutions of the past have failed to fulfil their promise. While public aspiration remains, public confidence in the capacity of government to

deliver has gone. Public doubts have replaced public confidence.
The task is the government of an uncertain society:

uncertainty as to the issues raised in a rapidly changing society
uncertainty as to the response to those issues
uncertainty amongst the public in the capacity for that response.

The government of uncertainty has its own requirements. It
demands a high capacity for learning both of the nature of the
problems faced and from the approaches adopted. But learning is
not enough. There is a need for a high capacity for change and
adaptation as learning grows. Yet public uncertainty can only be
resolved if the public are involved in the learning and in the
choices necessary for change and adaptation. The importance of
local authorities in the government of uncertainty is their potential
for societal learning, for adaptiveness and for involvement.

Societal learning comes from diversity not from uniformity. In
uniformity, the variety of problems and needs can be unseen.
From uniformity in approach one may merely learn of failure,
while in diversity can be found new possibilities for success.
Central government provides for the uniformities of society, while
local authorities can be the government of difference both in
response to diversity in needs and in building diversity in differing
aims. Local authorities have the potential for change and adaptiveness. They are built on a scale in which change can come more
easily. They can be closer both geographically and organisationally
to their citizens, who can be more readily involved in the choices
necessary for change.

If the case has been made for the potential of local authorities
for learning, adapting and involving, the reality can be very
different. The case for community government lies in the need to
realise that potential for the government of uncertainty.

Building community government

The case has been made for the role of local authorities as
community government. The changes required to establish community government depend in part upon legislation and in part
upon action by local authorities themselves. In effect what is

proposed is a new reorganisation, but a reorganisation that does not focus on structure, but on role, responsibilities and methods of working.

The role of local authorities as community government

The role of local authorities as community government has already been described. What is required to establish that as the primary role of local authorities? The critical change is to give local authorities the power of general competence – the right to act on behalf of their communities. Such a power could be given by extending the provisions of S 137 of the Local Government Act, 1982, set out above. Local authorities are given powers to incur expenditure on behalf of their communities up to a specified limit. That limit could be removed, recognising the right of a community to incur expenditure on its own behalf.

This would be to achieve the power of general competence within the doctrine of *ultra vires*. No body constituted by statute can act beyond the powers given by statute, but general competence can extend the powers. No power of general competence can be unlimited, and in Western Europe limits are set to prevent local authorities infringing individual rights, to prevent them carrying out functions given to other agencies of government or to regulate the terms on which they can engage in commercial activity. The importance of a power of general competence lies in the recognition it gives to the role of local authorities as community government.

The concept of community government has wider implications. There is a case for extending the quasi-legislative role of the local authority, giving it much greater powers to lay down regulations or vary the penalties to be imposed for particular offences.[7] Local authorities have two ways of gaining such powers – either as by-laws or by private bill legislation. It is right that powers which can be used against the individual citizen should be set within a national framework of law, but greater variety could be allowed than has been normal in this country. The principle should be that the case has to be made for uniformity, rather than at present where there is a presumption against diversity.

The recognition of the role of local authorities as community government gives the local authority a special concern with all the activities of government in their area. An increasingly fragmented system of government needs to be appraised in its impact on local communities. A concept of community government can be given expression in a right of inquiry by local authorities and in a duty of consultation upon other agencies. If community government is the expression of the community governing itself, then the community has a proper concern with the multifarious activities of government in its area.

Local authorities are charged with the provision of certain specified services and have the duty to carry out certain functions. The power of general competence could give them the right to extend the services provided. It is still appropriate to ask whether the established responsibilities of local authority support the role of community government. The issue is whether functions presently carried out by other agencies of government should be carried out by local authorities or equally whether any of the functions currently carried out by local authorities should themselves be given to other agencies.

The range of local authorities' responsibilities often appears more as a result of historical accident than of any systematic consideration of their role. It is difficult to see by what rationale local authorities have been given responsibilities for the education services, while responsibilities for the health services are given to appointed boards.

The concept of community government suggests two criteria that should be important in determining the functions to be given to local authorities rather than to other agencies of government. The first is local choice. Where there is scope for local choice within a national framework, there is a case for considering the allocation of such functions to local authorities. The second criteria is the interrelationship of the functions with other governmental functions since community government has a capacity to look beyond particular functions and to consider that interrelationship.

It does not follow that all the present activities of local authorities would meet these criteria. Where a local authority acts as a regulatory agency according to narrowly prescribed national standards, it is hard to see the case, other than administrative convenience, for it being a local authority function. There is, however, a case for functions presently carried out by special purpose agencies, normally controlled by appointed boards, being made the responsibility of local authorities. That case is strong in relation to the health service, the probation service and many of the functions of the Training Agency. To take the health service as an example, the scope for local choice is recognised in the powers given to local health authorities. Equally important however, is the close interrelationship between many of the activities of health authorities and those of local authorities. It is not merely the well-understood, if not necessarily always well-developed relationship on issues such as community care or environmental health. It is that in any policy directed at health promotion, the whole range of local authority activities have a role to play.

The development of community government requires a reappraisal of the complex of agencies that are involved in the government of local communities. In recent years there has been a growing tendency for the fragmentation of government (see Chapter 9). The growth of special purpose agencies builds organisational barriers into the working of government at the community level. It reduces the capacity of government to learn, because learning does not flow easily across organisational barriers; it reduces the capacity of government to adapt, because adaptation to emerging problems cannot usually be contained within the boundaries of single-purpose organisations, defined for past problems; it reduces the capacity to involve the public who have little respect for or even understanding of organisational boundaries. Special purpose agencies may be appropriate where problems are known and policies clear, but that presupposes a certainty that does not belong to present society.

The enabling authority

Community government cannot be built through existing patterns of working, since the organisational assumptions built into that system of working reflect traditions of local administration.

The first requirement is to recognise that although the responsibilities of local authorities as community government are much wider than those as local administration, those responsibilities do not need to be exercised directly. Once it is accepted that the role is defined by the needs and problems faced by local communities, then it is obvious an authority cannot and should not always act directly. It has to work with others.

Over recent years local authorities have shown a capacity for this role as community government.[8] They have responded to crisis in their local economies and to the growth of unemployment in their areas. At a time of financial pressure, they have established a new function of economic development, using their existing powers including S 137. It is significant, however, that this new function has involved them in working in a wide variety of ways to assist other organisations and individuals rather than acting directly. In this development of community government, one can see the enabling role at work.

The issue is what is the most effective way in which community needs can be met. That may involve direct provision, but a local authority can regulate; can provide grants; can use its influence in the local economy as a major employer or major purchaser of goods; can assist others through the knowledge, skills and information it deploys; can bring together organisations, individuals and groups; can build or assist new organisations; can contract with other organisations for the provision of goods and services; can involve users in the running of services; can speak on behalf of its area and those who live within it.[9] A dependence on direct service provision alone limits the role, as does the assumption that the only alternative mode of action is through private contractors.

The enabling role will and should be built in different ways by different local authorities, but national action may be required to increase their capacity by extending their powers. An enabling authority needs leverage and leverage implies powers and resources. One such resource is the ability to use contract conditions as a means of meeting community aims. Contract compliance has been restricted by the government and that restriction limits the capacity to act as an enabling authority. Community government requires an extension of capacity not a restriction.

The responsive authority

Community government has to look outward, yet past organisational assumptions in local authorities have built an organisation that looks inward. Too often in the long years of growth the provision of services became their own justification. They should adopt a public service orientation that recognises that the value of the service lies in the value seen both by customers *and* by citizens – whether those services are provided directly or through other agencies.

An increasing number of local authorities have come to recognise the need to review their working to ensure responsive services.[10] This involves far more than improving reception arrangements or training staff in dealing with the public, although both are important. It can involve the whole organisation, because the actions in the field and on the counter are conditioned by the rules and organisation governing them. It can involve the public beyond the organisation, upon whose judgement service must rest.

These developments are taking place in some yet not all authorities, but if community government is to be meaningful, these developments must become general. Central government cannot create more responsive service in local authorities – indeed it faces the same needs in its own working. It can, however, do much to encourage it.

The Scandinavian governments – reflecting a wide range of political views – have launched programmes for transforming the public services, directed as providing better service for the public. They recognise that the capacity to effect change at the centre is limited. The emphasis of the programme is on setting a climate for change through staff training and development. Beyond that, all four Scandinavian governments are committed to reducing controls on local authorities that hinder better service, and have launched the 'free commune' experiments, in which selected authorities are invited to propose controls to be removed by central government – itself an example of learning.[11]

New patterns of organisation

The development of community government requires from local authorities the capacity to work in many different ways. If they are to work with others to build responsive services and to strengthen local accountability, new patterns of organisation must be developed which do not necessarily fit easily into the traditional pattern of committee and departmental control.

Local authorities have already begun to develop new patterns of organisation as they have begun to develop new roles:

Local authority companies
Public and private sector joined in new organisations
Tenants co-operatives
User-control of leisure centres
Decentralisation to neighbourhood offices
Devolved management

The committee system itself should not be assumed to be sacrosanct or the best means of supporting community government. Local authorities should be encouraged to experiment. There are those who advocate the introduction of the directly elected mayor to give a public focus to the work of local authorities. That could be seen to be one expression of community government. Yet rather than requiring local authorities to adopt such structures, one should *permit* them to do so – if approved by or initiated by their citizens.

The accountable authority

Community government requires stronger local authorities, but stronger local authorities are only justified if there is stronger local accountability. It would be hard to regard the present local authorities as an expression of the community governing themselves. There is a weakness in their basis in local accountability. The turnout in local elections, although increasing slightly year by year, is only about 40 per cent. The local elections like Parliamentary elections can produce councils on which one party gains a clear majority on a minority of votes cast, or even without the largest number of votes.

The case for proportional representation is, if anything, stronger in local government than in central government. Because local authority areas are relatively homogeneous, the distortions caused by the first-past-the-post system can be greater. There are authorities where one party has gained the whole of the seats, leaving two fifths of the electorate totally unrepresented on the council. There are many authorities where one party is continuously in control for election after election, even though it fails to gain a majority of the votes. Certainty of power can easily lead to an arrogance which does not express accountability in practice. The development of community government can be supported by a system of proportional representation which can ensure the presence on the council of the range of political views in the community.

Electoral reform is a necessary but not a sufficient condition for local accountability. The election is the test of local accountability, but accountability requires the development of an active citizenship with the scope to play a part in local government beyond the periodic election. This will both strengthen accountability in its own right and, by promoting involvement in local government, encourage turnout. The use of the referendum by local authorities or on the initiative of a specified number of electors is one approach. The development of user involvement in the provision of services or in estate management enables citizens to play an active role in community government. The encouragement of elected neighbourhood councils for the expression of community views and as a source of community initiatives would spread involvement in a country which has less councillors in relation to its population than other countries in Western Europe (one councillor per 1800 citizens in the UK compared with a norm of between one per 250 and one per 450 in Western Europe).[12]

Conclusion

This chapter has set out a concept of community government. It has focused not on issues of structure but on the nature of local government itself. By emphasising role, functions, ways of working and the basis of accountability, it has shown that there are other alternatives to local government apart from that which we have known in the past or that emerging from the Government's programme.

Such changes will not be easily achieved. Central government will have to abandon policies adopted not merely in recent years but in the past. If the development of community government is seen as a means of social learning, then central government can achieve a new role in relation to local authorities in developing that learning. Change will be required in procedures, controls and in the civil service itself to release the capacity for community government.

It may be hard to see any central government ready to devolve power, but wisdom and political sense may lie in a central government that focuses on issues requiring its commitment, rather than on dispersing energy on issues which can be devolved to local authorities. At present policies are in the reverse direction, for the result of the Government's policies has been a concentration of power in central government, despite a commitment to reducing the power of the state. The continuation of those policies may seem inevitable, but that very concentration can create its own problems in lessening the effectiveness of a central government that has over-reached itself. Trends elsewhere are to strengthen local authorities rather than to weaken them. Other countries have learn the lesson that may have to be learnt in this country.

A reversal of past policies demands an alternative scenario for the future. It is not sufficient to expect the restoration of local government to its previous position. The case for community government is a case for local authorities with a new role and a new way of working. Such a case can be argued, but example is more powerful than argument.

It has already been pointed out in this chapter that some local authorities have responded to the challenge faced by building up a role that approaches community government. In response to the problems faced they have established a new role in economic development and a new way of working as an enabling authority in support of that role. Some are developing a public service orientation in building responsive services. The best argument for community government will be made by local authorities which take such measures further and strengthen local accountability by involving their citizens in the choices that have to be made and in the control of their services.

The Government's programme may seem to make such changes more difficult, but that programme makes such developments more necessary. The introduction of compulsory competitive tendering focuses attention on the governmental choice of what is required from a service. A local authority will only maintain control of services by showing its capacity to respond to the public's needs. A positive case for community government can be built on such necessities. Each local authority that seeks to build the case for community government needs to review its organisation and its way of thinking, to ensure not merely that it can meet the requirements of the legislation, but that it

has the capacity to speak on and for the community beyond the requirements for the services provided
uses to the full all the methods available to it to work as an enabling authority on behalf of the community it serves
builds a public service orientation as a responsive authority
involves the public as customer and citizen in the choices to be made, laying the basis for the accountable authority.

In present actions, the case can be made for the future of local government as community government.

Notes and references

1. Alan Norton, *Local Government in Other Western Democracies* (Institute of Local Government Studies, 1986) p. 24.
2. Ibid, p. 20.
3. Ibid, p. 42.
4. Michael Goldsmith and Kenneth Newton, 'Local Government Abroad', p. 140, in *The Conduct of Local Authority Business*, Research vol. IV, Cmnd 9801 (HMSO, 1986).
5. Nicholas Ridley, *The New Right* (Conservative Political Centre, 1988).
6. *Paying for Local Government*, Cmnd 9714 (HMSO, 1986) p. 9.
7. See David King, 'The Next Green Paper on Local Finance', paper given to an Institute of Economic Affairs Conference, 1988, for examples of possible powers.
8. See John Stewart and Gerry Stoker, *From Local Administration to Community Government* (Fabian Society, 1988) for illustrations of this argument.
9. See Michael Clarke and John Stewart, *The Enabling Council* (Local Government Training Board, 1988) for a development of this argument.
10. See Local Government Training Board, *Getting Closer to the Public* (1987) for examples.
11. See Lennart Gustafsson, 'Renewal of the Public Sector in Sweden', *Public Administration*, Summer 1987, and John Stewart and Gerry Stoker, 'The Free Commune Experiment in Scandinavia', *The Political Quarterly*, 1989, for descriptions of these programmes.
12. Goldsmith and Newton, 'Local Government Abroad', p. 141.

Index